I0797771

MISUNDERSTOOD

MISUNDERSTOOD

ALLEN IVERSON

WITH RAY BEAUCHAMP

GALLERY BOOKS

New York Amsterdam/Antwerp London
Toronto Sydney/Melbourne New Delhi

GALLERY BOOKS/13A
An Imprint of Simon & Schuster, LLC
1230 Avenue of the Americas
New York, NY 10020

First 13A/Gallery Books hardcover edition November 2025

13A is a trademark of Charles Suitt and is used with permission.

GALLERY BOOKS and colophon are registered trademarks of Simon & Schuster, LLC

INTERIOR DESIGN BY KARLA SCHWEER

Manufactured in the United States of America

10 9 8 7 6 5 4 3 2 1

Library of Congress Cataloging-in-Publication Data has been applied for.

ISBN 978-1-4767-8439-7
ISBN 978-1-4767-8442-7 (ebook)

CONTENTS

PRACTICE

The reason I did that press conference—you might know the one—was that I was good for the first time in a minute. It was May 7, 2002. My sixth season in the NBA had just finished in disappointment. Although I was already a two-time All-Star, an MVP, and nearly an NBA champion, rumors were circulating that Coach Larry Brown and I weren't getting along and that the 76ers would soon trade me. Trade me from the city I loved, the city that had embraced me from the beginning, the city that was home. Now everyone wanted to know what was next. Would Coach Brown return? Would I return?

I had been dealing all year long with hearing those rumors. *Where's Allen Iverson going to get traded? The 76ers don't want Allen Iverson anymore. He's not getting along with Coach Larry Brown.* Even my kids had to deal with it in school. Teachers: *Tell your dad don't leave.* Classmates: *Can you beg your dad not to leave?* My family too. They're telling me: *Chuck don't leave.*

It was pissing me off. So we set a meeting with me, Coach Brown, and our general manager, Billy King, where we're going to get this shit straight. Whatever is going to happen is going to happen today.

The message in that meeting was simple: *You're not going anywhere. Coach Brown's not going anywhere. You're here to stay. Coach Brown is here to stay.* Then we talked. We got back to being the loving family. We relaxed and were back to normal. I admit that it was bad before that. I didn't think they wanted me. The season had been long. I expected the worst. To me, loyalty is everything. Everything. So when they said it—you're not going anywhere, the family is staying together—yes, I was happy. The rest of that meeting was like making up with a girlfriend you're beefing with. At this point, you know you're sticking it out, so you can make your other points, like this or that can't happen anymore. But it was back to the way it was. I'm telling stories like I do. Coach Brown starts telling stories in his old-school way. Then everybody hugged. So like I said, I was good.

Once the decision was made, we all agreed to call a press conference. I could let the city know, let the whole world know. I'm staying, we're all staying. We have good news.

So I got in the press room. It was just me at the long table, microphones below, cameras pointed, the reporters staring up at me. All the Philly press came for this one. I'll be honest, I didn't always get along with the press. Never have. These motherfuckers had been telling the world what a terrible guy I am since I was a kid. And there they all were. They were unhappy because we'd lost. Unhappy because I wasn't the man they wanted me to be. Unhappy—hell, I don't know all the reasons they were unhappy.

Anyway, I was good. I figured I had good news. It was good news to me. *I'm staying. I'm coming to say I'm going to be here—that's it. City has nothing to worry about, teammates have nothing to worry about, family has nothing to worry about. I have nothing to worry about.*

But then the devil entered the room with a microphone. *So what about the situation with the practices?* Practice. It was one of the first questions. In response, I said the word *practice* a lot, as everyone in the whole damn world knows, but this was the main part that gets replayed over and over:

> *I'm supposed to be the franchise player, and we're in here talking about practice. I mean, listen, we're talking about practice. Not*

a game! Not a game! Not a game! We're talking about practice. Not a game. Not the game that I go out there and die for and play every game like it's my last. Not the game. We're talking about practice, man. I mean, how silly is that?

I never considered that this press conference would change my legacy. To that point, it was my moves on the basketball court that went viral—before going viral was a thing. But after that press conference, "practice" became as recognizably me as any crossover, any jump shot, any championship, or any heartbreak.

When I think about that press conference, the reality is there was a lot of other shit going on. To me, practice shouldn't have been the focal point. We had a bad end to the season, and there was my future I was trying to clarify for the world. But it was more than that even. If you listen to the whole press conference, the parts that didn't get repeated, I tried to explain. "I lost my best friend," I said. And between that and a disappointing season, I told them I was feeling "that everything is going downhill for me as far as my life. I'm human. I am just like you. You bleed just like I bleed, you cry just like I cry, you hurt just like I hurt." I said that, yet the reporters kept asking me about practice.

"I lost my best friend." In fact, at that exact time, a trial was going on in Virginia. They were prosecuting the killer of that best friend—Rahsaan Langford, just "Ra" or "Ra Boogie" to us. Me and Ra were like brothers. Ra got killed about seven months earlier, in the early morning of October 14, 2001. That was during Sixers training camp.

I didn't know it at the time, but if you look back at that trial, the prosecutor—from the same prosecutor's office that put me in jail nine years before—was busy telling the jury how much they weren't going to like Ra and his friends. My friends. Me. "A murder is a murder," the prosecutor said, "even if you don't like the victim and his friends." I shouldn't act surprised. The truth is, so many people never liked me and my friends—my "posse" or "entourage," they'd call it. It wasn't just all the reporters in the room. It wasn't just that prosecutor. So many people hated the dudes I grew up with, the life I'd come from, the streets I'd survived.

My whole life, on one side was my home, my upbringing, my people, and then on the other, basketball and everything that comes with that. One pulls, the other pushes. One thing I never did, that I refused to do, was to let go of home. Everyone told me to. A million times they told me to move on. But would I put in the rearview the people and the place that had my back from the beginning? The people and place that were the foundation of what I became?

That whole 2001–02 season, home pulled hard. *I lost my best friend.* I said it right there in the press conference. That shit broke me. And after losing Ra, we lost the goddamn games—the games I'd gone out there and played like they were my last. *I lost the games.* That shit broke me too. We were out of the playoffs in the first round after making it to the Finals the year before, after my MVP season. It hurt so fucking bad because the games meant everything to me.

So in that first press conference after ending our season, after losing, not one question about those games.

They wanted to talk about practice?

Let me tell you about Ra's murder. Because if you want to know about the press conference, about practice, about me, you need to know about it.

So, I wasn't there when Ra got shot, but I was supposed to be. We were going to go out to a nice club in Hampton, Virginia, to watch the Mike Tyson fight against Brian Nielsen. The same night, the Yankees were playing the Oakland A's in the playoffs. Ra was from the Bronx and was a Yankees fan. We were planning on doing it "upper-room style." That's what we'd say. We were "upper-room brothers" like Martin and Eddie in the movie *Life*. But I missed my plane from Philly to Virginia. I can't even remember why.

That night, without me, he'd gone to one of the worst places you can be in Hampton. It was a place I avoided. Yeah, I had gone there when I was young, when I wasn't afraid of anything. But not anymore.

He came to the spot with a few people, including a young dude that we called Fiend. All this I heard after the fact, of course. I was in Philly. We were in training camp, but I was nursing an injured elbow so I wasn't yet playing. From what I was told, the killer came into the club. He had a lazy eye. So when he came in, you know Ra was a jokester. Ra was like, *Fiend, you hanging with blind dudes now?* And the guy went crazy. *Motherfucker, you don't know who I am. I do this. I do that.* Ra was like, *Calm down, it's all good.* So Ra kept watching the Tyson fight. But the dude was staring at Ra the whole night. He couldn't let it go.

The Yankees game ended (the Yankees won—the game where Derek Jeter made the backhand throw to home against the A's) and the fight was over (Tyson could still fight, so he had no problem). Ra got in the car with Fiend, and it turned out the dude had been following Ra out the club. And so they said Ra turned around and smiled at him. Pulled off. Fiend stopped for something along the way, and while Ra waited in the car, the dude came up, opened the door to Ra's car. Ra got out the car, and the dude let it go. Shot him right there. Then he took off.

Hearing the shots, Fiend ran out, saw Ra's body on the ground, and got in the car and also drove off. Screeching tires. Ra left alone to die. That's all I could think about. Him alone on the ground, his blood staining the concrete as his life left him.

When I found out that Ra got killed, my heart broke. I should have been there. He shouldn't have been in that spot. All those thoughts come to your mind. What-ifs. And you know, he was one of the baddest motherfuckers of my friends from home. When we were kids, he was hustling and keeping me out of trouble. Ra actually helped push me off the streets. He said, *Don't ever come back here. You focus on sports.* And then when I was in jail and before I could cash a check in the NBA, he and my other friends from home helped my family survive.

When I made it, I brought him with me. He was there with me every year since. He was at my wedding. I was at his. He pursued his passion with music. And I helped him along that path.

This was the man shot to death.

That whole fall, from October 14, 2001, to the new year, I was dealing with this murder. With the funeral. With my grief. And I had a whole new family to take care of. Ra had three kids. He had a wife. Of course I was going to take care of them. I ended up paying for their home, their car, their school. How could I not? And if that makes me irresponsible with my money, so be it.

Meanwhile, the season wasn't going well either. Playing without me, we started the season slow. Once I came back, things improved, but not enough.

In January, they finally caught the killer. As the season went on, the trial approached.

We faced the Celtics in the playoffs, and they had home court. We lost the series in five games, 3–2. I averaged 30 points a game that series, but I didn't shoot it well. I attacked (of course) and took more than 12 free throws a game. I put it all out there. No one could or did question my effort or intensity in the games. It just wasn't enough.

So my first time back in front of the press after that series, after that season, after all the trade rumors, after losing my friend, they just wanted to talk about *practice*. The practices I missed. The practices I was late for. The practices I admit I didn't always focus on. Not even the games. All they wanted to talk about was practice. They were good at irritating me. I'll give them that.

So I said what I said in that press conference. And that's where it all came from. And everything in my life has been like that. People wanting something from me that I couldn't understand. And they misunderstood me—that where I came from, what I'd been through, made me different. I mean, to me, practice wasn't that important. Not compared to the games. Not compared to my friends and family.

*

This motherfucker right here, writing this book, almost didn't make it out of middle school. I could have died hustling before I even played a game. I could've been in prison for all fifteen years that the judge sentenced me to, stuck shooting hoops in a prison yard during my senior year of high school. I could have lost my sister when she was sick. I could have just given up when no one wanted to recruit me anymore. I could have given in to the negativity that greeted me when I entered the NBA.

Instead I became a state champion, an All-American, the league MVP. I took the 76ers to their first Finals since Julius Irving, the great Doctor J, was playing. And there in that press conference, at that moment, I had agreed, along with the coach and general manager, to stick with the Sixers, with the city of Philadelphia.

Yet all the media wanted to do was talk about practice. It still seems silly to me.

More than who said what and when, more than some missed practices, I think it all goes back to where I came from. What I went through coming up. What I had to overcome, and maybe what I couldn't overcome. Everyone knows that I fucked up more than my fair share. I'm human, like I said in that press conference. And I ain't perfect. So I'm telling you here about the beginning. Back home. In jail. At Georgetown with my mentor, my guide, the man who saved my life, Coach John Thompson. And my introduction to the NBA. So maybe you can understand.

To understand me—Allen Iverson, Bubbachuck, AI, the Answer—you need to hear the beginning. With my family. With my friends. In Newport News and Hampton. The seven cities of Virginia. On the Peninsula.

I

GROWING UP AND SURVIVING

ONE

NANA AND MOM

I was born on June 7, 1975, in Hampton, Virginia. My mom, Ann Iverson, was fifteen. My biological father was in Hartford, Connecticut. And from the beginning, my family didn't have much.

I grew up on "The Peninsula," with the Chesapeake Bay on one side and the James River running along the other. Hampton and Newport News are like sister cities there. I lived in both at different times. Really, I can say I grew up in both places. I was a Newport News dude, but I also grew up in Hampton.

But before I get to that, the story really begins in 1971 in Hartford. That's where my mother had been raised. By then, just twelve years old, she had three younger siblings: Jessie, Steve, and Greg. Her mother—my maternal grandmother—was thirty, raising the four of them by herself. She didn't want more kids, so she got her tubes tied. When she got home from the procedure, she wasn't feeling well, and after a while couldn't even stand straight. My twelve-year-old mom was on the phone with a sheet over her head to keep out the background noise—small house and lots of kids running around—when my Aunt Jessie interrupted her to say their mom didn't look right. They called an ambulance to come get her. My mom wanted to go to the hospital, but the last words her mother said to her were "No, you watch Jessie and Stevie and Greggy for me." Her mother never came home. It was an infection from the surgery. My mom could tell you to the penny how much the hospital gave as compensation: $3,818.18.

"Don't forget the eighteen cents," she would say.

My mom and her siblings were now motherless, but they were blessed to have a saint of a grandmother (my great-grandmother), whose name was Ethel Mitchell—"Nana" to all of us. Nana agreed to raise those four grandkids. Story goes that Nana's husband had enough with raising kids. So Nana was on her own.

After a couple of years, Nana started thinking about a change. My teenage mom was playing basketball then. (She said she had her coach telling her to "slow down and pass the ball." Sounds familiar.) She was also finding trouble—thirty-eight fights, she counted. After the last one, Nana was done. The family had moved to Connecticut years before, but she was originally from Virginia and still had family there. Once she saw a future raising those four grandchildren, and looked out her window at a Hartford neighborhood she didn't really like anyway, she decided to move back home. And maybe it had something to do with me too.

See, 1974 came, and Nana had already been taking care of my mom and the others for a little while. My mom was fifteen by then. She had been dating Allen Broughton for a couple years. Broughton was a star basketball player, just one year older than my mom. (He was only 5'5", but they said he played bigger than his size. Also sounds familiar.) All I know is that by the time the family moved to Virginia, my mom was pregnant. They made it to Virginia in time to enroll her into high school—at Bethel, where I'd end up winning a few games. That January, she ran the point, five months pregnant with me. Of course, I don't remember that!

*

So as I said, I was born June 7 of that year, 1975. When I was born, my mom says she knew after taking just one look at me—she saw my long arms and immediately said I'd be a basketball player. She just knew. And whatever anyone can say about my mom, she believed in me that day, and every day after that. I only made it where I made it because of her. Because of her belief in me.

Not long after I was born, I got the name everyone called me. You may know me by "AI" or "the Answer," but all that came later. Everyone in the family was trying to come up with a nickname for my baby self—"What are we going to call Allen?"—because in my family your name wasn't necessarily what you got called. For instance, my mom was "Juicy," and her sister was "Lil Bit." That's just how it was. So story goes that two uncles up in Connecticut were arguing over what my nickname would be. One uncle was called Bubba and the other was Chuck. Well, they got to arguing that I should get one of their nicknames as my own, and my mom said, "You know what, you both can be right. Bubbachuck." And so that's what it was from that day forward. Everybody called me Bubbachuck, sometimes just "Bubba," or mostly just "Chuck." You watch my games from when I was a kid, even the announcers called me that. And to this day, among my family, my friends, and when I go home, it's "Bubbachuck."

My first memories are from living with Nana on Jordan Drive in Hampton, in the Aberdeen section of town. She had a little one-story house with vinyl siding, set back from a creek. I don't remember it all of course, those early years. But I do remember it being crowded. It's hard to say how many of us there were. It had two bedrooms. We made room for ten or twelve people depending on the time. There was Nana; there was my mom; her little sister, Jessie; her two brothers, Stevie and Greg; and then me, of course. Others came and went. We didn't have a lot of money either. Now, that ain't no excuse for anything. It's just how it was.

Mom was still a kid then. Looking back, I can see that. So I was raised by the whole family.

Those first couple years after I was born, my mom kept playing basketball. She was the point guard her junior and senior years in high school. Then she graduated from Bethel High—something I never got a chance to do after they threw me in jail.

My mom was still a kid, so it was Nana who managed the house. She was the parent to all of us—obviously to my mom and her siblings, but also to me. She was just the backbone of the family, but it was hard trying to be the person that wants to and has to do everything, but you just don't have the finances, you don't have everything to be able to do it. The best way she could, she did. Everybody in the family respected her and looked up to her. She had strict rules, as a churchgoing, God-fearing woman. So we weren't playing music in the house. We had to keep it clean. People had to be home at a certain time. And everyone came to her to sort their shit out. Because she just had the ability to break things down and make sure everything was handled the way it was supposed to be. In her life, she had three kids. My grandmother, you know about, how she passed after going to the hospital. But for Nana, all three of her kids died before she did. So my mom, and Aunt Jessie and Uncles Steve and Greg, they were like her kids. And then there was me. I was the youngest, so Nana spent a lot of time looking after me, making sure I got dressed, got fed. She really took care of everyone, but me being the youngest, we had a special bond. I was her baby.

Back then she drove a big old burgundy car from the 1970s. I wish I could remember what it was. But I do remember that it had a big door handle that came in from the side far enough that when I was real little, I could sit on it kind of sideways. Kick my feet up on the seat. I don't know why, but that was just the way I liked to sit. Nana would be like, "Get off that door before you fall off this car." I would for a second, but then seconds later I used to get back on it. Well, one day I was in the car with her and my cousin, sitting like that. We were on the interstate. There was traffic, so we were hardly moving. Sure enough, the damn door popped open. Out I fell right onto the highway. My cousin grabbed me up quick and got me in the car. Thank God for the traffic jam. I started crying like a baby. Nana was so worried I might have done something really bad. But my cousin was like, "Aw, he just crying 'cause he scared." I never sat on the door handle like that again.

Nana watched me close. And we just got along so well. It's hard to explain, but we had the kind of relationship that when I was away from her, I would just look forward to being with her again. You know when you first get with a girl? All you want to do is see her all day? That's how it was. Like when I was on the bus coming home. Just looking forward to seeing her. To spend time with her, sit up under her. When we were together, she would take me wherever she had to go, in that burgundy car—to the store, to see family, everywhere.

Family time for me wasn't like it is today. When my kids were smaller, I would take them to Great Wolf Lodge or something and when we were in the car to go home, they'd ask, *When are we coming back?* That's the way I like it, I guess. I want them to have what I never had—a stable family life, presents under the tree, you know, nice shit. But it wasn't like that for me. Now, that didn't mean I wasn't having fun and being loved. It was just that I followed my family's schedule if I was with them. So when I spent time with Nana, it was going wherever she was going, to the store, to church, wherever.

(The funny thing is Nana *was* out having fun. I just didn't know it. I found out years later that she drove that car of hers from Hampton to Atlantic City a lot of those weekends of my childhood. She'd drive up there, play whatever games she played, and be back before I noticed. That's a six-hour drive!)

In those days, I had a lot of energy. When you're a kid, all you want is to be outside. I mean, there wasn't anything to do inside. Again, it wasn't like it is today, where kids have videogames and all that, big-screen TVs, and any damn show they want. For me it wasn't like that. The one thing

I would do inside is draw. If it was raining outside, or I was stuck in the classroom. I would draw all kinds of shit. What I would see or learn, I would re-create it. Teachers and adults would look at my artwork, and they'd be like, *Son, you got a future*. I loved doing it, and I loved the recognition. But for the most part, inside was boring.

So I would go outside. Nana's house in Aberdeen was right on that little creek, and I'd go down there to catch crawfish and to play in the water. It'd be fun down there, but it made Nana a little nervous, I think, especially when she wasn't around. We had such a good relationship, so much love, so that's why I remember the one time she laid her hands on me. I must have been four or five years old at most. She was going to church. So she said to me, "Now Chuck, don't go down to the creek while I'm gone. You stay in the house."

I nodded like, *Yeah no problem*. But I had no intention of staying in the house that whole time. I watched her drive the car away, down the block. Didn't wait more than a second after she got out of sight. I went out the back door right back down to the creek. Well, I guess she had a hunch. Because a few minutes later I looked up and saw her staring down at me. My heart just sank, man. I didn't want to let Nana down. So she gave it to me good.

It wasn't a feeling I ever wanted again—to let her down. And like I said, that was the only time that she ever put her hands on me. Nana was someone I wanted to do right by. She was the person I wanted most to make proud. That's why I remember that day so well, and I never disobeyed her like that again. It's something I think so much about, because she saw me go to jail, but she never saw me play in the NBA.

For the most part as a kid, I was allowed to go outside and do what I wanted. As soon as God opened my eyes in the morning, the first thing I'd do was hop up and go outside. I had Stevie and Greg, my two uncles, to push me around. Those two guys were everything to me. I looked up to them because they were out there doing all the things I wanted to do eventually—playing football, number one. Stevie was the younger one, and he was close to Nana as well. He was the closest to her of the four kids. Nana loved him. And he was the one who took care of her when she was dying. I don't want to even think about those days. They came much later.

Stevie and Greg both played football at Bethel. They were good but weren't pros or anything. I liked watching them. Then as soon as I could run, I demanded to play with them. They could see my quickness. *Just give me the football.* I'd take it and just go, freedom in running wild among the older dudes—we'd see if any of them could knock me down. Of course they could. They would tackle my ass again and again. Didn't matter how many times. I just said, "Let's do it again," because I wanted to do it until they couldn't fuck with me anymore, until I beat their asses. That was something I always did: just kept going until I could win.

One game we played was called hot ball. That's where you throw it up, one guy catches it, and everyone tries to tackle him before the guy can get to the end zone. I played that game hundreds of times—at my Nana's and later when we moved to Newport News. I got so damn good at it, I was dreaming of a future in professional sports.

I'd reach that dream eventually, but when I was little I almost lost the chance. I was at the bus stop, in the fourth grade. It was raining. And you know how when you're little, you want to be at the back of the bus? That way you're farther away from the bus driver, so you can act up? Well, the way to get the seat in the back was to be the first in line to get on the bus. No one was going to stop me from being in the back of that damn school bus.

So I was standing there as the bus pulled up. Someone from behind pushed me a little, like jostled me, and I slipped. My foot went into the street, and the bus ran right on over it. In fact the wheel was on top of my foot as the bus came to a stop. The other kids in the line started screaming at the bus driver, "Ms. Barrett, you just drove over his foot!" but she was just saying, "What?" She couldn't hear, and for some reason she wasn't opening the door. She finally came to realize that the bus was on my motherfucking ankle. She put the bus in drive and rolled on up over and off of it.

What I did then was I just stood up to get on the bus. I was going to be first on that bus. Nothing was going to stop me. Ms. Barrett was like, "No, you can't get on here." She looked scared. Then I sat back on the ground and realized what was happening. My ankle was all bent up. I was in shock, I guess. And then everything cut out. I don't remember the ambulance, though it came. The next thing I remember I was in bed.

My ankle was broken bad. I was crying, and I told Nana I didn't think I would be able to play sports anymore. She just said, "It's all right, it could have been your chest or your head. You could be dead." She wasn't going to let me have a sympathy party. And she was right. So I decided it wasn't going to stop me. I could recover. Later, I had to have a checkup with a different doctor when I was still wearing the cast. My ankle was already healing some, and I was feeling a lot better. The doctor sat me down and gave me a Snickers. He said, "Tell me the truth. There is no way your ankle could have gotten ran over by a bus. It would be crushed. You're in the fourth grade, man. That little-ass ankle." I told him it happened. He just shook his head. I'm not sure he believed me. But it sure made me feel better that it was healing.

Things were looking up. When I got back to school I did get my sympathy party. I took full advantage. When we had to line up, I went to the front of the line, like at the cafeteria. People were signing my cast. And before long my ankle was healed well enough that I was back at it. It didn't stop me from playing football a month later. I came back better than ever, glad I'd survived fourth grade.

My mom would watch me play football sometimes, and she'd smile. I think she knew it was basketball that I would play. I mean, she said it when I was born. But she'd watch me run through her brothers and a lot of the older kids, and she just could see that I had talent.

With my mom and me, even early on, sometimes it felt like we were friends, or brother and sister, as much as she was my mom. I don't mean that in any kind of way. I just mean that she was so young that we would just have fun together, whether it was listening to music, or sharing our love for jewelry, imagining the gold, the diamonds, the sparkle, the bling. In a way, we grew up together.

But she struggled to do all the things most other parents do, like pay the bills. A lot of bills didn't get paid. She had so many jobs. She worked as a forklift driver in the Avon warehouse and as a cashier at a supermarket. She worked as a typist at Langley Air Force Base. And she even worked at the shipyard, the big spot in the Peninsula. That's where a lot of people could get real jobs that paid all right. But she was out of work as often as not, and we didn't have much. She once put it like this: "I'm trying to keep a roof over their heads and mine. *Tight* isn't the word for our money. If there's another word past *tight*, use it." To get shoes for me as a youngster, she'd take me to the store. We'd walk up to the display, where they had all the shoe boxes on top of one another, and she'd be like, *Try these on.* Once she saw they fit, she'd tell me to walk on out of there with them. I hated that shit. I wanted to get shoes the regular way!

Before I have any memories, like when I was an infant, my mom met Michael Freeman. He became my dad. I didn't have a life without one. That's not my story. I mentioned Allen Broughton—well, evidently that was my biological father, but I never met him in person.

Michael Freeman was doing all right when he met my mom. He was working a real job in the shipyard. He was a small dude and went by the name "House Mouse." He could play basketball himself. A Sixers fan, his favorite player was Mo Cheeks. Maybe that was why it was meant to be, me going to the Sixers.

Unlike my mom, my dad never laid his hands on me. His way of putting down the law was just like a look. A look to tell me, *that wasn't right*, whatever I was doing. Once he got involved with my mom, he really was the one to take care of things when he could.

When I was about four, my mom got pregnant with my sister, Brandy. At that point, I think my mom was probably ready to move out of her grandma's house. We all loved Nana obviously, but I think my mom wanted her freedom. Nana had her rules, being home at a certain time, not listening to music too loud or too late, allowing only some friends over. My mom wanted to live by her own rules. And I guess you could say maybe I got that from her. She also never liked taking criticism, even if it was constructive. Now that she was going to have another child, this one with my dad, it just made sense to move in with him.

So we moved into a two-bedroom in the Pine Chapel apartments, which was still in Hampton but nearer to the Newport News line. I can't remember too much about that place, but I can remember my white sheets and the green curtains. I can't remember things like even Brandy's first day back from the hospital, but I can remember the color of the curtains and the sheets. The random shit I remember—it's strange.

I think my mom was glad to have her freedom. Now she could smoke cigarettes if she wanted to, and she could play music. She had a brown clock radio and she'd blast music through the apartment all the time, every day. It didn't have a record player, or anything fancy like that. The music we listened to back then was soul, R&B, all that stuff. It was something new for us, and it just floated through the house all the time.

It was around then that we began to listen to Michael Jackson. Man, I loved his music so much. It's something my mom and I shared, and as I was growing up each new song would come out, and it would be the most exciting thing. Everyone knew that about me—obsessed with Michael Jackson. Later in life, I would sing "Man in the Mirror" on the bus after games, teammates getting sick of that shit. But I'd just raise the volume.

I remember years later, I was playing in Denver. I was on the training table and I had my headphones on, and Carmelo Anthony came in. He took one look and told some of the other guys, "You don't even have to ask what AI is listening to. All he listens to is Michael Jackson. He loves that man!" Everyone cracked up because they knew he was right. That all started with me and my mom—like everything else.

When we were in Pine Chapel, I used to cry and ask for my Nana. But Mommy was like, "Your Nana ain't here. You living with me now, and I don't wanna hear that shit." I still got to visit Nana, but it wasn't the same. My mom probably was focusing on the baby. And my dad was around, but it wasn't like it was smooth. It was never normal. Him and my mom, they always had their things. So we all moved in together, but he was sometimes there, sometimes not.

One night, some fucked-up shit went down. My parents were in the "off" part of the "on-off" cycle, and my mom had a dude over from across the street. The two of them were talking and whatnot when my dad came by. Voices got raised. Me and Brandy were in our room, just being quiet—she was still a little baby. But I could hear the argument.

I heard it escalating, so I went out of my room and looked in the kitchen, where my dad and the neighbor were standing chest to chest. Then it came to fists getting thrown, and I scrambled back to my room. Seconds later, I heard the gun go off. I came back, and my dad had hit the man with a gun, and evidently it discharged. The dude was on the ground. It looked like half his head was gone, man. Blood everywhere. That's what I remember. The blood pooling on the floorboards. That color of red sticks with me like the white sheets and green curtains. I ran back to my room again to get away, to put that image out my head. Fucked-up. But I had to learn right then, at that moment, that it was just a fact of life, that you can't stop and dwell. As a kid, I'd cry every time my team lost a game. But for this kind of shit, I had to not think about it, not talk about it, definitely couldn't cry about it. Thank God my kids haven't had to experience shit like that.

The police ended up coming around and they picked Daddy up. The dude was hurt but he didn't die. It was self-defense, so my dad wasn't locked up for long.

After that, the family was ready to move again. Mom found a new place, over in Newport News, in a project called Stuart Gardens.

It wasn't the most stable situation, but my mom was there for me. I remember I was talking to her one time when I was still little. I said to her, "Mommy, you think I could play in the NBA or NFL?" I was just a kid. I hadn't even won a trophy yet.

She looked at me and said, "I know you can. You're going to do it."

I actually believed it. So I would tell the other kids about my plans. When everybody was laughing at me and my dreams, I used to basically say to them, "You laugh all you want, but my momma told me I could." Like that was the gospel, man. *My mom told me this, so you can laugh all you want.*

To this day, I will never forget her saying that. She believed in me totally. That meant everything to me, even if it wasn't perfect all the time.

TWO

STUART GARDENS

I remember when we arrived in Stuart Gardens for the first time. The house was right on the water. I mean, out our window we could see where the Chesapeake Bay met the James River—Hampton Roads, they called it. On the other side of the water was Norfolk, Virginia. My mom loved that view, and she was happy to have a bigger place.

The way Stuart Gardens was set up was it had one- and two-story buildings with a few homes in each. A little plot of grass surrounded the buildings. When you looked at it, the grass and the water, it looked nice. But it was still the projects. I ended up getting into fights. I watched as my friends and family turned to dealing drugs. Later, I saw dudes get killed on those streets, in between those buildings. A nice view of the water can't change the way blood looks soaking into the concrete.

I would actually walk away from the water to get a different kind of view. Walk one neighborhood over and you got to the single-family homes, each sitting on its own plot. Definitely *not* the projects. Me and my friends would go over there just to soak it all in, to feel like we lived in a place with regular houses. When we walked on those streets, people used to call the police, ear in one end of the receiver, yelling at us, "Y'all ain't supposed to be around here!" But they were poor folks too. That was still the hood. I figured this all out later. They were just poor people who lived in houses in the hood.

I was just a little dude when we moved in. And my mom was happy because it was our own place. Downstairs was a little kitchen and living room. Upstairs was where we slept. The spot had three bedrooms. One for my mom and dad, one for Brandy, and one for me. I learned quick that Brandy's room was good to sneak out of. I could open her window and get up on the roof, hang from the gutter, and from there I could hop on down, or do the reverse when I was coming home. I did that a lot.

You know how we are as kids, sneaky and you think you can one-up your parents, but the parents always one-up your ass? My mom knew how to one-up us kids. An example of that was when I came in late one night, lifting myself into the window from the gutter, and Mommy was just standing there, like Nana looking down at me in the creek. I have no idea how she knew. So she whooped my ass. And it wasn't the only time. Brandy would cry when I got my ass whooped—that's how close we were.

Stuart Gardens was kind of an enclosed neighborhood. One border was the water. You could go into it, to go crabbing or fishing, but you couldn't go past it. On the opposite side was Sixteenth Street, which ran parallel to the water. The other two borders were Anderson Park on one side and Roanoke Avenue on the other. Basically, Mom would tell me and my sister, "Don't go past Sixteenth Street." (If you can believe it, part of Sixteenth Street got named ALLEN IVERSON WAY.) Other than minding those borders, we were free to go where we wanted. That could be crabbing or fishing in the water, playing sports in Anderson Park, or just hanging out in the neighborhood.

Of course, I got to pushing those boundaries immediately. The real border was actually simpler: It was as far as I could go and still hear my mom's whistle. Her whistle was louder than any whistle that I ever heard.

Growing up in the basketball and football world you hear a lot of whistles, so that's saying something. So as loud as that shit was, if you didn't hear that whistle, then you were too far away. Before long, it even went past that. Because all my friends knew the whistle and they knew to come get me if they heard it. But then my mom could tell basically how far I was by the timing it took for me to get back, like, *I know you were at such-and-such place because it took so many minutes to get back.* She had my speed down to a science.

Not everyone in Stuart Gardens welcomed me. At first I was the new kid. And people would come messing with me, testing me. One time, I remember all these dudes came to the house to beat my ass over some stupid kid shit. I was so scared. My dad was there, and he just acted like he had it taken care of. He came outside, and all these dudes were talking shit. And he said, "Let's just play a football game." It doesn't make sense, but I swear that's exactly what he said, and that's exactly what happened. And I'd never seen my dad play football in the slightest, but that dude went out, and he was like Tony Dorsett. He was all over the field. It was a touch-football game, and the man was blocking for me as I ran with the ball. Somehow that calmed everybody down.

Fighting was a part of life there, but after a while, I got to know people, so it wasn't like I was the new guy, and nobody was messing with me anymore. But it was just a fact that you had to be tough. It was a toughness you built up from an early age. It was Newport News, full of tough motherfuckers.

So I ended up with a lot of friends there in Stuart Gardens. There was Tony Clark. This was my buddy. He was smaller than me, but older than me. A real tough guy. Wasn't anyone who wanted to mess with Tony Clark. He was also a swindler. He could talk another kid out of anything. The kind of dude who could convince you to give him a bike in return for a radio. To get the radio, he might have convinced another kid to take some candy. And he probably took the candy from a corner store on the other side of Sixteenth Street. So he walked out of his house with nothing that morning, and at the end of the day rode his new bike home. He could convince anyone of anything. He was a good friend to have.

And my best friend from the beginning was Snapper. He lived four or five buildings over. He was my exact age, but he was even smaller than me. Early on, we played basketball together—just two project kids who rode over to play sports in Hampton.

Most of my friends that I grew up with, they ended up in jail, or worse. Snapper is one of the ones who got into some trouble when he was young, but he's a different, unusual story in the sense that he's married with kids now, the trouble behind him. He works every day. He's one of the rare ones who I thought was heading for destruction, got to the brink of it, but somehow turned back and overcame it. I'm assuming that was God having his hand on him. Everything that everybody else was doing that was getting them killed or sent to jail for the rest of their lives, he was doing it.

But that was way later. Back when we were kids in Stuart Gardens, we were just getting up to normal kid shit.

One thing we liked to do was go crabbing. Crabs are a big thing down there. The Hampton High team was called the Crabbers. And like I told you, the water was pretty much right outside my house. It wasn't that hard to catch a few of them crabs. All you needed was one of these crab traps, some line, a bucket, and some time. The trap was made out of this metal wire, and it had little openings so the crabs could come in but couldn't get out. You had one of those traps, you were set. Oh, and you needed some bait. The perfect bait was a little bit of chicken wings to put in the middle of the trap to lure those motherfuckers in. If you had some chicken, you could get some crabs quick.

I remember one time, I was at home alone, and we had some chicken wings in the house, which wasn't always the case. So I grabbed the chicken, my trap, and a bucket, and I went to the bridge where you could drop your trap into the deep water. I started early and kept at it, and before not too long, the bucket was full of crabs. *Dinner for the family,* I'm thinking.

So I brought the bucket home and put it next to the refrigerator, feeling pretty good about myself.

Back in the day, I used to cut people's hair in Stuart Gardens. It was like art for me. I could see someone's hair in a picture, on TV, or in the street, and I could just do it. And of course I had a precise, steady hand. Eventually I got some clippers. People would come over, get in the chair. I could make a few dollars. So later that day, after catching all those crabs, my friend came over. I'm about ready to shape him up. He's in the chair. And just then my mom comes in.

Now, I had a bucketful of crabs. I had brought us dinner. Well, that wasn't the way she saw it. She was wondering where the chicken was. She was like, "You tryin' to get us some fucking dinner. Well, that chicken was *guaranteed* dinner." She walked over to me and she slapped me upside my head, right as I'm taking the clippers to my friend. He wound up with a part as wide as two fingers together. Dude said, "What'd you do, Chuck?"

I said to get some glue, stick it right back on there.

There was a store around our way. It was bigger than a 7-Eleven but smaller than one of your big grocery stores. It was where you could go to get pretty much anything. It had a fish and meat section in the back, and a big candy aisle. That was the aisle we were really interested in as kids.

Snapper was the one who perfected the art of stealing candy. He'd stand in the candy aisle for a minute, considering his options, and then he'd grab some Skor bars, some Reese's Cups, whatever that day seemed best. He'd look both ways, and he'd put the stuff in his waistband real quick. Then he'd walk out and we'd have ourselves a candy party.

That kind of thing, mischief, it just seemed natural. That's what we were, kids on the street, the project kids. It wasn't really anything big. And it was a lot less than the older kids were doing. I never thought of myself as being a tough guy. But I wasn't afraid either, just like Snapper. You couldn't be afraid.

Something we got to doing was going over to the mall and just trying to steal stuff from cars. We weren't too complicated about it. There was a big parking lot, and so a lot of cars were just sitting there. Me and my friends would try opening all the doors. When one was open, we would climb in and grab what we could: the quarters, the sunglasses, and whatnot.

The thing I think about sometimes now is, you would think we would be careful. But that wasn't the case at all. Even then, when you started trying to open doors, you were going to set off alarms. So we would set off all these alarms, and we would just run to a different part of the parking lot and try other cars. I mean, we would be in there with multiple alarms going off and we would keep at it. Just kind of laughing our way from one section to the next. Why would we do that? First thing is, we had nothing, just as kids, ten, eleven, twelve years old. We didn't have moms giving us money to go get shoes or catch a movie. So if we wanted to do something that might cost a couple dollars, that was one way to get it. Second thing is it was just fun.

Now, I said we weren't careful, but I did get to be careful about one thing. I started wearing gloves. I laugh now, because were they really dusting for prints? I thought I had these detectives figured out, man—gloves would keep me from getting caught.

Well, one day that decision came back to haunt me. It was a hot day. One of those Virginia days where it's 90-something-degrees and humid as a motherfucker. Just sweating. Me and Snapper and some other dudes went to the mall. I had my black leather gloves. I think by that point people must have complained about the project kids coming in there and ripping off their shit, so the police were onto us. But before anyone showed up, I got into a car or two and got some change and other shit. We decided to leave. We kind of all separated.

I was walking down this one block, not too far from making it safely back to Stuart Gardens. Still wearing the black gloves. And I saw this police car. I'm thinking to myself, *Just keep cool and keep walking.* And then when I got to the corner, I'm thinking, *I'm going to run.* That's my plan. At that point, maybe I was eleven or twelve, and I was already a fast dude. So the cop kind of started following me, and sped up as I sped up my walk.

Before I got to the corner, he and his partner stopped me. *Fuck*, I'm thinking.

"It's a little hot for some gloves," cop said to me.

I have no idea why I didn't take them gloves off, making me look like a guilty motherfucker. The cops started searching me, and of course they found all the shit I took, change and all that. Craziest part was Snapper and them were across the street just laughing at me.

The cop lectured the shit out of me. He didn't bring me in. He just told me how I was ruining my future. I was smart enough to listen until he stopped. But you know what I was thinking? I was just mad he took back the shit I stole. When he left, I was mad as hell. But I was glad he didn't take me to the precinct—or worse, go find my mom. That would have been real trouble.

The other time I got caught for something was like that too. I told you I liked crabbing, but I was also into fishing. With crabs you needed chicken. Well, with fishing what you needed was worms. For the most part, to get worms I would just look for some wet dirt and dig. You do that, you find yourself some nice nightcrawlers. But the nightcrawlers weren't going to catch the best fish. To catch the best fish, you needed the bloodworms—bigger, nastier, and more effective. Those were at the store, and the only people you saw with the bloodworms were the real fishermen, the dudes with jobs, who took it seriously on the weekends and after work. If you had bloodworms, you were no joke.

Well, one day I got it into my head that I was going to get me some of them from the store. And I actually had a couple dollars. So I went back to that same store I was telling you about, where we used to swipe candy. Back by the fish section, that's where they sold bait, including bloodworms. I went there and picked out a little tub of them. Took it to the fish counter. Lady tells me I pay for them at the front counter. So I walked through the store right by the candy aisle, and I just got to thinking, *It's just like candy.*

So I stopped and looked both ways down the aisle. The coast being clear, I tucked that tub of worms on the inside of my pants.

After that, I walked down the rest of the aisle toward the exit. Right before I reached the door, there's the lady from the back. *Fuck*. Evidently she'd seen me do it. Caught again. I just stared at her. She did a little lecture, walked me to the cashier, and watched as I paid for those bloodworms. There were other customers there, and I don't think they expected me to pull worms out of my drawers.

Me and Snapper would wander around with our friends, going into other neighborhoods and getting into fights with other kids. We were getting into all the kind of shit you expect of kids before they get into the real shit. But there weren't any guns. Nobody was dying. The crazy times came later, when the streets got hot. Nah, when I was little, it was simpler. Ripping off a few cars and the candy store was about it.

Drugs was one thing we heard about, though, something talked about on the street. And it was something I was always real scared about, especially when I was little. Just terrified the shit out of me. I didn't even smoke any marijuana at all until I got to college—"reefer" was what we said. Reefer was some shit you wanted to avoid! And forget about the other stuff. I wasn't getting close to that.

But man, it wasn't much later that kids around me, twelve and thirteen years old, started sniffing powder. I remember these dudes, they were like, "Hit this, Chuck, hit this."

I was like, "Nah."

"Man you a little bitch, Chuck."

I was terrified because I always heard that drugs were bad, to the point that you could die from it. If you did drugs, you couldn't play in the NBA or NFL. So I didn't mess with any drugs.

THREE

RAIDERS FOOTBALL

So those first couple of years in Stuart Gardens, I was out running around. From time to time my mom would set me straight, but for the most part I could do what I wanted. I played a little organized football, but not much, until late one summer when everything changed. When sports got serious.

It was at the end of the summer I turned eight. That whole summer had been fun. I went to Magruder Elementary most days, played basketball or football in the morning on their courts, and then spent the rest of the day in the pool. I'd have to take my sister with me. Brandy was four. I had to take her everywhere, and we got along, but obviously she couldn't move as fast as me, couldn't ride a bike for example, so that got old. But at least we were going somewhere to have fun. And the thing about Magruder is that while I ran around outside, they had things for my sister to do. Arts and crafts, all the shit she enjoyed.

My mom worked for Avon then in a giant warehouse. It was a fulfillment center—packing up orders from the Avon catalogs. She was still in her early twenties, just trying to make ends meet. She was a packer, and she drove a forklift. The company hired a lot of women, especially single moms.

At that warehouse, she met a man named Gary Moore—just "Mo" to everyone who knew him. Mo worked there, but his reputation was for a different kind of work he did: He was a sports guy. He did it even at Avon. He coached the women's softball team and encouraged the workers to be involved in other sports. But what he was really passionate about was kids' sports. He believed that kids in our community needed sports, needed something to do, something to burn off the energy, but he also believed in sports as a way to instill a positive work ethic.

He talked about that passion a lot in the warehouse. And my mom was, as I said, beginning to see that I was racing around all the other kids in the neighborhood, so I guess she got to talking to Mo about me. "Mo, you got to come see my boy."

Mo, he was like, "Aw, your son ain't shit." You know, he didn't believe her, or he was just shit-talking. But eventually, after my mom just kept on him about it, he agreed to come take a look.

I remember the day Mo came to Stuart Gardens. He showed up in his Chevy and talked to my mom from the driver's seat. Then he just watched me play through the windshield. As usual, we were playing hotball, tossing a football into the air and trying to tackle whichever dude caught it. I was just doing my thing out there, but I knew Mo was watching. I mean, I didn't know who he was yet, but I knew my mom cared. It always mattered to me who was watching. No different when I was eight. Time after time, I raced around these guys, through them, past them. When someone else caught it, I took down the unlucky motherfucker.

So after watching me for a couple minutes at most, Mo turned to my mom—Mommy told me he was like, bug-eyed—and he told her, "Aw shit, you got one." He wasn't talking trash anymore.

As I mentioned, I had been playing some organized football in Newport News. The first team I was on put me at wide receiver, and the whole year they threw only one pass to me. I remember it because I ran, got open, and the quarterback threw it straight up in the air. Here I am thinking, *This is my moment*, and the dude just threw it straight up in the air. The offensive line had a better chance to catch it than I did. We lost every game. *Every. Game.* And I would cry each time.

So next I played for a different team, the Trojans. On the first day of practice there, they had everyone try out, and I figured I'd try out at center. I just wanted to get on the field. So that year I was double zero, and I played center. Allen Iverson, offensive lineman. That's where it started. Obviously, that wasn't meant to be.

But when Mo got one look at me that day in Stuart Gardens, that was enough. He wanted me on his team, which was in the Aberdeen section of Hampton. It was a little far from where I was at in Newport News. But the Aberdeen Sports Association was known as a serious program. A man by the name of Butch Harper had resurrected it, and he brought along Mo as one of the coaches. At that time, Mo coached the intermediate football squad. That was for kids ten through twelve years old. So Mo had to figure out a couple things when it came to me.

The first was me not living in Hampton. Well, Mo arranged it one way or another—maybe we used Nana's address, I don't know. The second thing was my age. I mean, not only was I still eight, but I wasn't a big eight. In my MVP year in the NBA, I was 165 pounds "soaking wet," they said. At eight, I doubt I was 65 pounds soaking wet carrying two ten-pound dumbbells. In reality, I should have been playing Pee Wee football for another couple years. But Mo was adamant that I play intermediate. He managed to convince everyone that my little self was worth making an exception for. And the way I was, I always wanted to play up. It was true with all sports, from growing up with my uncles, Stevie and Greg, to eventually playing junior varsity at Bethel High when I was just in the eighth grade, to being the first ever to leave Georgetown early for the NBA. And it was also true of the friends I hung out with. I never really thought the kids my age matched up.

I was eight. And I was ready for intermediate football.

As I said, Aberdeen was a little way away from Stuart Gardens. It wasn't a walk. My mom got Mo to come that day to check me out so I could play in Aberdeen, but she wasn't about making sure I could make it to the practices or the games. I always had to figure that part out. And usually that meant Mo coming to get me. We were drawn to each other. He didn't have a son of his own—he had a wife and daughter, but no son. He had been an athlete. Baseball was actually his best sport, but he'd grown up playing football too. And he had this interest in helping kids of all kinds, but especially me.

When we first met, I just looked up to him. I looked up to my dad, of course, but my dad ended up being more of a street guy. He worked at the shipyard for a long time, with a real nine-to-five, but eventually the streets took over. Mo wasn't like that. He was a workingman. A family man. And I admired that about him. Truth is, I've not been perfect, but what I always wanted more than anything was a family that was strong and stuck together. And I do have that. Mo was an example from day one.

One of the biggest lessons he taught at the beginning was "If it's between you and me, it's me." What that meant was if it's you and me and the end zone, I'm making that tackle. Or if I have the ball, I'm scoring that touchdown. It was just knowing that out of all these people in the world who are talented, out of all of these people who are gifted, all these people fighting for the same shit, why can't it be me? It was about putting yourself first when it came to sports, but also in life. It was about having confidence. In the hood, there is fear. There's hesitation. And you had a lot of kids with low self-esteem. And what it comes down to is just asking yourself, *Why can't it be me?* Scoring the touchdown. Making the tackle. Shit, becoming president.

I've talked about growing up in Newport News and Hampton. Growing up in the streets. Being a project kid. I've talked about how it just seemed natural to steal some candy, get in some fights, all the shit we were getting up to. What didn't always seem natural to us was a better future. So those times, man, those times when you caught a glimpse of something better, it changed you. Raiders football gave us that glimpse.

So, as I was saying, to get to Aberdeen, Mo had to come pick me up. On my first day of practice he came to Stuart Gardens driving his ugly-ass red Chevy Blazer. It was a piece of shit, but none of us could say anything because it got around just fine, which was more than enough back then.

I remember getting to the field and seeing a bunch of big-ass dudes. The bigger guys looked down at me, and then up at Mo. You think they didn't question what Mo was thinking? *This little dude?* Inside, I was actually thinking the same thing. But I kept it inside and showed no doubt whatsoever. *Just give me the ball.*

I think within a few minutes of my first practice they began to see what I was about. I was running all over the place. A ball went up in the air, I was going to go get it. Something about being the little dude meant I never lost that edge. I always showed I was tough. Even in the last football game I ever played, the state championship my junior year at Bethel High, the play I remember best, everyone remembers best, was a hit I made playing safety. We will get there. But that pride, that toughness, it comes from the Raiders.

Come to think of it, it comes from Newport News too. Here I was, the smallest guy on the field. One early practice, I was playing defense. I ran down the quarterback from behind. I grabbed him by the jersey and just threw his ass to the ground. Everyone was staring at me like I was crazy. But here's what I was thinking: I'm from Newport News. These dudes are from Hampton. They're soft. Now, fast-forward to now, if you think that about Hampton dudes, you're gonna end up under the dirt. But that's the way I felt. Even when I was in high school. The Newport News guys would talk all kind of shit about Hampton, but they always knew I was one of them, which made them lay off me, and it also gave everyone on my team a little bit of confidence and credibility from that street mentality.

There was only one problem there with the Raiders early on. I was already a Dallas Cowboys fan—still am. A massive fan. The best player in the early 1980s, of course, was Tony Dorsett. He wore number 33. So I said I wanted to wear 33. So what's the problem? Jermaine Marshall wore that number. He was a young star. And he was a running back. So what could I say to that? I just wanted the number. And I stuck to it. I remember as the first game of the season approached, I just kept bothering everyone about it. Finally they were all like, "No, Chuck, you eight and you not getting that number."

I was eight years old. I had already seen a man's head nearly blown off. I was running around on the streets taking care of myself and my four-year-old sister. I was tough. But not getting number 33 made me cry. I literally cried right in front of everyone, so much I was getting dizzy. These boys were about to be men. I remember Mo shaking his head. The rest of the guys were just watching. Not long after that, Jermaine pulled me aside. He said "Bubbachuck, you care so damn much, you can have the number." That was the kind of guys we had on that team.

That first year, I was no star. I was just a little guy who was learning the ropes. The team was already on its way to being good though. When Mo first got the team up and going, that wasn't the case. They'd had a few bad years, but along the way, Mo had learned what he wanted to do, and the team was beginning to get better. We had talent, and we were starting to gain some attention. I just loved it. I loved the practices (yup, I did, fuck all y'all, lol), I loved the uniforms, I loved the perfect black and silver Raiders helmet that dwarfed my eight-year-old head, I loved just being around the guys.

But we didn't get a championship that first year. I had to wait for that. We lost in the playoffs. And after telling you so many nice things about him, I can tell you that Mo fucked it up. It was fourth-and-one, and we were down by six. We had one of the best running backs in the whole league in Jermaine. And Mo tried to outthink those guys, but really he out-thunk himself. Using Jermaine as a decoy, Mo called for a handoff to the fullback, who got stuffed. Season over. I cried as I always did when I lost back then.

But we won every championship after that. Four straight.

The next year, Mo made me quarterback. No quarterback wore 33, so then I moved to number 10, and later it was number 1, which I wore throughout high school.

That next year another thing happened. I met two dudes that were my best friends for years to come: Michael and Eric Jackson. They were actually cousins, but two very different people. They were kind of my good and bad angels for a long time.

Michael was the kind of dude your mom would be just so happy her son was chilling with. This dude came from a good family, and he was smart, and he never did any bad shit. Now he's an educator in Ohio. This man has a PhD. You told us that when we were kids, truth is we would've believed it because he was smart as hell, and disciplined. Nobody had anything bad to say about Michael Jackson. This would have been 1984 or 1985, so *the* Michael Jackson was legendary already. It was easy to pick a nickname for this dude—he was "Thrilla."

Thrilla could really run. He was, and still is, the only person who ever beat me in a race. He went to Bethel High with me; he ran track and played football there, by that time growing into his body and becoming a running back. For Mo, for us Raiders, he was a lineman. I don't think that ever sat well with him, but you would never hear this dude complain about anything.

Thrilla was the model friend. He had a way of saying my name. A way of saying it when he knew I was fucking up—"Buuuuubb," in a low kind of way, and then repeating it, "Buuuuubb." It used to get on my nerves. What he meant was "Calm your ass down," or "Chill the fuck out." He always looked out for me like that. He blames himself for not being there years later, the night that led to my arrest.

Eric, like Thrilla, was from Hampton. He had a good upbringing, but he ended up finding himself more on the streets. He was raised by a single mom but lived with his grandmom too. It was like if me and my mom had stayed with Nana in Hampton. Even then, we just called Eric "E." He was as small as I was, and fast. He played wide receiver, flanker, and sometimes, when Mo wanted to let me just go get the ball, he'd have E play QB. *Just throw it as far and you can, and let Bubbachuck go get it.* That was a play we had.

That second year, we just started killing, man. It was a show. We'd play on a Saturday, and there might be four or five games running at a time on a big field, split up for the intermediate league. If you wanted to know where to find the Raiders, you just looked for the game that everyone was watching. No one would watch the other games, even the parents of the kids in the other games. Supposedly there are tapes of those games. We've tried to get our hands on them, but people being crazy, they want like a million dollars for the Bubbachuck tapes. But man, we were just out there having fun.

And some days were not all that fun. Mo decided after we won one championship, he was going to get us playing the top competition in the region. So this time he put together a game against Petersburg, a town about an hour away. The day of the game came and it was one of those real rainy days. Rainy and cold as hell. It was so muddy, you hit the ground one time, and your whole uniform was black.

When we got there, *oh shit.* We looked across the field, and these motherfuckers were so big. They had gold teeth in their mouth. They were crazy looking. I was the youngest dude on the team, the smallest, and I was the QB. We ended up beating them 7–0 or something like that. After the game it got crazy, and there was a huge fight. One dude had a yard marker that he was fighting with, just swinging it like a sword or one of them bayonets. The rain, the mud, and a fucking brawl. We got the hell out of there. The next year Mo asked, did we want to play them again? We were like, "Hell no." That shit was too violent.

After our fourth straight championship it was over. We were all legends. Next, we were supposed to go to high school. From a football standpoint, we were ready. Thrilla and E went on to Bethel that next year. I got hung up with some problems of my own making.

But before I get to all that, I haven't even talked about basketball.

FOUR

NO, NOT BASKETBALL

Playing football was my first love. I didn't play basketball at all at the start. It was something I always thought was soft. Football was the best way to show how tough I was, I guess. And that's what most of the guys around the way would play.

Well, one day, I must have been about nine or ten, Mom came to me and told me she was taking me to basketball tryouts.

I was like, "Hell no."

Man, when I got something into my head, it was hard to change it. I focused on football, and I even played some baseball, but I wanted nothing to do with basketball. Part of it was I wanted to chill out after all the football stuff was done. I loved my freedom.

But my mom wasn't taking no for an answer. And she put me right in the car and drove over to the gym. Now, I can't remember where it was we went exactly. It was some kind of tryout for the rec league. And she literally had to drag me in there. I was crying, sobbing.

We walked onto the court. And I didn't even have to start playing. That's the crazy part. I saw all the dudes I knew from around the way, from playing football, and here they were in the gym. And I was just thinking to myself, *why not me?* So I just sat there watching. I must have watched for ten, fifteen minutes. I had to see the moves they made, the way they shot the ball. And then I was ready. It was the way I learned—visually. It's still the way I think and learn. It was like this: Since I was little, I was an artist. I could see something and draw it, recreate it on the page. And that's how it was with sports. I would watch, then imagine myself doing it. Then go out and do it.

So I stepped out on the court. And I repeated what I'd just seen. Natural.

It was over. Basketball was my game. It took about a week. I would start each practice just watching. Here's a layup. That's a jump shot. Here's how you stand on defense. Okay fine, I didn't pay that much attention to defense at first.

All I could say to my mom was, "Thank you Mom, thank you Mom, I appreciate that." She knew better than me. You know when your mom tells you something, and goddammit she's right? "Eat this, it's good!" And then, *Oh shit, it's delicious.* That was me with basketball.

So over that first week or two I managed to master the basics. Within a month, I was the best dude on the team.

But basketball didn't end up being like football in those early days. I didn't have all kinds of success winning championships as a little kid.

My coach up until high school was Bob Barefield. Like Mo, he was over in Aberdeen, in Hampton. He was an older dude who knew everything about basketball, and everything about kids in Newport News and Hampton. So he would come to the neighborhood and pick me up. He had a little van. He'd roll around Stuart Gardens looking for me, asking where I was. Got to the point that people recognized the van, like they recognized my mom's whistle, and they'd come get me.

In the beginning he would pick up me and Snapper. Coach Barefield knew that we were different. We were the project kids. He would make us comb our hair before he allowed us to get out of the van. The other kids on that team were from Hampton—they had parents who could get them to the game, get them to comb their hair right. Mike Jackson was on that team, even though basketball wasn't really his sport. So this was lesson number one with Coach Barefield: combing our hair.

Playing basketball wasn't really like how it was with Mo. Maybe it was a lack of discipline. But I really thought I was Michael Jordan. So let's say I got a steal or something. I'm in the open court. And I'd go and rock the cradle, do it just like Mike, but then I'd miss the layup. I would lean in on my layups like he did on his dunks, and obviously I couldn't dunk yet, but I'd lean in like I could and bang the layup off the backboard. I couldn't do anything regular. I remember all the coaches, they'd be like, "I'll buy you a pack of Now and Laters if you can just make a regular layup, don't try anything fancy." But I would never do it. And it would be frustrating as hell to the coaches.

Coach Barefield wanted more from me than just winning games. We never won any championships anyway. He would talk in those van rides about the blueprint. He had this Southern accent and a high-pitched scratchy voice, a country kind of way about him. He talked in that way about how we were going to stay out of trouble, keep from dying or going to jail. That's what he had in mind when he had us comb our hair.

And there it was again. Another person who believed in me. Another person who had charted his own life and was doing good—and made me believe I could do the same.

He would give me tough love. But it was more for messing up in school than for messing up on the court. My mom would tell him if I was failing a class or not going to school. And he would threaten me that I wasn't going to get to play anymore. As bad as I sometimes was, he never followed through on those threats. He was too nice. He hated to see me get upset.

From the beginning, it was important to me how I looked on the court. That's the way my mom taught me. So I had the Jordans from the beginning. And I wore these high-ass socks, with knee pads. I look back at the picture now and I have no idea what it was with the knee pads. But I set it up so the sock went right up to the knee pad, like one big part of the uniform. Like a sleeve for your leg.

As I got better and better, there was the issue of being on the travel squad. Finally, they asked me to travel with them to a tournament in Kansas. I don't remember how we did, whether we won or lost our games. What I do remember is that I was obsessed with getting these Nike Air Force Ones. We had no money, but I was just bugging my mom. To me, I couldn't go to that tournament without those Nikes. And so that month we had no electricity or hot water. But she got me my kicks.

When I think about my early basketball education though, it was the Aberdeen playground where it was really at. Basically the littler kids would play during the day, in the summertime, when it was hot as a motherfucker. Then when the sun was about to go down, that's when the games got real. I remember, all I wanted was to play in those night games, but if you weren't ready, well, you weren't getting on that court.

So I spent my summers figuring it out as a kid. Learning how to really play the game, about getting to the hole and finishing. It wasn't about some cheap fouls. And it wasn't about a jump shot either. You had to bring it. Of course, you wanted to stay on the court by winning.

It was about when I was in eighth grade, around thirteen or fourteen years old, that I started playing during the night games. And it was like overnight, going from not even being allowed to get on there to all of the sudden I was the best player out there—the guy who got picked first. That was about as happy as I ever was. My uncles Stevie and Greg were out there playing then. That was me, always playing up. That's what I was all about.

To give you an idea how big those games were, there was one weekend at the beginning of summertime. A few days before that, I had broken my thumb. So my dad took me to the hospital, and they put a cast on it. Fast-forward, it was just a perfect day. It got cool as the night came. Everyone was there. I'm not just talking about the dudes playing the game. All the girls were there too, chilling, enjoying the late light and the cooler air. Packed in on the benches, leaning against the fences. And watching. One thing about me, there's a reason you could count on me bringing it when I was playing in LA or Atlanta. Lots of fine people to impress.

I wanted to play so fucking bad. So you know what I did, I went home and put the cast in some water, and took the damn thing off. Wrapped my hand up with some ace bandages, and just went out there and played. It hurt so bad. But my team kept winning. I refused to relinquish the court that night, game after game. Coming home I was crying. And Daddy was like, "You're just going to have to let it heal on its own now." He wasn't taking me to get a new cast, that's for sure. That thumb still hurts sometimes to this day.

That was the summer before I was supposed to start high school. It was a crazy summer. I had become a good basketball player, but I wasn't any kind of playground legend yet. In football it was different. Everyone knew me, and so the plan was Notre Dame, I think even then. But basketball, I loved it. I dreamed of playing in the NBA, but that seemed like a distant hope.

FIVE

SURVIVING MIDDLE SCHOOL

School. I never liked it. I hated it, I guess you could say. And it's something that's hard to explain. But the hours didn't agree with me. I didn't like getting up early. I still don't. And I didn't like sitting there listening all day.

So as soon as I could figure out how, I started skipping school. I would leave the house, find my friends to hang out with, a lot of times some older kids like Tony Clark, the swindler, or other kids cutting school like Snapper. And it wasn't hard. My dad was out on the streets more and more, and my mom, she would be out as well. So I had a lot of autonomy, I guess you could say. My mom would come home, not always sure from where, and she'd find out I'd missed a day or two—or more. She would whoop my ass. But then she would be gone, and I would take off again. I would just tell her I was staying with my friends. Something like that.

While my body didn't feel right in the morning hours, when night came, I felt alive. I was just like my mom in that way. We would stay up late together, and as I got older I would hang out until the late hours with my friends, just talking, chilling. As a kid, you couldn't get me to shut up. I'd be joking around, making impressions, cracking everyone up. I was like the class clown—minus the "class" part. It would be late as hell, in the streets, as often as not. That was a pattern that never left me, from when I was young enough to slip out my sister Brandy's window in Stuart Gardens, to wandering the dorms late at night at Georgetown, to chilling at the TGI Fridays on City Line Avenue in Philly.

When I did go to school, I got along with everyone. The teachers liked me. I wasn't a troublemaker, a bad kid, nothing like that. It was more about me just making it *to* school. By seventh or eighth grade, my teachers and everyone knew about me. They knew I was a football star. Remember what I said about the crowds for our Raiders football games. The teachers all knew, the kids knew. And everyone always liked me, which made the teachers pay more attention and become more of a pain in the ass to me. It got to the point one year that the principal came to me. He said, "Son, you got to start coming to school. If you come ten straight days, I will take you shopping." He knew I didn't have much. And it worked. The next ten days I was in school, and sure enough he lived up to his end of the bargain. He took me out and got me some clothes.

The next day, what do you think I did? I didn't show up. He was mad as hell. Who wouldn't be? That doesn't feel good to be played like that.

It was tough at home too. My dad was in and out. He had his own spot in Glen Gardens by then. My mom was hanging out with this other dude. They had gotten into a fight, and he'd hit her with a broom, injuring her pretty bad.

My dad heard about it and came to the house. He found the dude in the bathroom. So then the man ran out of the bathroom and down the steps to get away. Before chasing him, Daddy busted into my room looking for something. He was looking for my baseball bat, but he grabbed my fucking football helmet. I'll never forget it.

"Daddy, no, not my helmet!"

I got to back up for a second to explain about that helmet. Mo was cool with a guy who owned a car-detailing spot. This guy used to paint our helmets to perfection: a deep, spotless black with the silver contrast. He had them looking just like the NFL Raiders helmet. I had just got mine done, got a brand-new double quarter cage, everything. Man, my favorite goddamn helmet. So that's why I wanted to protect that motherfucker.

My dad ignored my plea, grabbed the helmet, and chased after the dude, out our front door and into the street. All of us—me, Brandy, my mom—peeked out the window, and we saw Daddy on top of the dude. All you could see was my helmet flying up in the air, like pieces of it. Shit was flying up in the air, Daddy was just smacking him in his head, and the helmet was just popping into pieces.

That wasn't too long before we got evicted from Stuart Gardens.

So with me being a night owl, and the chaos I sometimes found at home, I never went to middle school every day. But two things really made it go wrong during my first eighth-grade year. Yup, *first.* It took me three years to make it through seventh and eighth grades. I probably attended classes the equivalent of one year total.

The first thing that threw me off was basketball. The second was a girl.

So that fall—this would have been 1988—I played Raiders football. Come November, there were basketball tryouts for the school team. But I was missing school, like I did, and sure enough, I missed the tryouts. I came back to school a couple days later and went to practice. You got to understand, I was so much better than everyone else on that team. But the coach said no. The principal said no. I had missed the tryout and they were going to be strict as a motherfucker about it.

Being strict as a motherfucker never worked with me, man. Never. (Ask Billy King and Larry Brown.) I just said *fuck these motherfuckers* and walked away, and I stopped going to school entirely.

The other part of it, as I said, was a girl. She was older—an eleventh grader. She was something to look at and she was fun as hell. But more than anything, she was my first. Man, I just fell in love with her. I was young. All I can do now is laugh.

She was in eleventh grade, or should have been. She wasn't going to school either. So what I did was I just went over her house. I would go there, lay down with her, and go to sleep. She lived in Stuart Gardens as well. Her mother just let me lay up there all damn day, a fourteen-year-old basically living at her house, neither of us going to school.

My mom was out more and more. Brandy would stay with friends, or I'd help take care of her. We never had any goddamn money. Like with my shoes, sometimes certain things got bought, which meant our bills didn't get paid. One advantage for me was that our phone was always off, so the school couldn't call. And with my mom out, I could always get the mail before she did. In other words, she had no idea how much school I was missing.

Then, because football season was over, I wasn't seeing Mo as much, so he didn't know either. And it was just so easy.

But it came to an end. Real fast. I was over at this girl's house. This was pretty close to the end of my first eighth-grade year. I was just chilling and someone started knocking on the door. She got up to get it and in walked my mom. I was lying in bed like a grown-ass man. Just my boxers on. To this day, I have no idea how my mom found out I was there.

She came in mad as hell. "Why ain't you in school?"

I was quick as a motherfucker. "I was at school. School is over."

She looked at me like, *Boy, I'm still your momma.* Then she informed me of the time—it wasn't even eleven o'clock yet.

So I said, "School got out early today." She said to stay right there. This house, unlike my own, had a working phone. She called the school right then. She got on the line with somebody from the office, who I guess told her all the other kids were still in school.

My mom grabbed me and just started screaming and swinging. You know what I did? I ran. I ran right on out of that house and away from there. She yelled after me, "Go on ahead and run! You'll be back!" She was right. That night I was back home. Everyone was fucking disappointed in me.

They came to find out I had missed sixty-nine days of school. That's the number I remember.

A couple days later, Mo came over. He was like, "Chuck, what the fuck is this? You missed sixty-nine days?" Evidently, he and my mom had been talking. At this point, it was obvious I was going to have to repeat eighth grade. And he and my mom made a decision together. I was going to go live with Mo in Hampton, and I was going to go do eighth grade over again at Jefferson Davis Middle School. It wasn't like I had a choice in the matter, so I didn't complain. And I was a long way from straightening out. But I don't know what would have happened if I didn't have that place to go, to get a new address, and to try again at a new school.

It's hard to keep everything straight though, because it was right around then that we had to leave Stuart Gardens. It was also right around then that my dad got locked up on a drug charge. He hadn't exactly been living with us for a while anyway. He was, like I said, living over in Glen Gardens at that point. Glen Gardens was another project—a much worse project that was near the border between Newport News and Hampton, but definitely on the Newport News side. It wasn't as spread out, and later it became a symbol of all the shit that was just hitting the Peninsula—the real drug shit had arrived. They eventually bulldozed that shit down later in the 1990s, but at this point it was the late '80s, and it was going strong. That's where my dad was at, and where I'd go when I was tired of staying at Mo's.

My mom and Brandy, who was ten or eleven, were kind of going from place to place figuring it out. One thing about Brandy was she would just leave, and my mom wouldn't know where she went. So me and my mom would go looking for her, crying, worrying someone snatched her up. But we always found her. She'd be at some friend's house. And we'd lecture her about letting us know, but she kept doing it. One time we were out looking for her for hours. Phone didn't work, so the only thing we could do was search. We always found her, and she'd get her ass whooped.

So then I started living with Mo, his wife, Phyllis, and their daughter. They welcomed me. It was the first time having a phone, having heat all the time, having food all the time, all the shit that's supposed to be natural. I had to get used to that. I felt like I was Prince Akeem from *Coming to America*.

Mo's wife was the stricter of the two. They had rules, like I couldn't come home too late. And as I've mentioned, rules never really worked with me. So even though I had normal shit that felt like luxuries, I would let myself out and be gone for a couple days at a time. Looking back, I know that probably pissed them off, especially Mo's wife. But it was hard: As much time as I had spent with sports in Hampton, my other life, the less "respectable" side, was in Newport News—my friends and family there, my freedom there.

I did a little better at Jefferson Davis for my second attempt at eighth grade. But I still missed days. The same shit. In the fall I was better because I played junior varsity football for the high school, and the coach kept an eye on me. Then I played basketball in the winter, and Coach Mike Bailey, who would become my high school basketball coach, and everyone else had their eye on me from that. But come the spring, I had no sports teams and the weather was getting nice. I wasn't going to school much. I wasn't staying with Mo enough. And it was the end of the year. We had some final tests. I didn't even go. I just blew off the whole thing. I had other things I was more interested in going on. I didn't go to the last day of class. Didn't pick up my report card. Didn't even know if they passed me. I just kind of shoved it down and ignored it. I thought I might have to do a third eighth-grade year.

*

It was around that time that I began to see the drugs, and the other side of it: the money, the opportunity.

This is probably the hardest part to talk about. Who knows the truth about it? Mo. My mom. The people in Newport News.

My Hampton people, a lot of them, my coaches and all that, they don't know about it. But what happened, well, it was a terrible time period, and then it was over.

It started for me in maybe 1989. The beginning is a blur. Basically, crack had come into Newport News and Hampton. All I knew was that it was new. You'd hear it on the street, and the way people talked about it. Cocaine had been around for a while, but it was expensive. Then it was this thing called crack, cheap as hell and twice as good.

I was still terrified of drugs. So the part that resonated for me was the fucking *money*. There was so much money in it. And growing up without, that's what I wanted.

There was this older Newport News dude. He was one of the main guys who helped us get started eventually. He was from the Woodsong projects, not Stuart Gardens. He was one of the first guys I saw with a pimped-out car. He had this lime-green Chevy Blazer, with the rims, and the roof cut. Watching him drive that thing around, it was a big deal. It was like something totally different. He'd made it. Mo represented something different too, a real job, a real house, a real family. But so did this dude, man. He just seemed to have it figured out. He's in prison to this day for some shit he didn't even do, if you ask my opinion. I paid a bunch of his legal bills over the years, but it hasn't helped yet.

Arnie was one of the other guys. He was also a few years older than me. He's a dude who, to this day, is hard to talk about. We ended up splitting on bad terms much later, after he came with me to the NBA. But back then, he was my brother. Then there was E. He was the one guy who really wasn't from the neighborhood, being a Hampton guy. But he was drawn into it too. There were other dudes on top of that.

Mike Jackson, Thrilla, he never saw any of this. I hid it from all my coaches and dudes I was chilling with in Hampton. It was like two sides of my life. It's all so hard to talk about because I never have. I never wanted anyone to know.

The epicenter was in Glen Gardens, where my dad was, and where I'd stay sometimes. He wasn't doing great then, when he was out of jail. Glen Gardens was where a lot of the Newport News guys would gravitate to hustle. That was just a hot spot for all the activity. I had my own little setup.

At the time, I loved it. I had money in my pocket. I bought what I wanted. I had the shoes. I had the clothes. It was as great as I could imagine. You have to understand, I never really had anything, and now I could get what I wanted, when I wanted.

It didn't take long to identify the people that were fucked-up on the shit. It also didn't take long to figure out who was bringing it in. With their gold chains and cars, they weren't exactly trying to hide it. That was what I wanted to be. I was never interested in the drugs themselves. Maybe when it first came, I was too young. And I got scared off by seeing a bunch of people close to me fall hard to addiction. Like for example, when I was staying at Glen Gardens, I would sometimes stay with my homeboy, and his mom would come in when I was asleep. She would come in and constantly wake me up and be asking me for it because she knew what I was doing out there. It was like I could never get any sleep. Shit like that, so from the beginning I decided it wasn't for me.

It was also knowing I was worth something. I had football and basketball. And there wasn't a day that I didn't believe in my heart I'd make it big. So I wasn't fucking that up with drugs. That's the one smart decision I started with and ended with.

This is how it worked: One of the older guys, the guys who were really making it happen, would give me $100 of work. That was like maybe twenty bags at $5 apiece. After I sold that off, I'd get another $100 worth of work. For each $100, you paid $70 back and kept the rest. It wasn't a big margin, so you couldn't be taking any shorts.

During the week, it was the older guys who controlled things in Glen Gardens. The little guys like myself would be stuck with the crumbs. Our time came on the weekends. That's when the older guys would go to the clubs to spend the money they'd made. Meanwhile, we little guys would have the whole weekend to ourselves, and I might end up with $1,000. Imagine that, fourteen or fifteen like I was, coming from flat broke, now with a thousand dollars in my pocket.

It was a terrible, terrible summer. But as it was happening, I didn't see it like that. Every day, I woke up, money in my pocket, and we would go to TJ Maxx and pick out our outfit for the day. We would eat at Red Lobster. We were renting cars. It was just so different, so much more than what I knew or grew up with. After a while, I had regular customers. Some of them are good, respectable people to this day. They had my beeper number. That was the easiest money I made.

It was spring and summer of that second eighth-grade year that I was most involved in that business. The truth was I was already getting a sports rep. I played JV football at Bethel as an eighth grader, pretty much unheard-of. And Coach Bailey was already invested in me. That same summer, he was trying to get me to do Summer League, and he'd come to Glen Gardens searching. I also had Mo, who had already nearly killed me after finding out about me missing most of the preceding school year.

Unlike Coach Bailey, Mo knew what I was doing and exactly where I was. So I just tried to avoid him. I might avoid him for days, but he'd always be back. Again and again and again. He showed up in that Chevy. It got to where everyone in Glen Gardens knew that damn car. E would be like, "Goddammit, Mo is back." And E didn't feel too good about it either. E was a Raider and revered Mo. Every time Mo showed up and saw E, it hurt the both of them, I think.

I remember one time I got in Mo's car just because he was irritating everyone on the whole block. My crew came to me a few times. They were like, "Mo's got to get offa here, and there ain't but one reason he's here, and that's your ass." I wasn't hearing it from them, and I wasn't hearing it from Mo. I had a taste of money, a taste of hustling. I was trying to provide for my sister. I was taking care of my mom as much as I could. No one was getting me out of there. But they started saying it more and more. So this one time I was like, *Okay, let me talk to him and get him out of there.* Soon as I got in the car, Mo started talking to me about what it was that I was giving up, all the talent I had. He asked me what I was up to. He knew. But I talked to him a little bit about it and told him about my customers. I'll never forget that man's face as I told him some of the names.

The thing about Mo was he was always happy once we'd driven a few blocks away, just to be chilling. And as much as I hid from his ass, I liked escaping with him too. It wouldn't take long to get over his angry stuff, and then we'd be onto something funny. And even that day, we just started laughing about these sorry motherfuckers who were coming to me for their fix. Sad as shit. But it was funny in that moment.

It wasn't just Mo trying to get me out. My homeboys were urging me off the street too. It was because of the attention I brought. But there was something else. I think they saw what Mo saw. This wasn't my path. I had a different future. In a way, the only person that needed convincing was me. No one else was trying to keep me there. And the shit just got to adding up.

One time outside Glen Gardens this dude drove up and asked me what I had. I showed him in my hand, and motherfucker grabbed my arm, but I would not let go. I wasn't going to be short. So he put his car in drive and dragged me down half the goddamn block. I shook loose, body still intact. The older dudes were just laughing at my ass.

Another time, I handed the shit to this other dude before he paid me. When I asked for the money, he tried to get in my face and fight me. I ended up beating his ass real bad.

The worst was one day when I was in a darkened hallway in a Glen Gardens building. Somebody had smashed the light years ago. Or maybe it just stopped working and nobody gave a shit. It was Glen Gardens, after all. It was the middle of summer. There was a constant line of people, a line of cars, the flow of people wanting a fix was just constant. People wanted what they wanted.

This dude came up to me in the hallway. He was twice my age probably. I was still just a teenager. He asked me for something, so I turned around to get it. I turned because I didn't know any better. Next thing was, in the dark hallway, I felt cool metal touching the back of my head.

"Gimme the fucking shit, man."

And there it was. I was done. Dead. I remember that moment like it was yesterday. I was still a kid and I'd already fucked it all up. I hadn't even gotten to high school, and already it was over. What was my Nana going to think? My mom? Mo? I wasn't even going to make it to motherfucking high school.

So I did the only thing I could think to do. I emptied my pockets. I had whatever was left from the stash, and what I was thinking was, *How am I going to make this money up?* But at the same time, another thought in my head was even louder: *I'd rather live another day.* So I gave him what he was asking for. Never turning around. Just waiting to see what he did. And as he grabbed my shit, the cold ring of the gun's muzzle pushed harder against my skin.

Finally, the pressure eased back. I couldn't believe I was still alive. After a second I turned to look, and I saw the dude's back. He was running. I didn't even think. So as fast as I was, I chased his ass down and I was screaming at everybody that he had robbed me. It was real bad on him after that. An ambulance had to come to take him away.

It was a bad summer.

*

My mom found out about it. Of course she did.

She came down to Glen Gardens one day. My heart sank as I saw her.

"I know what y'all out here doing," she said.

And I was like, "What am I supposed to do? I don't have shit. I gotta eat and I want shit for school coming up. I'm about to start ninth grade."

She goes—and I'll never forget it—"Well I know what you're doing. I know you messed up 'cause I'm not here to watch over you. All I want you to do is make me one promise."

And I said, "Alright, what is it?"

"I want you to stop once the school year starts."

"Yeah, as soon as the school year starts I'll stop. I promise."

Man, this motherfucker didn't know if he had passed the eighth grade, whether he would even be let in the front door of Bethel High. But I meant it when I agreed to that promise. I knew that had to be it.

One day near the end of that summer of 1990, I ran into my sister Brandy. She was staying with one of her friends, and she had nothing for school. I had a rental car—no license, but I had me a car. So I took her to the mall. I told her to get whatever she wanted. She went to the TJ Maxx and picked out all her school clothes. She went and got her schoolbooks and supplies. She had this smile on her face. It was the two of us, brother and sister, almost regular. It was one of those days I remember because it felt so good to have something, to help her get what she needed.

The dudes from Newport News, they were basically like, *We got you, Chuck. You will be able to get your sister clothes and get yourself clothes. Chill with us. But your days hustling are over.*

Mo. My mom. The crew. My sister. All saying the same thing—hustling was not my path.

I showed up at Mo's the day before school started. I went to bed, and the next morning I went to Bethel High for the first day.

I walked up to the building. I looked at the student list. And there it was. My name. Allen Iverson. I had been accepted to high school.

II

MY TRIALS ON AND OFF THE COURT

Jail

Sitting in jail for the first time, the motherfucker was hot.

It was late summer and it was Virginia. They had just pulled me out of the courtroom, everyone crying. And I crossed this line. All of the sudden the air-conditioning stopped. They put me in a van, and as it drove away from court, people outside started following it until it drove faster than they could run. I watched their faces get smaller as the van brought me to jail.

They put me in a holding cell first. I don't know what they were doing as I sat in this little room. All that lay before me was time. Time to think. Time to get used to the fact that my time wasn't my time anymore. But you can't think about anything when it's hot like that. The air wasn't moving, no windows or open doors.

I was still wearing my gray suit. My lawyer told me to wear a suit. I had to look respectable for the judge on sentencing day. My mom had picked out the suit for me. I put it on that morning and looked at myself in the mirror. That's a handsome dude. Everyone smiled at me, like, all grown-up. Not a thing they can do to a respectable young man like that.

Right.

Now I was in jail, wearing the damn thing in the late summer heat. It felt like hours waiting. I had no idea when it would end. So I took off the jacket first. Then rolled up the shirt sleeves. Then I took off my shoes. My socks. Before long, I took the shirt off, leaving just my undershirt. Then my pants came off, and who knows what I looked like at that moment, but I wasn't as hot.

Eventually an officer came in. He looked at me, a kid, just in his undershirt and drawers. He laughed.

When it finally came time, I left the cell with the suit all bunched up in the corner.

Man, I wore suits after that. But what good did that suit do that day? Was that bunched-up, useless suit the reason why I never wanted to wear that shit again? I don't know.

So how did I land in jail? Better yet, how did I get out? Put it like this: It's a good thing I accomplished everything in my junior year of high school. Because my senior year I was a jailbird.

SIX

HIGH SCHOOL FOOTBALL

One thing never changed about me and school. The hours didn't agree with me. So most mornings, it was me sleeping until Mike Jackson arrived in his little black 1981 Toyota Tercel. I was living with Mo in Hampton, just a short way from where Mike lived. Most of high school, he'd come rolling down the street to pick me up. And most times, it wasn't like I was dressed and wearing my book bag ready for school. I'd be asleep as likely as not. Mike, he was straight A's, so he didn't want to be late. But if I'm being honest, with him bringing me, he often was.

Bethel High School was a beautiful place. People from all over went there. My mom had gone there, and there were plenty of dudes like me from Hampton. But there were white kids, there were Asian kids. It was like the United Nations. It was poor kids and rich kids. When we talk about what eventually happened at the bowling alley, and when we talk about Virginia, there's a whole race element to it. But at Bethel, at least when I started, it didn't feel that way. I had great relationships with everyone, including my coaches, who were both white men. And I had friends of all colors.

Bethel football started right up as I began my freshman year. They had me on varsity, of course. But for some reason, maybe my size, the coach didn't really see me as a quarterback. Now he didn't see me as an offensive lineman either. He had better sense than that. I think it just made sense to put the fast little dude at wide receiver. Of course, I was accustomed to being the quarterback, but that's how it went. The problem was they felt like they had more prototypical passers ahead of me. I also played safety, which, because I was a Raider, was really what I loved: to hit people. Tackle people. While I wanted the ball in my hands, you can get the ball in all kinds of ways—interceptions, kick returns. And any way I got it, I made it my mission to score.

Now, the year before, remember, they had moved me to Jefferson Davis Middle School. And they had me playing JV football for the high school that fall. So everybody knew me when I started at Bethel. In fact, people used to come watch the JV games. Those would be in the morning. They weren't meant to be something you watched. But people started hearing murmurs about me, and they started showing up. I was just a wide receiver. And I put on a show. I used to tell the older guys, "Watch, I'm going to return this kick for a touchdown." And I'd do it. But that was junior varsity. Once they let me in the door at Bethel, it was varsity.

Our coach was Dennis Kozlowski, or "Coach Koz" as we called him. He was a great coach, but we fought at times. I mean, things had changed. I lived in Hampton with Mo. I was in high school now. I didn't have excuses. But even then, it's not like I went to school every day. Sometimes Thrilla drove to school by himself, especially on Mondays. I didn't want to end those weekends, man! And the teachers, they would kind of warn me before they went to Coach Koz and let him know. But I would push and see how much I could get away with. The teachers were just regular people, and they began to see the level of excitement I brought, so they didn't want to get me in trouble until they had to. They enjoyed the show themselves.

So there was a push and a pull. With Mo, with Coach Koz, and with Mike Bailey, my basketball coach. They'd try to get me in school, for me to be eligible of course. But they also truly cared about me, and they knew school was important to whatever future was in front of me.

When Coach Koz was on me, I would give him excuses. He'd try and work with me. Then he'd get frustrated. He was also the track coach. That caused some friction itself, because of course he wanted me running track. But track never appealed to me. Running for no particular reason? Nah, give me a ball and a place to put it, man. So I didn't have any interest in plain old track.

I remember one time he was on my ass because I was missing school or something like that. So he said to me he was going to kick my ass off the team unless I ran track. So I'm thinking, *Okay then, I will just run track.* I had been the fastest motherfucker on every team and still was. Thrilla, the one dude who had beaten me in a race in my whole damn life, was on that track team too. How bad could it be?

It was bad. Coach Koz was like, "Okay, now run a 400." One time around the track. I remember Mike was there watching. So I ran. And I ran my ass off too. But it wasn't like returning a kick or interception. It hurt so bad. And that was that. My one and only day running track.

Football was another story. But before I get too much into it, I have to explain the dynamics of the whole thing.

In Hampton, there were two big rivals, but it wasn't exactly even. There was the Hampton High Crabbers, and *then* there was the Bethel Bruins. Like the little brother. In fact, Bethel had only existed since 1968, when it was created because Hampton High had grown too big. So it was like a little brother from the beginning, just there for the Hampton overflow.

Every year, the Hampton–Bethel game was by far the biggest. It'd be like a Cowboys–Eagles game. It didn't matter what else happened. If you lost that game, it was a bad year. Now, the old money was from Hampton High. You talk to some people, they will tell you that's what me going to jail was actually about. See, we were about to flip that rivalry, and some people, powerful people, didn't like to see Bethel on top. I don't know about all that.

But coming into my freshman year, the fall of 1990, Hampton had won nine out of the last eleven games between the two schools. Worse than that, they had won the Peninsula District title thirteen straight years! Meanwhile, we hadn't even made the district playoffs since 1976. Coach Koz was quick to remind us that he'd won two state titles in 1974 and '76. But that didn't really mean anything to us. That was a long-ass time ago.

Coach Koz had me at wide receiver and defensive back. I wanted to play quarterback eventually. But like I said, I had two dudes in front of me. Paul London was the starter and a star, and another underclassman was the backup. London's main position was defensive back. And his best sport was baseball, if you can believe it. That year, he won Athlete of the Year in Virginia.

So I had to pay my dues. But I got on the field. My first big game came against Ferguson in mid-September 1990. We mostly ran the ball that game, and got out ahead. But in the second half the Ferguson dudes started coming back. Down just a touchdown, 21–14, they were driving to tie it up. That's when I got an interception with fourteen seconds left. Game over. Everyone started coming up to me cheering. You know I got my ass out of bed and came to school the next week because everyone was patting me on the back.

Even when we lost games here and there, I started getting comfortable. In a big loss against Phoebus, I remember Paul tossing me a fifty-yard pass and just gliding into the end zone. It's something that I'd keep feeling going forward. The moment you know you belong. The moment you realize. It's like the world around you is chaotic, loud, uncontrollable, and then you get out there among the other dudes and it quiets down, and the body takes over. It would just happen. It was like when I was watching those dudes playing basketball the first time, and then I was able to own the court moments later. Now a freshman, the interception, and the fifty-yard reception. A few years later, the moment I crossed over Jordan in the NBA. Okay, I'm getting ahead of myself.

Back to football. That 1990 season didn't end well for us. After we lost a couple close ones, things took another turn at the end of October. Paul injured his collarbone. So Coach stuck with the backup, even though he knew that I could play quarterback too. "Big strong arm. He can go deep," he'd say about the other guy.

First game without Paul, we played Lafayette, which was not a powerhouse, let's put it like that. They won two games that whole year. But we were only winning by a touchdown late in the game, so Coach gave me a shot at QB. Then I threw an interception, and they came back and tied up the score. So of course, I had to make up for that. First I returned the kick to the thirty-five-yard line. Then we moved the ball down the field. Finally, the line gave me some time, and with about a minute left I threw the only pass I completed the whole game: a 34-yard touchdown.

Everyone was elated, and I was thinking maybe I'd get more chances at QB.

We were 5-4. The next week was our last game of the year. At that point we were already eliminated from the district playoffs, but we could still earn a winning record. More importantly, that final game, as always, was against the Hampton Crabbers, who were motivated. Besides trying to beat their rival yet again, they were looking for their fourteenth straight division title.

In the end, it didn't matter who played quarterback. We were missing London, and Hampton hadn't been champs so long for no reason. The less said about that game the better. We didn't score a goddamn point. Not one. And they scored 53 of them!

53–0.

We wouldn't forget it. It wasn't going to happen again.

Sophomore year was pivotal. Obviously we wanted to be better. And I wanted to be quarterback. But the greatest blessing probably came when

Mike Jackson, by then a junior, joined the team. As the track star, he was Coach Koz's favorite. Coach was more proud of the fact that his mile-relay team had placed second in the state than of anything else. Mike had been on that relay team. At the same time, no one could blame Coach for loving Mike, since Thrilla was everyone's favorite.

As we started up practices, there was still the question of quarterback. When you're in high school, every decision just seems so big. We talked about it, dissected it. I cared about it more than anything. And it seemed like Coach wanted to do anything but name me the starter. He probably had his reasons. "Too much too soon," some shit like that. But that's not how it feels when you're sixteen and fucking brimming with confidence and lust to get in there.

Coach Koz couldn't decide, so he said me and the rival QB would both get reps in the games. That's all I needed to hear, because I knew that as long as they let me play, my play wouldn't let him keep me off the field.

But it was the defense that carried us early on that season. We started the season with four straight shutouts. The first game, against Norview, we won 34–0, but there were two parts of that game I really remember. The first was that because our senior running back, Steve Rimpsey, got injured, Mike Jackson got a shot and busted out with more than two hundred yards and a couple of touchdowns. The second thing I really remember was that I had five interceptions by myself. *Five interceptions!* And that was all I wanted—for them to have to account for me on both sides of the field.

We finally gave up a point in our fifth game to Kecoughtan, but still made it to 5-0 with a 35–14 win against them. That was the game where it started clicking for me on offense. By then, the other QB had gotten hurt, and once the job was mine alone, it stayed mine. Against Kecoughtan, Coach Koz finally unleashed me. I ran for 88 yards and two scores, and threw for 174 yards and another TD. I also intercepted two passes.

We had been feeling like we weren't getting respect all season, but people started noticing then. People started talking. And Coach Koz kept on me to come to school. He saw it was important for me to be in the lineup, which I could only do if my attendance record was good. Rimpsey was back so Mike was more of a backup, but the two of them were chewing up yards. The defense kept making plays. The next game, against Phoebus (remember, they had beaten us the year before), we had a close one. They got up on us 14–0, so we were behind most of the damn game. Didn't matter. I threw a 24-yard touchdown pass to Kelly Rodgers with about five minutes to play. That put us up one. Then, with them driving down the field to take the game, I intercepted a pass to seal it.

It was fun coming to school when people started really seeing what I could do. What I could bring. Now, I wasn't all bright-eyed and bushy-tailed when Mike came calling in the morning. But when he said it in his voice, "Buuuub. Buuub, come on," that irritating voice, "we got to go," I was more likely to listen when we were kicking ass on the field.

After starting the season without a whisper, we had moved up to being ranked seventh in the state.

The next three weeks, we beat up on three lesser teams. I was throwing for touchdowns, running for touchdowns. And by the time our record had gotten to 9-0, I had thirteen interceptions on the year.

So game ten approached: Hampton. I remember as we played the week before, Coach just on our asses, like, *Don't you start looking ahead. Don't you start thinking about the Crabbers.* But goddammit, that whole season was Hampton! Man, Bethel was fire that week. All anyone could talk about.

Me, in particular. See, as the season wore on, it became less and less about the other guys, and more and more all eyes on me. Even Coach couldn't avoid it. Early in the season, he'd be talking about Mike Jackson, the sprinter turned halfback, about Rimpsey, about the offensive line, about our defense, the line, the linebackers. But now he had to talk about Allen Iverson.

Of course, Hampton didn't win all these district titles for nothing. They had the defense, and they had their own dual-threat QB. While we were ranked in the top ten in the state, Hampton High was all the way up there at number one.

In Hampton and on the Peninsula, it was a real problem to some that we might be flipping it to Bethel High. The week before the game there were even some threats. That's how much this rivalry meant, man. It really had people hating us, a bunch of kids basically.

We played the game at Darling Stadium in Hampton, and it was packed. Supposed to have a maximum of 7,000 or 8,000 fans, it was standing room only, and they said it had over 10,000 people piled in. The damn game was on live television. Two best teams. Both unbeaten. One city. A bitter rivalry.

The game turned into a defensive struggle. They would move the ball, get close to the end zone, but they could never get a touchdown. The best chance for them was when, in the first half, they had a first-and-goal from the one-yard line. We stuffed them twice, I remember. Then on third-and-one, Tim Johnson, a great linebacker on that team, the leader of the defense, guessed right when they tried a little misdirection, and wrecked their running back for a loss. Hampton settled for the field goal, and that ended up being their only points.

In the third quarter it was 3–3. We moved the ball down the field. Thrilla was the tailback that day because Rimpsey had gotten hurt again. But they seemed to always have an answer to stop our drives. This time we got on their side of the fifty, and I remember I took off running on a bootleg, and got down to the twenty-five for a nice gain. There was excitement in the air. The crowd was tense. The problem was getting time for me to throw—these Hampton dudes were flying after me! So Coach Koz called a little play action, and it gave me the second I needed. I saw my teammate Kelly Rodgers streaking down the side and threw it up to him. He went and got it, and suddenly we were up 9–3.

When that pass connected, the crowd, all bundled up on a cold November day, went nuts. It was pandemonium. And we realized, as a team all together, that we could beat them, end their streak. People don't believe this, but I sometimes think that was the highest-pressure, most exciting shit of my entire life. I mean, I didn't feel anything but joy—on the field—back then.

Toward the end of the game, Hampton got their shot. Time was running out. They got to about our ten-yard line, but they couldn't get that last snap off. The game was over. Our whole team rushed the field, and then our fans joined. People just spilled out of the crowd onto the field, man. It was my first time being a champ in a moment like that—center of the big-ass crowd, making motherfuckers happy as hell. And it felt so fucking good.

Now, I said we had been looking ahead to that game. But the truth is we may have stopped looking ahead after beating Hampton. The district title might have been enough, and we forgot about the playoffs. Because the next week, we lost to Norcom. And it became really about stopping me. Every time I got back there, they were in my face, in particular blitzing right over the tight end. I had no time to pass the entire game.

Shit ended real quick. Remember what I said about beating Hampton being the main thing, what defined a season? Nah, man. We won that shit, but then we didn't advance in the state playoffs. So I said to myself two things. First, we have got to win it all. Second, the only way anyone is going to beat us is by stopping *me.*

So, the answer was easy: *Nobody is going to stop me anymore.*

SEVEN

HIGH SCHOOL LIFE

While all this football stuff was going on, life was tumultuous as hell. I started off freshman year still living with Mo and his family. They had a room for me in their house in Aberdeen. I couldn't ask for anything more—a working phone, heater, hot water. But I wasn't the sitting-still type, remember? And I was still a night owl. I really didn't need sleep. It'd be late as hell, and that's when I felt most awake. I never wanted the night to end. But in Mo's house, the night had a defined end point, a time to be home, a time to be quiet, and the next morning, a time to leave the house to go to school. So I was there, but I wasn't always there. I still had my life, my mom, my dad, my sister, my friends, Newport News.

My freshman year, it got chaotic for the family. We had been evicted from Stuart Gardens. My sister was staying at one place. I wasn't always sure where my mom was. My dad was at Glen Gardens until he wasn't. I would stay with him some of the time when I left Mo's, and there was another spot, a friend's, in Glen Gardens that I could stay at sometimes. I had my freedom there.

That February of my freshman year, 1991 it was, Daddy got convicted of a drug charge, distribution of cocaine. He got a ten-year prison sentence, and before he went in, he told me I had to "hold down the fort" until he got home—except there really wasn't a "fort" to hold down.

Sometimes I ran into a little trouble of my own. We'd be renting cars, driving around, like when I took Brandy out shopping. I didn't have a license, but that didn't stop me from driving. That's how I caught my first arrest. Another time, there was a drug investigation that they said got me on video hanging out. I didn't get arrested or charged, but someone, I don't know who, alerted the school to it. You have to remember, I wasn't yet on the map as the next superstar when I was fourteen or fifteen years old, so I was just out doing what I wanted.

Just before Daddy got locked up, my mom got pregnant, and she gave birth the fall of my sophomore year. Right when we were in the middle of going 10-0 and beating Hampton, Iiesha was born—nine days late, and after a difficult pregnancy and birth with all kinds of complications. The birth was at a hospital in Norfolk, and they told my mom not to expect Iiesha to make it. Then they moved her to Georgetown University Hospital. The baby had seizures. But they figured it out and she made it out of there. She's strong now. But then, even when she came home, there were still the seizures for quite a few years.

My mom finally got a spot on Victoria Boulevard in Aberdeen. I don't want to make it sound like some nice-ass shit, because it wasn't that. It had a busted pipe under it and smelled terrible, especially during the summertime. I never liked seeing Iiesha, struggling like she was, raised in that house. But damn, if that wasn't home. It was a place we could all be. After my mom got that house, I would be there as often as Mo's. I took care of my sisters when my mom wasn't home. That's just how it was. I might have become a *Parade* All-American (and we will get to that), but I still changed the baby's diaper. Sometimes the lights would be out. Or the gas. The phone damn near never worked. If we had a phone longer than a couple of months, then we felt like we were rich. But as little as we had, it was still our home.

EIGHT

BASKETBALL HIGH

Mike Bailey coached basketball. He was more like a father to me than Coach Koz had been. And I don't mean that as anything against Coach Koz. It was just different. Coach Bailey took me into his life, let me get to know his wife, Janet, who was one of the nicest people I've ever met. At times, I actually stayed in his home. He would drive to places I shouldn't have been, looking for me if I wasn't at the place I was supposed to be at—school, basically. They got to know Coach Bailey's car, and they'd whistle so I knew to get out of there if I didn't want to go with him. It was just like with Mo.

One of the things I always loved about Coach Bailey was how he wanted us to run. "Get the rebound and sprint out," he'd say. Back in those days, the transition game was associated with Loyola Marymount University, where Bo Kimble and Hank Gathers and all those dudes played and scored like a hundred a game. He studied that offense. He wanted that to be our mindset, which of course appealed to me. So that season, not only was I entering the mix, but he had installed this new transition-based system.

Bethel basketball was in worse shape than the football program had been. It didn't have the history of any state titles. In fact, Bethel had never won more than sixteen games in any prior season. The team was coming off a 1-18 season overall, 1-15 in the district. The thing with me is I paid no mind to that. That wasn't how it was going to be once I stepped on the court. Sure enough, we won our first game my freshman year, matching the previous season's total in a day. I scored 15 points.

Now, from the beginning, it was me and another guy, Tony Rutland. He was a guard like me, he could score like I could, and he was a freshman like me. And he felt like he should be the guy. Not only that, but since he didn't play football like me, he had been practicing with the team before I joined.

So we battled at times. I loved this dude. He was my partner throughout high school. But we battled. Coach Bailey early on called us his "terrible twos." We both wanted the ball, both always thought we were open. And Coach's big thing early on was finding a way for us to coexist. In that first game, Tony only had 8. When we played our next game, he had 34 points, and I only had 8. This was kind of how it went freshman year. By the time January came, Tony had become the district's leading scorer. Meanwhile, I missed some time with a bad ankle that never really got right that season. We were 7-4 heading into the first Hampton game, which surprised everyone. Nobody expects much from you when you only won one game the year before. And I hadn't really dominated in the summer league or middle school. People knew me, but they didn't necessarily see me as the up-and-coming basketball star.

Once again, the Hampton Crabbers showed us what was what that first year. They beat us by 27 points the first time we played them. They had this sophomore, Damon Bacote, who lit it up, which he would for years to come.

After some wins and losses, our regular season concluded that year with another game against Hampton. Number one in the state, according to the press. We were 12-7 at the time, and 10-7 in the district. It was already our best record in seventeen years, since 1974. But the Crabbers clobbered us. We lost that one 128–89. Maybe that's better than the 53–0 whooping we got at the end of my freshman football season. A couple days later we lost to Kecoughtan in the first round of district playoffs, and Bethel basketball was done for the year. I averaged about 12 points a game. Tony averaged almost 18. Not bad for a couple of freshmen.

So we had improved. I learned I could hang with these guys (I led the team with 21 points in the second game against Hampton). I had a great coach and a great running mate in Tony, but just winning some, losing some, being respectable—that wasn't what we wanted.

Sophomore year of basketball, coming off that 10-0 football season, we were so much more confident. And success came. Early on we beat Gloucester High School and I had 19 points in the third quarter. A few days later, we lost a close one to Kecoughtan. We were both unbeaten coming into the game. While we lost that game, me and Tony combined for 49 points. By the middle of the season, we were the top two scorers in the district. I was getting my shots more and more. I was hitting threes, driving to the rim, getting out on fast breaks. And this year, Coach Bailey was pretty clear that we had to get better on defense. It wasn't just the Loyola Marymount, get-it-and-go system. Giving up 128 points to Hampton, as we did my freshman year, wasn't going to cut it. As the season wore on we won some, we lost some.

Mid-January 1991 came and we had our first game against Hampton. Remember, we had finally beaten Hampton at the end of that football season. Their whole school was riled up and mad as hell about us taking the football crown. I was determined to make it happen on the basketball court. But we were small. People talked about me and Tony in the backcourt, perimeter guys. But could we hold up inside? I think that day might have been when I really started seeing it on the basketball court—again, that moment you know you belong. There was absolutely nothing

I could not do. I scored 39 points in that game, in every way you can imagine, and we won 83–72. But here was the part that really had me fucking hyped—I had 13 rebounds. Even though we were small, we beat them on the glass that day.

Back at school, in the neighborhood, in the papers, that's when people started getting excited about basketball. Like, *Damn, this motherfucker is doing it on the court now?*

That excitement built in the school and in the community, but more than anything, it built in myself. We blew out Phoebus, and I scored 37. We won a tight one against Lafayette, and I scored 18 of my 22 points in the fourth quarter. I felt a need to one-up myself. By the end of January, I was the leading scorer in the district, with nearly 25 a game. While Tony had led the team the year before, it had slowly shifted to me as the focal point and scoring leader. We were still a two-man show, mind you, but it was different.

The top team in the district that year was the Kecoughtan team that had beaten us earlier. They had this dude, Faisal Abraham, who just kicked our ass. The excitement had built to the point that for the first time ever, we sold out our gym. Fourteen hundred people piled into that little pressure cooker. The next year we moved over to a much bigger venue, that's how crazy it got. But this was the first taste. I scored 35 and we almost had them. But Abraham was just a little too much at the end.

While we didn't win the regular season title, we still had the district tournament.

That started well when we beat Menchville, and I remember that game because I scored 42 points—the most anyone had in the district all year.

But then in the district semis we played Hampton again. They had the better record, even though we beat them twice. And this time they had our number. Teams had been playing crazy defenses against us all year, blitzing me as I brought the ball up court, box and ones, diamond and twos—anything to slow me and Tony down, and this was no exception. It was another bitter loss to end the year. And another time where I felt like they put everything into stopping me, and once they accomplished that, they won.

It was like football all over again. We had achieved a lot. But it wasn't enough for me. I couldn't stand to lose. I hated it. And I was determined not to let it happen again.

NINE

THE SUMMER OF 1992

So I practiced and I played. I played and I practiced. The court in particular, for the next few months of 1992, was my sanctuary. And it was for the rest of my playing days—the drama and the chaos disappeared as I stepped onto the blacktop, eventually wood surfaces, in air-conditioned gyms, then arenas.

But that summer . . . Damn that summer. Sometimes the moment I stepped off the court, life smacked me in the face.

My life that summer was surrounded by death.

I lost a whole bunch of dudes. I lost count, and that's the worst of it: I can't even remember exactly which ones happened which year.

The worst was Tony Clark. The trickster. The swindler. The fighter. Dude who could leave his home in the morning with nothing and hustle his way to a new bike to ride home. I remember it like it was yesterday. His cousin came running up, and she was like, "He dead."

My heart sank. "Who?"

"Tony, Tony dead."

I hustled down there, following his cousin. They had already moved the body, but there it was, the bloodstain on the driveway of a Stuart Gardens house. That one, it still hurts. It was crazy too. It wasn't a drug war or any shit like that. His girlfriend stabbed him in the throat. She said he had been beating her and it was self-defense.

Another killing was this dude from the neighborhood. I'm not going to say his name. He was a bad motherfucker, and he was always drunk. He used to mess with this crackhead. He would just beat the shit out of this crackhead for no fucking reason. So one day I was coming back from playing basketball in the park just as it was getting dark, and I saw this dude stumbling. I'm thinking he's drunk, as usual. Nah. He had evidently gone to mess with that crackhead, and the crackhead just shot him, one time in the heart. Sometimes I wonder how I got through shit like this, the stuff my kids never had to deal with, thank God. Well, it was like when I was a little kid peeking out of my bedroom door in our Pine Chapel spot, seeing that man's head bleeding all over our floor. You couldn't stop and dwell. If you did, you were done for.

Then there was another guy. He came from a good family. They had a funeral parlor, their own business. So this dude was different. He had money, and he was always walking around with chains on. He had beef with some dudes, and they came to arguing about some bullshit, and what I heard was they were just trying to mess with him. They shot him in the arm, but the bullet went through his arm and caught him in the chest. That day, I heard the commotion—this was in Glen Gardens—and I ran over and saw his body on the ground. At the funeral, his little boy, his son, was crying like a motherfucker on top of the casket.

I can't recount them all. Like I said, can't even remember them. But it got to be regular. And while I was done hustling, my dudes on the street weren't. They were out there running around, and all kinds of shit was going on. People were hiding their guns in my house, and there were robberies, shoot-outs. It felt like anyone could go at any moment. Ra could go. Arnie could go. E, too. That's just the way it was. What hurt so bad later when Ra did get killed was that we had gotten out. We were *in the clear.*

One thing about me, I knew that all that shit was dangerous, but in my mind I was just thinking, *It ain't gonna happen to me. I ain't fucking doing nothing to nobody.* I knew everybody who was anybody. I knew who the killers were and weren't. I knew who wanted a problem and who didn't. I knew who was robbing and who wasn't. I knew who was selling drugs and who was not selling drugs. I knew who was using them. So I knew how to avoid trouble. And I had no interest in making any enemies on the street.

But I swear to God, it comes back to what my mom told me when I was eight years old, "This is what you gonna do! You want to play basketball? Football? If that's what you wanna do, you can do it." She was telling me I was worth more than all that street shit. And I fucking actually believed it. Like damn, Mommy said I can do it. So, I was out there putting the fucking work in to become that. I was out there doing it, doing it, doing it, even with all that shit going on around me. I would go out there and put the goddamn hours out there on that goddamn court until it got dark.

I was hungry as a motherfucker. *I'm gonna play basketball.* There ain't no food in this goddamn house? *I'm gonna take it out on somebody.* My friends dying in the streets? *Let's play football, goddammit! I'm mad! I wanna hit somebody, I wanna do something.*

That summer of 1992, I channeled that anger and took it out on the whole damn country.

Once high school basketball stopped, it was time for Summer League. This was the Amateur Athletic Union (AAU) summer season. Back then it wasn't like it is today. You didn't just get to play. You had to be among the best, and you had to prove yourself to get on that AAU motherfucker.

So all those dudes I'd been playing against? Now we joined forces and became one team. So we had me and Tony Rutland, and remember Faisal Abraham from Kecoughtan? Damon Bacote from Hampton was on that team. Another dude that came from Maury High School in Norfolk was Joe Smith. *The* Joe Smith that would end up going to the University of

Maryland, winning all kinds of accolades, and who was the first pick in the NBA Draft the year before me. It was the summer before his senior year of high school, and at the time he wasn't heralded like that. He shocked the world when he went to Maryland and won all that shit.

Anyway, this was Boo Williams's team. Boo Williams had run the summer leagues in Virginia since the early 1980s. He'd been a baller himself, playing for Phoebus, in Philly for St. Joe's (there goes that Philly connection again), and even internationally. He came back to Virginia and set up the summer leagues, building it from nothing into something you couldn't even believe now. He's got himself a multimillion-dollar complex with all this sports shit now. It wasn't like that yet in 1992. But it was big, and how it worked was you played in the summer leagues, and if you were the best, you moved up and played with the travel squad (the Hoyas). You had to earn that shit. By the summer of 1992, I had earned it. They couldn't keep me off it.

Bill Tose was the coach, and he was a tough guy. The big thing for him was the Hoyas had done it before—they had won the whole AAU national championship with a guy you might have heard of, Alonzo Mourning. So Coach Tose wasn't taking shit from us. Any time we said anything, he was all about that national championship in '88. But I didn't want to hear that before-shit.

That AAU season started in April with the Boo Williams Invitational. It was the local AAU tournament and teams from all over came. It was our first taste of playing together that year.

The thing about basketball, you get a group of guys, they can be from the neighborhood, they can be from your school, or they could be a group of All-Stars from the area, like this was. However you get the guys, you start playing, and you see who can do what. The leaders become defined, the best players become defined. It's just natural. It happens in practice, it happens in games. It just happens. You work so hard to make it to that next level, and that shit happens again. It's how you realize how good you are—or ain't.

In this first tournament, we were still feeling things out. But I had my moments. A couple dunks, a couple threes, a couple steals. We lost in the final to a team from Florida, in a real close game, 79–76. I came away with what was now a familiar feeling. Man, I couldn't defer. I couldn't allow them to stop me. I had to be the guy. Making that realization and putting it into action, that's what I had to do.

That May, I started getting some more recognition. Nike invited me to their camp, one of 120 dudes across the nation, and one of only 25 rising high school juniors. I got that invitation, I was like, *Damn, I'm the real shit.* And people were surprised, because I hadn't yet gotten that national recognition. Just me and Joe Smith got the invite from our squad.

Later that summer, we won the Boo Williams Summer League, and I collected 35 points in the final along with the MVP trophy.

From there the team traveled to a tournament in DC. We beat a DC team for the title, and this time there was no deferring. I led the team with 36 points and got me another MVP. What I remember, though, was Alonzo came and spoke to us. It was like a little pep talk. Man, seeing him there. He was doing everything I planned to do. He had just finished his Georgetown career. He had been drafted No. 2 by the Charlotte Hornets, right after Shaquille O'Neal. He would go on to finish second in rookie of the year to Shaq as well. As I traveled farther with the team, I got exposed to more shit like this. I was seeing my future. That day Alonzo told us what it meant to win the whole damn thing. Now, let me tell you, nobody, and I mean *nobody*, thought we were going to do all that. But I just said to myself, *We going to win this motherfucker.*

The AAU Nationals were held in Winston-Salem, North Carolina, at the end of July 1992. Everybody was there. In the first game, I paced myself with 21 points and we pretty easily beat an Oklahoma team. The next game was crazy. We played these dudes from Cleveland, and they gave us a good one. When we were down two points right at the end of regulation, I passed the ball to Faisal, and he dunked it to get us to the first overtime. After we tied the first overtime, we had a three-point lead in the second when this dude hit nearly a half-court shot to send it to triple overtime.

I just said to myself, *I got to take over this game.* In the third overtime, I scored all seven of our points (making it 33 for the game) for the W.

Next we blew out these dudes from Wisconsin. We then won two more against Arkansas and Memphis, games where I scored 37 and 26. As we moved along in the tournament, the competition kept getting better and better. I had to adjust, maybe to a defense laying off me by shooting more threes, if the dudes inside were bigger, sometimes passing more to my teammates. Whatever it was, I figured it out. I got more dominant, became more the team's focus, as our competition improved.

As a team, we found ourselves in the final. And I found myself the focal point. When you're at a big tournament, when you're playing like that, everyone starts looking at you. You walk down the hallways, and people start pointing. And remember, I didn't come in with this big reputation. No one was thinking about Boo Williams winning the whole thing that year. Nah, man, the team that everyone started out talking about was this group from North Carolina. They had three real dudes. I'll put it like that. Jeff McInnis, Jeff Capel, and, of course, Jerry Stackhouse. All eyes were on them the moment they walked in the place. In the final, that's who we faced.

That final game was as intense as any AAU game I ever played. They got ahead early, but we came back, and right before halftime, I hit a long three to give us a one-point lead. In the second half they were hounding me, trying to keep the ball out of my hands. I had to work hard for my 25 points, and I led the team with 6 assists. On the defensive end, I had to guard McInnis. Dude was bigger than me. And he would back me down even though he was a guard. It was a way I would get attacked later in my NBA career. In this game I collected fouls, and sure enough, with a three-point lead and about two minutes left, I got me my fifth and fouled out. Now, you know how hard that must have been for me to watch the end from the bench. But after they tied it up at 78, Tarik Turner made this spin move to score. Now ahead by two, we made just enough free throws down the stretch to hold on.

As they missed their last shot, we jumped into a pile. We were hugging. We were dancing. When I say "we," I mean Tose, I mean Boo Williams. All of us. We were just so happy.

And then they announced that I had won the MVP. There were fifty-six teams in that tournament, and most of those dudes were rising seniors. All of them were bigger than me. Many of them came in with more fanfare. But none of them walked out with it. When I say everything changed with that tournament, it's no exaggeration. All of the sudden I was the No. 1 rising junior in the country. The best guard. All that.

TEN

JUNIOR YEAR

I haven't even gotten to the most important part. When I was still sixteen and a sophomore, I met Tawanna Turner. The first time we met, we just exchanged a few words. She was a student at Kecoughtan. She came from a real nice family. Then, a month later, I can't remember where it was exactly but I was talking to some friends in a hallway, and I just started backing away. And evidently she was behind me, doing the same thing, backing up. We just backed right into each other. We turned around and that was it. You know, like it was meant to be.

From then on, we spent almost every day together. And the crazy shit about her is that she actually used to be at my house more than her house, and I told you about the living conditions in my house already, but it didn't matter to her. She came from a family with a real nice house, like Mo's, running water, working electricity, a phone you could call, and no damn smell. But she came on over to my house anyway.

She had a car, and I remember my mom used it like it was hers. She even had Tawanna's extra set of keys. We would wake up and the car would be gone. Tawanna would just be with me all the goddamn time. We didn't do too much like going places and shit like that. We would just hang out there. She would bring me food and be waiting for me after most practices. I don't know, I guess we just liked being around each other.

She's part of the reason I don't want anyone to think, as tough as some things were, that I had it bad. Man, I had all kinds of fun. I had family. I had my girl. And I was a star.

From that point forward, Tawanna would come to all the games. The kids at her school would be talking trash about me. They didn't like that she was with their rival's star. But she'd defend me. She once got in trouble for defending me to a teacher after the bowling alley situation.

So that was just the beginning. We have had our ups and downs, as I said. More ups. But that's where it all started.

When I got back from the AAU, it was a different atmosphere. The talk was all about me and basketball. Football was the biggest sport on the Peninsula. The football rivalry with Hampton was the biggest game. But all of the sudden it was like, *Hold it, this dude has a* basketball *future.*

And so rumors started up. *He's going to stop playing football, and it's going to be basketball alone.* I don't know where that came from. For me, I had things left to do on the football field. So it was just a couple weeks after exploding onto the national scene with our AAU championship and me being awarded MVP that football practice was starting. And the attention was different. I remember I missed the first or second practice. I can't remember why. This was an August practice in high school. And the press covered that shit. That was the first time (but not the last) that everyone started being interested in me and practice.

There was an article about rumors that I was going to play basketball exclusively. In an interview to the local paper, Coach Koz said what he always said—I'd be treated just like any other member of the team who missed practice. The spotlight was so much brighter, and I would learn that year that being under the bright lights wasn't always something you wanted. Now people in the media, and all over the place, were talking about my grade-point average, my attendance record. I was a high school junior, man.

But fuck all that. I did play football that year. I had business to take care of. And it's going to sound funny, maybe, to hear all about that football season. But you have to remember, football was my first love. And football was the biggest thing. Football was it. The next four months of Bethel Bruins football changed my life. We became legends.

Our first game of the year was against Lafayette. I had injured my thumb in practice a couple weeks earlier, and they were keeping me out. Xavier Gunn, like me, was a star in football and basketball, and he took the snaps at QB. The plan was for it to be that way the whole game. I still played safety, of course. But at halftime it was only us leading 6–0, and we had been sloppy, fumbling the ball four times. So I told Coach to just let me in there. The adrenaline started flowing when I ran for a 14-yard touchdown in the fourth quarter. Mike Jackson by then was the main running back, and he rushed for over 100 yards, in a 21–0 win.

After beating Menchville, we faced Kecoughtan, Tawanna's school and always one of the top teams in the district. In the lead-up, I remember they were talking about how they needed to stop me, that was their focus. That was everything. They almost acted like it was simple.

So we won the flip and asked to receive the opening kickoff. I went back to get the kick. And I was telling everyone to watch. Now it's almost funny, but this team was so focused on stopping me that they kicked me the ball on the first play of the game. So I just caught the ball and ran it back for a touchdown. So much for stopping Allen Iverson. We won 27–0.

Now 3-0, we had held all of our opponents under 150 yards of offense. We were really doing it with defense, just like the year before. We had some powerful dudes on that team, guys like Bobby Simms, Barry Hargraves, Xavier. Man, I don't want to leave anyone out, because all them dudes were amazing. So the next week was more of the same. After going up 28–0 in the first half, Coach Koz sat me and a lot of the other starters for the second.

We were not catching anyone with any surprises this year. At this point we had won thirteen straight district games. We were ranked No. 3 in the state. Hampton, though, they were No. 1.

The next week, it was more about our offense. We beat Ferguson 56–29. That 56 points was a new Bethel record (it didn't last long). I ran for three touchdowns and passed for another. Thrilla had over 200 yards rushing. And if you think beating Ferguson ain't nothing, the man playing quarterback for them was Aaron Brooks, who played QB for a long time in the NFL. He actually had a hell of a game against our defense, but obviously it wasn't nearly enough.

Then the next week, we had a bad one against Denbigh. While I tossed a couple TDs in the first half to Kelly Rodgers, they beat us with a seventeen-play game-winning drive at the end. The Denbigh dudes were acting like they had won a Super Bowl or something. We huddled up, and Coach was just serious. Like we couldn't take this shit for granted. We had won fourteen straight district games. And now that streak was over. The next week against Gloucester, we got that message. We won 75–15 after being up 50–0 at halftime. I ran for a touchdown. I threw for a touchdown. I returned an interception for a touchdown. I returned a punt for a touchdown.

A couple weeks later, we faced Phoebus, a big game with the playoffs on the line. I had injured my shoulder, so Coach decided I shouldn't play quarterback. Take it easy. Man, that was something I wasn't capable of. As the first half unfolded, I was going crazy, with our offense unable to score without me. I begged Coach to at least let me return punts, and sure enough, I returned two punts for touchdowns in the second half—our only points of the game to that point. Down a touchdown late, Coach finally relented and put me back in at QB. In the games, I just had to do everything. It was like when I was a kid taking the cast off so that I could go back to Anderson Park to play basketball. Like, it killed me not to be doing everything I could in the goddamn games. So after going in as QB, I engineered a long drive and connected on a touchdown pass as time expired to pull within one. But we missed the two-point conversion as I got stopped on the goal line. Another loss meant that we had to beat Hampton to make it to the playoffs.

Hampton was unbeaten once again. They had the top-ranked defense. They had the top-ranked offense. The Associated Press had them first in the region, eighth in the nation. The game was in Darling Stadium once again. And people were going crazy again.

The November day, cold as shit, thousands on the Peninsula still packed into Darling Stadium. And from the opening, things just fell into place. There were a couple plays I will never forget. With us leading 17–7, Hampton got the ball down near the goal line. They handed it to their star running back, a dude named Myron Newsome. This guy went on to be a star linebacker at Virginia Tech. He was shorter than me, but he was thick and built. He was low to the ground. They handed off to him and had the side sealed just the way they wanted, so it was just me between him and the end zone. If it's between you and me, it's me, and so I tackled him short of the goal line. As a team we did it. Another play I remember is throwing a 16-yarder to our tight end Chris Gaskell. He dragged two Hampton dudes with him into the end zone for yet another touchdown. We could feel it.

To put the game out of reach, I had one of these plays that you can't forget. I dropped back to pass, rolled to my left, and immediately had defenders in my face—five of them! I was sprinting out, and they were coming after me. I kept moving, sideline approaching, and just as I was about out of room, either out of bounds or buried by these five guys, I saw Rodgers in the back of the end zone. Snapped off the pass to him as the five dudes were left clutching the grass and watching us celebrate. The final was 30–10.

Just like the year before, our fans went crazy. There was jubilation. We beat Hampton. But this time, I was just thinking about how we'd done that the year before. It was time to take the state.

Everyone was talking about Bethel football. It was in the papers, on the radio. There was a lot of shit-talking too—some said I was too old to be playing in high school. At one point, Boo Williams had to go and get my birth certificate to prove I was my actual age. What is it about needing birth certificates when you're beating people you ain't supposed to beat?

There was also talk that fall about my grades, my attendance, practice. People would actually be talking about all of this on the local sports talk (1310 on your AM dial), as if I wasn't a fucking kid.

And I laughed at it mainly. Like, did I threaten them that much?

But the attention was getting crazy. Football recruiters were coming, and the basketball stuff was still piling up. From the summer, every team started reaching out. Duke was looking at me, and so were Kentucky and Notre Dame. The attention was crazy. The Hampton University coach said, "He's the best defensive back I've ever seen; he's the best quarterback I've seen." That dude got in trouble because college coaches weren't supposed to make comments like that about kids not even seniors in high school.

It would only intensify as we made our way through the state playoffs. Whereas the year before we had gone undefeated, and then come up short in the playoffs, this year we had lost a couple games and didn't even win the district, but by beating Hampton we had a chance to make up for it in the end.

The first playoff game was against Lake Taylor, in Norfolk, Virginia. Me and Thrilla each had rushing touchdowns and combined for 150 yards on the ground. And our defense, led by Xavier that day just like the whole year, shut them down after an early touchdown. So we won 25–7, which set up a rematch with Norcom. They had beaten us the year before, and that season, they were undefeated. They were nationally ranked. All that shit. Do you think it mattered to me?

This time we were ready when they blitzed over our tight end. We would just leave the rushers unblocked and I'd pass it to the tight end real quick. So that kept them from doing what they did the year before. That's an example of how Coach Koz was a great coach. Now, one thing I haven't even mentioned is in addition to returning kicks and punts, playing quarterback and safety, I was also the holder on field goals. In that game, it came down to field goals. Early on, after trading touchdowns, we missed our extra point. I remember walking off the field after the missed kick, and I let our kicker Wilton Evans know that we trusted him. We were down 8–6.

The second half was a defensive battle. Early on in the third quarter, Evans kicked a 37-yard field goal for a one-point lead. They followed that with their own field goal, to get it back. Then in the fourth we moved into their territory, until the drive stalled. Coach Koz sent out Evans for the 40-yarder. He had never made one that long in a game. I remember I jogged out there to hold. And I just said to him, "Think of the ball going through the uprights." That's what I always did—visualized what I would do with my body to manipulate the world around me, then do it. Didn't matter if it was football or basketball or drawing. And so that's what I said for him to do. *Visualize kicking the ball through the uprights.*

I can't say for sure what he did in his mind. But in the game, he hit the ball true and straight, and it just managed to clear the crossbar.

That was all the points we needed. I wish I could describe what it was like coming back home, and to school, after that. People were going crazy. We had beaten three straight unbeaten teams. Two of them—Norcom and Hampton—were nationally ranked. It was such hysteria that they had to postpone the start of basketball season for us. The football team was all anyone could talk about.

Next up was Huguenot. We didn't know much about them. They were in the Central Region of Virginia. We had to travel to Richmond, and we had to play for the first time on artificial turf. Maybe that's what slowed us down, because we couldn't do anything for most of game. The first half ended 0–0. In the second half, they built up a 16–0 lead.

By the fourth quarter, it almost felt like it was over. The game being in Richmond, where Huguenot was located, meant it was more of their fans. There were a lot of ours who made the trip, but they were quiet at this point. It was wet 40-degree weather, with some drizzle. And it felt like time was running out. But a couple little things happened, starting when they punted, or tried to, with less than nine minutes to play. They snapped it over the punter's head, and all of the sudden we had the ball on their 28-yard line. Two plays later, I had a passing touchdown to Gaskell and a two-point conversion to Rodgers. We'd cut the lead to eight. Then with 3:30 left in the game and them at midfield probably thinking about running the clock out, we recovered a fumble. A couple plays later, we had a third-and-two. It was a designed rollout to the left. I was able to finally get to the edge, and I raced for 27 yards to the one. After I ran it in from the one for the score, I threw a pass to Michael Simmons for the tying two-point conversion. Overtime.

In Virginia, we only had overtime in the playoffs. And the way it worked was each team took a turn with the ball starting at the ten-yard line. And you'd keep doing that until someone won. Huguenot got the first chance, but couldn't score. So then it was our chance. Coach knew that all we needed was a field goal. So he wasn't messing around. He called Thrilla's number on first and second down, which got us to the two-yard line. Then Coach told me to keep it. But he wanted me to be careful with it. So I snapped the ball, saw a little space, and squeezed through the line. After I hit the ground, I looked and found myself in the end zone, in for the winning touchdown.

The whole team stormed the field. Ten minutes of game time earlier, we had been down 16–0. Pretty much dead. These motherfuckers had us on the ropes. It kind of felt like when we lost those heartbreakers in the regular season, we learned how to win the close ones.

Next up was EC Glass, in Lynchburg, Virginia, for the state championship.

These games were intense. The atmosphere. The pressure. And the ways we won. The state championship wasn't like that. In fact, all the drama was prior to the game.

It was now mid-December 1992, and snow mixed with rain heading into the game. Their field had been covered with three inches of snow, and was muddy as hell. Coach Koz didn't want any surprises, so he had us travel to Lynchburg early to check out the field conditions and practice. It was the day before the game. It was so fucking cold, and I just got mad. He had me fielding punts. I got one, and just had enough, so I didn't return it. We had played fourteen games over fourteen weeks in a row. I just didn't feel like it was right, having us practice like that. So I let Coach know it.

He did something then that I can't stand. He said "Do it"—basically just because he said so. I caught the next punt and didn't return it again. This kind of shit happened now and then, but damn, Coach got so damn mad. He sent me off the field and said I wasn't playing in the championship game. I went to the side. Practice continued. And Coach was acting like I wasn't playing.

Now of course my mom was going to be there. So was Tawanna. Everyone was going to be there. Lynchburg was even farther than Richmond, but it didn't matter. That night I was chilling with Xavier and Mike, and they just weren't going to let it go like that. Unlike me, they were seniors. They were leaders. And they went to the coach.

I'll never forget that kind of loyalty. They went to Koz and they told him, "We got this far as one team. We made it to the championship. And we cannot stop now." To his credit, Coach relented. He asked for the whole team to vote, and the whole team—to a man—voted that I should play.

I acted like I knew that was what was going to happen, but I can't tell you how that made me feel. To have the guys stand with me. Stand *up* for me. Those dudes were family.

So the next day we went out and beat the shit out of EC Glass.

We got a lead early, and I could feel all the momentum. We were far from home, but it was a familiar feeling—like when you know you're in the right place doing the right thing, that you are better than these motherfuckers on the other side, that this is your stage. The feeling took over when they punted a short one early on. I let it bounce. And then I grabbed it. You could see the two guys who'd gotten down there to cover it kind of relax for a second, and then buckle as I made my move. I beat them to the left sideline, cut back against the grain. Raced into the end zone with diving tacklers grabbing at the air.

It was over right there.

We won 27–0. We were state champions.

When the horn sounded, our crowd flooded the field. The song "Celebration" played on the speakers. Everyone was there. The TV crew came to interview me. I'll never forget it. Mo and many others will tell you that in that moment of victory, of conquering everybody, I actually arrived at the beginning of the end.

The interviewer asked me on the broadcast, since I was only a junior, what was next for me? I said exactly what was on my mind. It was something I think a lot of people didn't care too much for. And maybe it was why some people later wanted to put me in my place. I don't know.

So to answer the question, what I said was "Gonna go get one in basketball now, that's all."

I think they were expecting me to say something about football. Sad part is, I would never play football again. Not one game.

ELEVEN

SIX SECONDS

It took six seconds. Six seconds into the first game of the season. That was all.

The football championship had been Saturday, December 12. The first basketball game was rescheduled for Tuesday, December 15—rescheduled because our first three games that year had to be postponed due to the football hoopla. Me, Xavier, and Kelly Rodgers were the guys from the football team who were also on the basketball team. The other dudes had been practicing for more than a month. That Monday, we joined Mike Bailey and the team for practice—the one practice before the first game.

The press wanted to know if I was going to play with such a quick turnaround. Could I play without practicing? And you know everyone in school was running up to me—"You playing, you playing?" Damn right I was playing! Then people were like, *He's going to be tired from football. He's not going to have his legs under him.* Some people suggested they ease me in, like maybe off the bench.

I did not ease in. Nope. Three days after winning the state football championship, I did this: scored 37 points, got 8 rebounds, 9 assists, 7 steals, and 2 blocks. And we beat Tawanna's school, Kecoughtan, in their own gym, 73–68.

But it was in the first six seconds that I let everyone know. Yeah, it was the first play of the game. After they got the tip, they passed it on the perimeter, and I jumped the lane, stole the ball in stride, glided to the other end, and I just fucking jammed it. I looked at their crowd. What I saw, I could never have imagined. They were fucking excited. Like they knew, even from the other side, that they were seeing something.

I told the interviewer after winning state in football, it was time to get one in basketball, but with that dunk, it was my real announcement. That was six seconds into the game, six seconds into the season. *Damn, this motherfucker is going to do it, ain't he?*

That Christmas, there was a tournament for all the area teams, up in Fort Eustis. The games were played in Anderson Field House, which fit a few thousand fans. In a sign of just how crazy things were going to be that year, for every game I played, they filled that joint to the rafters, standing room only. In the first game, I put on a show for them with a triple double in the three quarters I played.

Later we faced Huguenot. And you know they were coming for us, and me in particular, after they gave up the 16–0 fourth-quarter lead in the football state semifinal. But that night, they weren't getting their payback. I had everything going. My shot, my drives, my steals, my dunks. In the fourth quarter, I was sitting on 46 points with a double-digit lead. The crowd started chanting for five more points—to get the tournament record of 51 that Hampton's Damon Bacote had scored earlier in that tournament. I ended with that same 46, but that was the kind of excitement there was.

Sure enough, we had Hampton in the final. That's just the way I wanted it: the challenge of the best competition. We had two district games coming up with Hampton, and a meeting in the district tournament was a possibility. So this was not the end of it, but you don't need me to repeat it at this point: Hampton was our fucking rival. And Anderson Field House was rocking.

On that day, they got us. We made it close. Down five in the last minute, I got the ball and hit a three. On the other end, they missed the second of two free throws, but Rutland's last-second three was off, and we had our first loss of the season.

I had been starting to feel invincible. Still, I knew this was a December game, and we had the whole rest of the season in front of us.

Our first game of the new year was against Denbigh, one of the top teams in the district. I had missed a practice, and Coach Bailey sat me for the game. I was mad as hell, man. But Coach Bailey talked to Mo and my mom. He got them on his side, and I just had to take it.

The whole team was down, but the most disappointed motherfuckers were in the crowd. There wasn't an announcement until right before game time. So everyone was mad as hell. Even *their* fans were pissed off. And we lost that one.

But there was a positive that Coach Bailey pulled out of the situation. By having Tony as the only real scorer that game, he damn near caught up to me in scoring, and we were both right about to pass 1,000 points for our career. So for the next game, Coach invited both of our families. I won a lot of awards that year, and plenty before that too, but this was an honor that I won't ever forget, because my mom got to experience it right there with me.

In the third quarter, I passed the 1,000-point mark, and they stopped the game, pulled my mom out of the crowd, and gave her the basketball. You should have seen her smiling. She had put me on this planet, she had taken me, kicking and screaming, to my first basketball practice, and she had said, "You're going to make it." Now she was here with me to accept it. A few minutes later, Tony passed that milestone as well, and he shared it with his family.

After a few more wins, our first rematch with Hampton approached.

Coach Koz was also the athletic director, and he had sense by then to move the game to Hampton University's Holland Hall, which seated 3,000. It turned out 3,000 seats was not nearly enough. There was a line hours before the game. And what awaited the crowd was our worst performance of the year.

It was close going into the half. They were up 47–42. But our team was not right, and Coach Bailey kept yelling at me. *Pass the ball ahead. Drive to the hoop. Stay in your spot on D.* It was getting on my nerves because I was trying to fucking win. As the second half opened they came at us hard, and before you knew it, they were ahead 65–51. I had scored 29 of our 51 points by then. I felt like I was keeping us in it by myself. And Coach just kept on me, like it was my fucking fault. And of course I was frustrated that they were beating us, again.

He kept telling me, *Pass it, pass it.*

So I told him to stop telling me what to do. I didn't whisper that shit either.

He took me right on out of the game. In the huddle at the next timeout, he got on me again, and I responded by saying something I shouldn't have. I respect Coach Bailey too much to even repeat it now. I was emotional. And so he sat me not just for a minute, but for the rest of the game. I wasn't ready for that. I just stopped talking. I went real quiet.

After the game, before opening the locker room or anything, we had a team meeting. Xavier said I was selfish. He was the one who had stood behind me in the football season, remember. So it hurt. And I was mad. Mad from losing. Mad from being taken out of the game. They'd proven they couldn't do it without me. It was 65–51 when I got benched and we lost 101–67. Here they were calling me selfish—I was leading the team in assists! I didn't say a word though, and I walked on out of there.

The next game we had Menchville, and I wanted to show them what it would mean for me not to be selfish. I wasn't going to shoot it at all. The whole first half, I passed, passed, passed. And where did that get us? We were down 41–25 at halftime. Coach walked into the locker room.

He was disheveled. His thick-ass glasses were probably fogged up. His hair all over the place. He was the quietest guy in the world, except on that sideline. He'd be on the officials, and on his own players, demonstrative as hell, and with me more than anyone. In the locker room, my teammates had their heads down. Coach turned his attention on me. He wasn't acting mad. He didn't ever really react in anger (except maybe when he benched me the previous game). He said to me in front of the whole team that he knew I was about winning, and he asked, was this how we were going to win? Were we going to win with me just passing?

The way I heard it was, *Don't be selfish.* Now it was, *Be selfish.* Two games, two different messages. It left me seething. What do you do when you feel you're the best? When you've come all this way to be the best? When you can feel the ability to control the game but you have to rely on your team? It was a struggle my whole career.

In the second half, I couldn't keep muting myself. Coach Bailey was right. I wanted to win more than prove my point, I guess. And I returned to the lesson as a kid, Mo's words from the Raiders: *If it's between you and me, it's me.*

The second half, it was me. I started shooting. I got warmed up in the third quarter, but we were still down 15 going into the fourth quarter. At the same time, everyone was kind of relaxing, like it was going to be normal. And in the fourth quarter, our whole team just took flight, man. I scored 21 in the quarter, and we outscored them dudes 37–10 in the final period. It was a win, but it felt like something was different after that. Like it was my team, and I was cleared to run it, to shoot it, even if they wanted me to listen. I didn't get it perfect by any means from there on out. But our team went on a rampage.

We won the next five games, and we were rolling. I remember in particular playing Kecoughtan in front of Tawanna again. I scored 42 in that one. I swear the crowds we were up against started cheering for *us*, the momentum building. Every game, my crew would come and watch. One time, I don't remember the exact game, my homeboys said if I scored 40 they would hook me up with my first real chain. It was a herringbone. So the first half I couldn't get it going and had maybe 14 points. In the third quarter, I looked up and them boys had the chain in its case and were holding it up. I just went crazy after that, and got my 40-some points. I wore it in my first *Sports Illustrated* shoot the next year.

The next big game was against Denbigh. They had beaten us earlier, but that was the game Coach Bailey made me sit. Still, they were in first place and we needed a win to tie them for the district lead. We had this one at our small-ass gym, which was too confined to fit the excitement. I looked at it like I had to put on a show. That night, that's exactly what I did. We ran out ahead early and never relinquished the lead. I had 41 points, 10 boards, and 13 assists. And steals? Six of those.

The win created a three-way tie at the top of the district with them, us, and Hampton. We finally moved into the rankings for the state, finding ourselves in ninth place. Wouldn't stay that low for long.

We won a couple more easy ones after that—the last on Friday, February 12, 1993.

With the seventeenth win of the season, we had the most wins in a Bethel season ever. I was leading the district in scoring, having overtaken Bacote.

That left just one game before playoffs started: a matchup with Hampton that would decide the regular-season district title. They had beaten us twice. They were tied with us for first in the district. They were ranked higher. They were fucking Hampton.

Man, life seemed so perfect then, like my game was fucking taking off and we were heading for this dramatic district game, the rivalry, then the state tournament. It was as good as things could be. But everything would change before we played that game.

TWELVE

THE BOWLING ALLEY

So now we come to the night of February 13, 1993—the night of the bowling alley. There was all this pressure with basketball, and my home shit was my home shit. And I remember Coach Bailey told me he wanted me to relax. As you know by this point, we had our fights that year. And there was drama. Sometimes we didn't speak, like after he benched me against Hampton. But he was like a father too. He had let me stay in his home parts of one summer in particular, when he'd gone out driving looking for me on the streets. He just cared about me. It was him caring that pissed me off half the time. Still, while I couldn't always communicate it, there was no one I trusted more.

I think back to it, and I think about how a couple weekends before that I went out with my crew. We were at a hotel in Hampton. There was a whole bunch of people there, but me and my friends went upstairs, just chilling.

While we were up there playing cards probably, we heard some shots fired. *Boom boom boom*. We had all heard that sound plenty of times—enough that we could tell it wasn't that close. Still, you didn't expect that sound in a hotel. We stayed upstairs, but after a while we came down and saw the police and everyone hanging around. Caution tape. All that. A dude got killed that night, some beef with a bouncer. And we walked out of there, glad we hadn't been where it happened—really not giving it too much thought.

But Coach Bailey found out I'd been there. The shooting was in the news, and then, because it was me, it was reported that I was seen at the hotel. He confronted me with this look on his face. He was mad I was there, but damn, the dude was worried about me. I'll never forget it. The situation seemed all regular to me, but he was like, *That shit ain't regular.* I think he could feel all the pressure I was under. And I think that's why Coach said to me right after our game that Friday, "You go do some regular kid stuff. Have some regular kid fun."

So on February 13, a Saturday, I went to chill with some friends—not my homeboys—at the Circle Lanes Bowling Alley. The next day was Valentine's Day, and that would be just for me and Tawanna. Mike Jackson was almost always with me, but he never liked bowling. He still blames himself for not being there. He just wasn't a bowler.

A whole bunch of us went that night, but three other guys are important: Michael Simmons, Melvin Stephens, and Samuel Wynn. These weren't my street friends. It wasn't the Newport News guys. It wasn't all the dudes that would become the focal point of my so-called hood friends. That's the ironic part. The bowling alley was in Hampton. *Ain't no bad shit happening in Hampton* was the way I thought about it.

So we were all bowling in two lanes. And with us, we just liked to have fun. We were loud as shit. That's just the way we were. It was like "showtime" in the school cafeteria, fucking around with one another, having fun. This one dude who worked at the alley claimed he came over and told us to be quiet and stop standing on the chairs—requests that were ignored. But again, I don't even remember that. He turned out to be real important. Until he testified in the trial, I don't remember ever laying eyes on this dude.

So, at one point in the night, I walked over to the snack bar to get something to eat. There were these white dudes sitting there. I later came to find out they were from Poquoson. Now, Poquoson was outside of Hampton; it was a real expensive neighborhood, not just stand-alone homes, but people with real money inside. All I really knew about it was that it was a place you didn't want to be if you looked like me. Remember, I really didn't grow up thinking about race. It wasn't white and black for me—and Bethel had people of all colors in it. But that race stuff got blown up the night in the bowling alley and for the rest of my life. Back then, you might even say I was naive. Still, there was stuff you kind of took for granted without even thinking about it, and one of those was don't go to Poquoson.

Now, what happened next, I've talked about it a million times. I testified at the trial. Every word and movement has been dissected. I honestly can't go through every moment like that anymore. And I don't need anyone saying, *You said this then, and now you saying that.* But what definitely happened is this one dude was standing next to me. He was a grown man, twenty-two years old, 6'2", over 200 pounds, by the name of Steve Forrest. He was drinking beer with his friends. When I went to the snack bar, he said some shit to me, some racial shit. After exchanging words and it becoming physical, my friends came over and defended me and took me right on out of there. And then it was just a big-ass fight. I mean shit started so fast, and then it was just like mayhem.

Crazy part of that whole situation is, my friend Michael Simmons had a video camera that night. You know, if you had a camcorder back then, you were something. Like that was the shit. So he had a camcorder and he caught the whole thing. You can't see where it started, but the mayhem that ensued, that shit was on there. And you could spend your whole life looking at it, and you ain't going to see me doing a thing. Not a goddamn thing. I mean, you could videotape every moment of that night from every single angle in the alley and you still wouldn't see me doing a goddamn thing.

Now I don't want to get ahead of myself, but let me ask something. They called us a mob that night. And by us, I mean the Black *kids* who were fighting the white *grown-ass men* drinking beer. If you're going to form a mob—I can't even repeat that "mob" shit with a straight face—but if you're going to form a mob, are you going to videotape that shit? Nah man, this was some kids out having fun. And then it just went crazy. And every motherfucker in that place just started fighting. As they were hustling me out of there, I saw all kinds of shit. People fighting with bowling equipment. Chairs flying. It was just crazy.

And I remember they got me into a car and we got on out of there.

Later we went to my friend's house. Mike Jackson was there. And I told them about what had happened. But honestly, you already know I'd seen all kinds of shit, death on the street and all that. So this chaotic scene, it just was like, *damn.* But it didn't even occur to me that night that this was going to be about me. You talk to those dudes now who I hung with that night, like Thrilla, they're going to tell you that I was just chilling.

When I called Mo, he wasn't so calm about it. With Mo, he was worried from the moment I told him about it. In his day, they wouldn't even go to that bowling alley because of the race dynamics. So when he heard it was a fight with white dudes, that's when he got concerned. Well, he was right. And I would hear from the police soon enough.

The biggest game of the year was coming just three days later. The excitement level was unprecedented. Even Holland Hall wasn't going to contain that level of excitement. So they moved the game to the Coliseum. That was the downtown Hampton arena. Nobody ever thought to have a plain old high school game there. But with the district title on the line, with all the hoopla surrounding us at Bethel, they needed a place to put all those excited motherfuckers. It was packed. They said more than 8,000 showed up.

Before the game, the cops contacted me. They said they needed to see me. They just needed to take some pictures, they said. Came to find out that this was a picture they were going to use in a photo lineup. But they didn't say all that. They said if I didn't go voluntarily, they would have to arrest me. And they knew exactly where I'd be that night. Everybody did. They'd put me in handcuffs right there in the Coliseum.

Wasn't any way I was missing the motherfucking game! That was my concern, for real. The games meant everything to me. So I went down to the precinct. They took the pictures, they let me go, and I went to the Coliseum that night. Now, I came to find out later about the photo lineup. They had me with like five other dudes. Remember, I was seventeen. The photos of the other dudes in the photo lineup had to be grown-ass men. So who do you think was going to get picked out? Not to mention, it was my face everyone knew.

Listen to what one person said about that night: "Had he not been a star at Bethel High, had he not been as well-known as he was, then he may not have been identified by anyone. He may have been like the twenty other people who were involved who were not charged."

You know who said that? The prosecutor who put me in jail.

Over at the Coliseum that night, there were 8,000 pairs of eyes all focused on me.

My focus, however, was on winning that motherfucker. Focusing on the game, that was unwavering. No matter what shit was going on in my life, with my coaches, with my school, with my friends, my family, with practice. At the games, no one questioned my focus. And honestly, like that night at the Coliseum and so many times before and since, it was easier to focus on the games than the rest of my life. The games were something I could control. The other life stuff might be spiraling. But the court, the baskets, my teammates and my opponents, the fans out of their damn minds—that was the quietest place I knew.

During the pregame introduction, I walked onto the Coliseum floor, witnessed the crowd filled to the rafters. I heard the cheers, pure excitement. The news hadn't really gotten out about the bowling alley, so it was the last game I'd play in high school without hearing from the crowd, from the media, about all that.

We had lost to these dudes in December. They had beaten us bad in January. The lesson from that January game was I had to stop being so selfish, but the lesson of later games was that to win it, I had to shoot it. I wanted to win it.

So I came in there hot as hell, and started the game cold as a motherfucker.

Hampton took it upon themselves to focus on stopping me. So they had one or two guys on me at all times. If I moved off a screen, both my guy and the screener's guy would follow me and trap. I kept shooting and missing in the first quarter, and we got down eleven.

In the huddle, Coach Bailey told us we had to adjust; if they got two guys on me then it was going to have to be the other dudes to make their open looks. Everyone looked at me. Coach Bailey's eyes were on me. Like this was the moment. This was the moment they had been talking about back in January. *Pass it.* Time to trust my teammates.

To prove a point, Tony Rutland took that shit personally. In the second quarter he started bombing. When they came at me with a second defender, I just passed it to Tony. He made them pay. He ended up with 18 in the first half, while I shot 3–13. If not for him, they would've had the game right there. Instead we came all the way back and held a lead at halftime.

It was more of the same in the second half. We took control in the third quarter and barely held on as they mounted a rally that fell short. It wasn't my best game at all. Yet we won. The other dudes had done it. And not just Tony, but the big guys won on the glass.

With the win we had assured ourselves a spot in the regional. And we had won the regular-season district title for the first time in Bethel history.

Later that month, I was named a *Parade* first-team All-American. I was one of just two juniors to receive that honor.

The next day, the Newport News *Daily Press* covered the win against

Hampton, but it also had its first article about the bowling alley. At that point it was just described as a big fight, but the paper found room to say that I was there. There weren't any charges yet, but of course having a chance to name Allen Iverson, they figured they might as well take it.

We began the district tournament after that, winning the first game easily. Then on the Tuesday after the Hampton game, we were set to play Ferguson. But first, I had to be arrested.

Since the week before when I went to the precinct to take the photos, Mo had picked out a lawyer for me. We didn't have any money, of course. Mo worked at Hampton University. He spoke to the president there, and they helped us land on Herb Kelly. Mr. Kelly was a lawyer who did work for the university. He had been doing it a long time, but I now know he hadn't tried any criminal cases in years. He wasn't that kind of lawyer. But he had one thing going for him—he agreed to represent me for free.

As a seventeen-year-old, I was technically a juvenile, but the crime they charged me with could lead to me being either charged as an adult or staying in juvenile court. That would be up to my eventual judge. For my first court appearance, we were still in juvenile court, and the press wasn't allowed in there. Even so, man, the press was waiting for me outside, to take pictures and write whatever other bullshit they wanted to write. Mr. Kelly arranged it so that I went in and out the back way, and I never got put in jail. I got me a small bond, got the charges read, and got right on out of there.

But before I get back to basketball, you got to hear what they charged me with—maiming by mob, which was a felony charge. I was just like, *Where was the mob?* It was a fight.

This shit was just so crazy. Four of us got charged: me, Michael Simmons, Melvin Stephens, and Samuel Wynn. All four of us were Black. Not one white dude charged. I learned much later some other real crazy shit—"maiming by mob" was a statute created a long time ago, like a century before, and it was designed to protect Black folks from getting lynched by white mobs. It was still on the books a century later, available to these prosecutors to charge me with a serious felony. Without the mob part of it, it was misdemeanors at most. So yeah, I was charged with breaking a law aimed to stop lynch mobs.

Mo came to court, of course. And I remember he just had this look on his face. Like he knew this was how it was going to be. He knew that this wasn't going to go all quiet. The man been with me since I was eight years old playing hotball in between the Stuart Gardens buildings. He was never righter than when he told me from the get-go that this bowling alley shit was a problem.

So I got arrested. Charged with felonies. Life was fucked-up. Where could I go for some quiet? Right back on the basketball court just a few hours after pleading not guilty. From one court to another court.

We had a second-round playoff game against Ferguson. It was back in Anderson Field House in Fort Eustis, with another capacity crowd expected. We raced up there to make it for the tip.

As always, loud as it was, excited as everyone was, it quieted for me as I stepped on the floor. Aaron Brooks, the quarterback I mentioned who went on to play in the NFL, was on that Ferguson squad, and he gave us a lot of trouble. Meanwhile, their defense was running two guys at me all game. But on this night it didn't matter. I hit threes from all over the place. Seven of them. I got 42 points, and when it got close, I scored 9 of the last 13 to seal it. As long as I was out on bond, no bullshit arrest was going to keep me from building my legacy.

THIRTEEN

BETHEL CONTINUES

With the win against Ferguson, we had assured ourselves a spot in regionals, but we still wanted to win the district tournament, and to do that it would take a win in our fourth meeting against Hampton. Three days later, we did exactly that, playing a Hampton team that was without their guy, Bacote. We got ahead 12–2 and didn't look back. I scored another 42.

As the calendar turned to March, we began our assault on the state title. After an easy one in the regionals we faced Maury, and they had Joe Smith on their squad. Since we'd both played together on the AAU title team, he'd come into his own and was a *Parade* third-team All-American heading to the University of Maryland.

And throughout, we had no answer for him. He scored 37 of their 50 points. They went back to him again and again. Meanwhile, neither I nor Tony could get it going. I ended up with just 19. Couldn't hit my shot. Not one three-pointer. Down the stretch we had to find a way on defense, and that's when I asked Coach to put me on Smith. Coach Bailey looked at me like I was crazy, but at the same time he knew we had to try something different. So in the fourth quarter, it was me, all six feet and zero inches, against one of the top centers in the country. I fronted him. I used my quickness. Basically just competed. My teammates came to help. And we kept him from scoring in the final minutes until he had a meaningless basket as time expired. We walked out of that defensive struggle victorious, 52–50.

With the win, we'd booked our spot in the state quarterfinals, and from the quarterfinals, just three games left to do what we had already done in football.

The state quarterfinals were in Richmond, at the Ashe Center, which fit about 6,000 fans. And we began our mission against Hopewell. We built an 11-point halftime lead, and though it got close in the second half, we held on for a victory. I scored 38 points with 5 threes. But it wasn't just the scoring. I also had 8 assists, 7 rebounds, 6 steals, and 4 blocks. I was just on this mission now. I had to do it all. I had played defense against Joe Smith, so now I was going to block shots, sky for boards, if that's what we needed. There was only one thing I wasn't willing to do: let us lose.

A few days later, we traveled to Charlottesville to face Woodbridge in the semifinal. On the season I had racked up 896 points. That made me tied for the Virginia record for points in a single season. The man who held that record at the time was none other than Moses Malone. All I had to do was score a single basket, or just one free throw, and the record would be mine. But in Woodbridge we faced a team that prided itself on defense. They hadn't given up more than 59 points all year. I paid that no mind. That's how confident I was. But I should have, because they locked us down.

In fact, early in the third quarter, we found ourselves down 17 points. Nothing was working. Me and Tony's shots weren't falling. They played it slow and kept going down low to Damion Keyes, their center who scored 30 on us. Once again I went down there, the littlest guy on the team, to guard the big man. He was a head taller than me, and probably had 100 pounds on me too. Along the way, I got myself in some foul trouble.

We were making it up slow, too slow, and with less than three minutes left, they were still ahead, 59–50. It began to feel like the football game against Huguenot, when we were down 16–0 in the fourth quarter. Me and Tony then just turned on the defensive intensity. We hounded them, got a couple steals. With 26 seconds left, we had clawed our way within three. I had the ball and I had two of their guys draped all over me. But I wasn't letting anything prevent me from rising up. I was about four feet behind the three-point line, rose up above, and let it go. I sank the tying bucket to send us into overtime.

I'd carried us into the extra period, but the dudes had to carry it over the finish line. I fucking fouled out after overtime started, and from the bench it was me and Mike Bailey together, barking out orders, encouragement, prayers to the team. I remember standing beside Coach, as powerless as I could be on the court, yet completely a part of the team.

Out of nowhere, our young big man, Lovett Gaither, scored 9 of our 13 points in the extra period, for a 72–65 win. Watching him and the other guys come through, and from the bench, I felt this pride and kinship, not just with the dudes on the floor but with Coach. This was his view? Damn, that shit was stressful.

The next day was the final against John Marshall. We could just feel it at that point. We got down early, but in the third quarter we made our now-familiar move. Me and Tony once again started hounding them. We took control with a 26–10 burst, giving ourselves an 11-point lead. But somehow, feeling the state championship in our grasp, we relented a little bit. And they came after us. With a little more than a minute left, they came all the way back to tie it at 69.

Their crowd was going crazy. I think we had tightened up just a little bit. I didn't feel any of that. I just sensed the moment. There was less than two minutes left and we had just turned the ball over. They had a chance to take the lead. Their guard was bringing it up the left side of the court.

I could see he wasn't comfortable with it. So I came from across the floor and just as he turned away from another defender, I saw my chance. Attacking, I swiped it clean off the bounce, took it the other way, and made a layup with two guys chasing after me. It was good for a two-point lead. It was one of those moments. Like it was just my time.

On the next possession, Tony hit a little jumper, grabbing us a four-point lead. It was almost done, but we needed an exclamation. A minute later, Tony missed a free throw when we were up four. But you know me. I was lurking, and as the rebounder turned around to take it up court, I snatched it.

Just like in our first game of the year, when it had taken me six seconds to steal the ball and announce my presence with a jam, I fucking two-hand-dunked it to let everyone know it was over.

I remember as the buzzer blared, everyone erupted from our bench, just jumping around. This was it. We had done it. State championship number two. For me, I stood tall, chest out, arms down, nodding my head, smiling. There wasn't any thought of a bowling alley. There wasn't any thought of a trial. There wasn't any thoughts of nothing—just the exhilaration.

This would be the last high school game I ever played. But I didn't know it at the time. I couldn't imagine it.

For my senior year, the only hoops I'd shoot would be in the prison yard.

FOURTEEN

THE TRIAL

Everyone had a fucking opinion. Everyone had something to say about Allen Iverson and the bowling alley. You heard it in the barbershop. In the classroom. On the streets. On the radio and TV. Wherever people talked, basically.

But most of all, it seemed, in the newspaper. The *Daily Press* carried it front and center. I'll never forget how they looked for me when I got charged in juvenile court. We had to go out the back way to avoid the cameras. Then they published my name, even though juvenile records were supposed to be sealed. What meant a lot to me was three girls from Bethel High, who I didn't even know, wrote a letter to the editor basically telling them that shit wasn't right to put my name in there. Three other guys got arrested, one was also seventeen, and they kept his name out of it. But they had papers to sell. And they said I was so famous, their readers had a right to know. But listen, this is how close me and Tawanna were. It was probably the only time she ever got in trouble at school, because she was a good kid. One of her teachers said some shit about me and the whole situation, and she had a mouth on her, so she got into it real bad with this teacher, standing up for me.

I was supposed to be a kid still—unless they could try me as an adult. And that was the first legal question. We had a hearing on April 12, 1993, for that purpose, and they had witnesses and everything. They brought the cops in. I knew something was up because my lawyer asked the cops about when they brought me in to take pictures. Mr. Kelly asked the officer if I was told to come into the station just to take pictures. The cop denied it. When he denied it—remember, he had told that to me—I started to see how things were going to be.

The judge didn't make a decision that day. What was on the line was this: As an adult, I faced five to twenty years on each count in adult prison. As a juvenile, I would be looking at something like six months at most in a detention center, and keeping my record sealed. I didn't think I was getting convicted either way, since I didn't do anything, the way I saw it. But damn, that was a big difference in how I could be charged and punished.

At the hearings, they laid the "facts" out. The big white dude testified that he was just having beer with his friends. So mind you, he was over twenty-one and was drinking; we were kids and there wasn't any drinking among us. He said I came over to him and his friends and just started cursing for no reason. So he got up to have words with me, and before he knew it, he got hit by someone else, and that's when the fight broke out. He admitted to throwing chairs and punches, but he said he was just acting in self-defense. He did go to the hospital with a broken bone. He did not claim I actually hit him or that he saw me do anything physical.

Then there was this one young lady, who I never even saw in the bowling alley. She said the fight started and everything went flying. She claimed she saw me, and came up to me and said, "Why are you doing this? Why can't you stop this? Why does it have to be racial?" Nobody ever said that to me, first of all. And she couldn't explain why she said that it was racial. See, I was the one talking about some racist shit he said to me (which he denied). His story was that I was just cursing at him for no reason. Yet here she was coming up to me crying about why did it have to be racial?

Then she said, "The last impression I had was the smile on Allen Iverson's face. Then I woke up. I was knocked out." She couldn't say who hit her though. She couldn't and didn't say she saw me do a damn thing. No, a dude who worked at the bowling alley and who had supposedly told us to quiet down earlier that night was the only one who said he saw me do anything violent—as he would testify to in the trial.

I watched this all unfold, and I couldn't believe it, man. I had been involved in fights before, all kinds of shit, but I never went out there and hit some girl. And for no reason? With a fucking chair? I remember one time as a kid, my sister, Brandy, she had a problem with some girl, and she came to me for help. I looked at her like she must be crazy. Couldn't fight no girl! What I did was I helped her learn how to handle herself. Which she then did.

The accusations were so beyond my imagination that in a way I walked out of there like, *No way in hell is the judge going to believe all that.*

Life kept going. And by life, I mean basketball. It was another summer AAU season. Just two days before that hearing, we won the Boo Williams Classic AAU tournament. Then, a couple days after the hearing, we won the AAU state title. I scored 42 in the clincher. That put us in the National AAU once again, beginning July 17. And of course, I had been invited to the Nike camp once again. That began on July 5.

I was thinking to myself, almost like making plans, *How can I one-up last summer?* Well, we would have to repeat as AAU national champs, first of all. Then I'd have to get me an MVP at Nike. The legendary Bob Gibbons, who'd been rating high school kids forever and helped Nike choose who got an invite, would come out with his senior-class rankings after that week. I had my eye on being No. 1.

So basketball remained my sanctuary. It was the good part of life. I was off the streets and succeeding—a kid reaching for his future. That's the way I saw it, anyway.

Yet on May 5, the judge made his decision about what court would hear my case. After the prosecutor characterized my actions as the embodiment of evil, the judge found that I should be tried as an adult. He scheduled the trial for July 9. Looking at it now, it's so fucked-up because I just never believed they could do this. I didn't believe it the night it all went down when I called Mo to tell him what happened. I couldn't believe it when I went to take the pictures at the precinct. I couldn't believe it when they charged me. And I couldn't believe it at the hearing. Man, these people were really after me.

That June, I was supposed to pick a sport to focus on. People told me basketball was my real future—my way out. Dudes made more money in basketball and had longer careers. It shouldn't have been a hard decision, but I wasn't ready to rule out football. College basketball and football—that was something I had always imagined.

I narrowed it down to fifteen schools. Schools like Duke were on the list, University of Southern California was on there, but so were a couple local schools like Hampton University. They were all still sending me shit in the mail, doing all that stuff, and maybe they were closing their eyes to the bowling alley situation. I was still undecided on whether to play football as a senior in high school.

The Nike Tournament was set to go from Tuesday, July 5 through Saturday, July 10 in Indianapolis. It was going to be my second year there, and, like I said, I wanted to make my mark. But the problem was that my fucking trial was right in the middle of it. So Nike offered to pay my airfare there and back. Thursday night I'd go back to Hampton. I would have the trial on Friday. Then I could go and play in the nationally televised All-Star Game the next day on Saturday. People acted like I was diminishing my trial, but to me, this was something positive to do with my life. Why wouldn't I want to do something positive with my life? Everybody was acting like I was jeopardizing my life, my future, by getting in trouble. But the second I tried to continue to make something of it, by sticking to sports, it was like I was doing something wrong. It basically felt like people were mad that I didn't know my place.

They had these columnists in the newspaper talking about how I was a coddled star. That I would be another example of a Black kid from the ghetto failing to reach his promise. I'm not lying, man! They were actually comparing me to these other playground legends who busted, like Lloyd Daniels. And what did they want me to do—quit *before* they threw me in prison? I was blessed to have defenders, man, like Mo, who wrote a letter to the paper. Friends and family encouraged me. Leaders in the community advocated for me.

The other part that's crazy is I was thinking to myself, *I actually already did what they wanted me to.* I couldn't say the shit out loud. I wasn't telling anyone about my days hustling. But in my head, I was like, *I did all the bad shit they imagined. But I dropped that shit. I focused on sports.* It was never enough. They wanted me to drop my friends too. Drop my words, my style, my thinking. I didn't realize this all back then. It took me a long fucking time to get it.

What I wanted to do was succeed and bring my friends, my family, my community, my way of being, along for the journey, for the rewards.

So you're motherfucking right I went to Nike the week of my trial.

And sure, I felt invincible. Against all the odds, I had just won state in football and basketball, and this was after dominating the entire nation on the AAU circuit the summer before. I'll never forget one quote that got out. Bob Gibbons said, "Every school in the country wants him. If he was John Dillinger, they'd take him."

That was the atmosphere as I got to the camp. Remember how at my first AAU championship, I walked in and no one was staring at me, but they all pointed as I left? This year, they were staring from the start. Everyone knew who I was, and the bowling alley shit just made it even more. The other kids out there competing, they weren't shaking their heads like, *He's ruining his future.* Nah man, that shit added to my rep, if I'm being honest. But I just wanted to play basketball. That's what I did, and I shut out all that other stuff, the talk and the coming trial, kept my head clear like I was always able to do, and sure enough, out of the 125 kids invited, I was among the ones picked out for the Saturday All-Star Game to be televised on ESPN.

But first I had to go to my trial. That Thursday night they drove me on out to the airport for my flight back to Hampton. The next morning, I was ready for court. Wearing that suit I already told you about. Just like I was supposed to.

While the trial was in adult court, it was a different judge. Judge Overton was an old white dude. And Mo will tell you we should have known when we looked at his résumé and saw that he was a proud graduate of Hampton High. That was where the old money was, the people who'd been in power for a long time. Judge Overton was part of that tradition.

We had to decide something before the trial, which was whether we wanted a jury trial. Obviously, I was seventeen at the time, and I wasn't really too sure about all the ins and outs of that. Mr. Kelly wanted to do what was called a bench trial, just in front of the judge. I'm really not too sure, looking back at it, why we didn't go with a jury. Of course a jury of your peers can mean a lot of things. It wasn't going to be my friends from Stuart Gardens on the jury, if that's what we chose. So he decided to do the trial just in front of the judge. Knowing what I know now, would I do that again? Hell no. I don't know, maybe it was that Mr. Kelly had not tried a criminal case in a long time. Or maybe it was that Mr. Kelly thought he was on the level with this judge. Whatever it was, it did not work.

There were two strategies to my defense. The first was we wanted to show that I didn't do any of the shit they said I did. So I was going to tell my side of it, and we had another witness, Dwayne Campbell, who pulled me out of the alley when the fight started.

The other part was Mr. Kelly's legal defense. The charges were three counts of maiming by mob. So what did that mean? They had to show that I was a "person composing a mob" and that I caused an injury "with intent to maim, disable, disfigure or kill" the person. And to be a mob, they had to show that a "collection of people," including me, "assembled for the purpose and with the intention of committing an assault or a battery." Mr. Kelly's whole point was even if you believed what they said, I wasn't part of a mob, because the whole thing started with a fight all of a sudden. So no mob ever formed. Remember, this whole crime was originally supposed to be about stopping a bunch of white folks from getting on horses together and deciding as a group to do some bad shit to Black folks.

Mr. Kelly, like Judge Overton, was an older white dude. He worked for some fancy firm, and he did business with Hampton University, so that's how Mo got him involved. He wasn't really a criminal lawyer. But he was well-known in court. With his white hair, his 6'4" figure, and Southern accent, the dude carried himself like he ran the place. He strode around with this cane. It had a silver top on it. He'd kind of hit the cane on the ground when he made a point.

So they marched their witnesses in. Steve Forrest told the same story he had in the first hearing. He said that after I cursed at him, he stood up from his beer and his friends and just all innocent said he wanted no trouble, they were just about to leave. That's when someone else came and hit him out of nowhere.

Then came the woman who claimed she asked me why it had to be racial. She described the scene: "It seemed like it was just Black people trying to injure whatever white people were around." And this time she said the last thing she saw before getting hit was my "smirk."

I remember turning around a couple times to see my mom just shaking her head. Mo was mad as hell. Behind them was an assistant coach from the University of Virginia trying to recruit my ass! Coach Bailey was there looking more worried than in the fourth quarter with us down a dozen.

The bowling alley worker was the next witness. He was white and he was a student at Bethel, though I did not know him. And he said some shit I still can't believe. He said he saw me hit the young lady with a chair. Then he claimed he asked me why I would do that. And after that, I supposedly hit him with the chair too. Listening, I just sat there stunned.

After that it was my turn, and I told my side of it: that Steve Forrest had started it by saying some racial shit he shouldn't have. I spoke back to him, and the next thing I know there's shit flying and my friends grabbed me and took me on out of there. Which is exactly what everyone knew to do with me if shit like that ever happened, because my friends knew who I was and fucking believed in me.

The truth is, shit had almost happened at times before. With Mike Jackson, he'd do his "Buuuuuub" magic, and stop things before they started. But when I hung out with Arnie and Ra and all them, and something happened—arguments, fights, what have you—the first thing everyone would do is grab me and get me out of there. It used to piss me off sometimes. That's what happened the night of the bowling alley, and that's what I told the judge. Then Dwayne Campbell testified that he was one of the dudes who grabbed me to get me away from all that shit, so I wasn't even there when most of it happened.

Then there was the part about the video. It showed a lot of the chaos. And the video didn't show me on it doing shit. But Mr. Kelly argued that it was not relevant to the trial, basically. So the video was not part of the evidence. That shit went right over my head, but after the fact and on appeal, they were like, how did your lawyer try to keep the video out of evidence, when it didn't even have you in it?

So after their witnesses and our witnesses, Mr. Kelly made his motion to dismiss. This was his big moment. He thought he could convince Judge Overton that they hadn't shown a mob. So he explained it. We were just kids who came there with an intent to have some fun bowling, not to fight. "Somebody hit somebody and then it turned into a fight." The cane tapped.

Judge Overton wasn't interested. He just denied the motion.

It was late, and so he scheduled closing arguments for the following Monday.

We all left the courthouse, and it was kind of like, *What just happened?* I was just seventeen, man. So you know what I was thinking? *Get me back to Indianapolis and the Nike camp so I can put on my show!* Nah, I was worried too. I remember sitting around that night with my friends. *Could he really find me guilty?*

Next morning, I was in the car, running to the airport.

This is what I remember about the big Saturday game. The opening tip came to me, I raced to the other end, passed it ahead for a layup, and we had the first two points. I was right where I needed to be. On the basketball floor, so it was quiet again.

The following Monday, we returned to court. All my people came back. The newspapers had run wall-to-wall articles. Even some of the national news had come. Mr. Kelly stuck to the script. They hadn't proven that I hit anyone. And it wasn't no mob. "There is no common purpose when people come running from everywhere because of the words 'fight, fight, fight.'"

The prosecutor focused on other things. She said I "had two choices—either stay and participate, or get out. He stayed and participated and became a member of the mob. . . . We don't care how good a basketball player Mr. Iverson is. . . . [T]he fact is, he acted like a criminal that night." She described what happened as Black people "started hitting whatever white people got in their way."

Then she looked Judge Overton in the eye. It was like her victory dance in the end zone. Because she knew a certain segment of the population was mad as hell I'd played in that Nike Tournament.

"Now," she said serious as a motherfucker, "it's our turn to *Just Do It.*"

Just Do It like Nike exhorted, except instead of excelling at sports, she wanted the judge to just find me guilty.

Maybe that's why I ended up getting a lifetime deal with Reebok.

Judge Overton just did it. He found me guilty of all three counts of maiming by mob. I heard that word. *Guilty*. Like damn, the judge decided I'd done these crimes. But it felt heavier than just that. *Guilty* meant I wasn't worth shit, like I didn't deserve a future. This judge had deliberated and reached a verdict: I was just another bad street kid. Just a word I swore I'd never say in this motherfucking book.

Again, I turned to look behind me. My mom was broken. Mo looked like he knew it was coming but he was still fucking mad. Coach Bailey and Mrs. Bailey seemed devastated. Tawanna, she was calm, stoic.

I turned back and faced the judge. He scheduled the sentencing date for late summer. He let me remain out pending that date. But he set an 8 p.m. curfew. That meant I couldn't travel for the AAU national tournament and defend my title the next week. It meant that except for going to the gym or the park, I couldn't escape in the game.

So what's a dude like me supposed to do with an 8 p.m. curfew? They took the one thing I was good at and said, "Sit at home waiting to see if you even get to sit at home anymore."

Remember the difference between being a juvenile and an adult? The sentence was like that too—all over the map. The judge could give me simple probation, or he could sentence me from five to twenty years in prison on each count.

The *Daily Press* made its position known. Through the editorial board, the paper said the court could "help Iverson with a firm sentence that ignores his star status." *Help* me. And that was really how a lot of people felt about it. This one writer, I won't name him, wrote column after column denouncing me and my friends. The letters to the editor were often about me. Shit like this: "I am so tired of the NAACP and a lot of Blacks turning every incident into something racial. Allen Iverson was wrong and fortunately the system worked." Another lady hoped "surely justice will prevail and he will play ball in prison instead of on the pro courts."

But I had my supporters. The mayor of Newport News was Jessie Rattley. She and a couple of local ministers, Rev. M. I. Jefferson and Rev. Alfred Terrell, sought a meeting with Judge Overton to appeal to his conscience and convince him that my future did play a part in considering whether prison was appropriate. But the judge just said no, "I don't take recommendations on sentencing. They should talk to his lawyers." A bunch of concerned citizens formed this group called SWIS (a letter for each of the four of us accused of these crimes at the bowling alley). They raised money for all of our legal defenses.

Everything was going crazy. The NCAA investigated whether it broke their rules when Nike had sent me back home for my court date. The rules allowed for Nike to pay for only one flight there and back, apparently. Then it was reported that Duke, Kentucky, Wake Forest, and even local schools like Virginia and Old Dominion were no longer recruiting me.

Damn, I thought. *Maybe they didn't have to put me in jail to keep me from reaching my dreams.* At the end of August there was a tournament in Virginia Beach—I could be home before my curfew. I said I would play. Then the press wrote a story about it, and even Boo Williams had to come tell me that I couldn't play until the sentence got figured out.

Not to mention Bethel football. Of course I dreamed of repeating as state champs. But I didn't get the chance to even decide—I was not allowed to play high school sports until the case was over. I sat at home as practices started up in mid-August, just chilling with Tawanna, spending time with Iiesha, watching her learn to walk and talk. This little girl had almost died after being born late, before she even had a chance to do the simplest things. Still suffering from seizures, the kid was strong as a motherfucker.

There we were on Victoria Boulevard. It wasn't much, but we still had fun. And I'd go spend the days with Ra and Arnie, and Marlon and E, all those dudes. Or I would chill with Mike Jackson. We'd play one-on-one Monopoly, buying every property we could, ruthless with one another. Like always.

Mike left for college that August. He attended Virginia Military Institute, where he'd run track, maybe even play football. When he packed his bags to go, it was hard to put into words what I felt. After that, something was missing.

By then, the sentencing had been put off to September. Everything was put off. A decision if I could even play high school sports was put off. I started considering going to a prep school. I was a little older than an incoming senior might be, having done two eighth grades, and my academics and attendance weren't great. Prep school was an option to get my grades in order and play high level basketball. I spoke to some schools that were more than willing to bring me on. One school was called Maine Central Institute. Faisal Abraham had gone there. He had gotten his shit together and was about to start as a freshman at Marquette. The local papers were so interested in me, they even covered this. So everyone knew I had a path forward, even if it wasn't playing sports on the Peninsula with Bethel.

FIFTEEN

SENTENCING DAY

September 8, 1993, was supposed to be my second day of senior year of high school. Instead it was my sentencing day. The night before, I remember chilling with my friends when it kind of hit me how much power this judge had over the rest of my life. He could give me probation or he could imprison me for years and years—beyond a time when I could still enroll in college and make it to the NBA.

Looking in the mirror and then in front of family, I practiced what I would say. More than anything, I wanted to get it over with.

The next morning, my mom got Iiesha all dressed up for court. She had two little pigtails, a dress. I put on that suit. That damn gray suit. I looked in the mirror. Collar straight, tie tight.

To get in the front door of the courthouse, I had to walk by all the supporters from SWIS, TV crews and photographers, and a big-ass crowd.

As the sentencing hearing began, I heard Mr. Kelly explain to the judge that I could go to this prep school in Maine that would have all kinds of rules and requirements, and ensure my education was being tended to. Two of my teachers at Bethel told the judge that I wasn't a bad kid. One of them, Ms. Abernathy, said I was "the kind of student you like to teach." But the prosecutor told a different story. Of course she detailed again all the things she said I'd done. She talked about that one prior driving-without-a-license case I mentioned—my "criminal past." And she claimed that I could be rehabilitated in jail. As she later explained, "There are programs. There is a GED program. Iverson can finish his education. There are recreational facilities. I don't think he'd be any worse off."

Then they asked if I had anything to say. Here is what I said: "I would like to apologize to my family and friends and the community, if I caused them any embarrassment. And I think I've got my chance now to talk, so I did feel bad for what happened to the people that night at the bowling alley. I wouldn't want that to happen to anybody in that situation."

Judge Overton gazed from the bench, over his reading glasses, considering me. A couple years later, people fought against his reappointment when it came to light that he was a member of two old-ass all-white clubs, one of them the damn yacht club. I guess he didn't like what he saw as he considered me.

He said it then: five years for each count, for a total of fifteen years.

The whole fucking courtroom gasped.

Fuck. My future. Was it going to happen right then and there?

But before that got answered, Mr. Kelly had one last card to play. See, the one of us who had done a jury trial and only been convicted of misdemeanors, Stephens, he had requested and received the chance to be out on bond while awaiting his appeal. So Mr. Kelly asked for the same, a bond pending appeal.

Judge Overton just said no. Not even that.

So that's when the officers came. They said quietly, "Hands behind your back." The cuffs slid on as I turned to look at my family. I didn't have no smile, but I didn't show tears either. That was me. Meanwhile, my mom cried her heart out. Iiesha sat there not knowing what to do or say. I could see how mad Mo was. Coach Bailey and Mrs. Bailey just grabbed hold of one another.

One thing I'll never forget is how my coaches had my back. Coach Koz went out there and said, "I'm appalled that they decided to incarcerate a teenager who had a possibility of a future, and now it appears dim. We've lost one of our family."

Coach Bailey spoke from his heart: "I've felt sad in my life, but this is a sadness that can't be expressed in words." Later I'd hear about it, how on the courthouse steps he told the press, "We didn't lose a tremendous high school athlete today, we didn't lose a member of our student body. We lost a friend."

Seconds after the handcuffs went on, they tugged me out the courtroom into the back. Then they put me in the van to be taken to the jail. I turned to look. Out that back window I could see everyone gathering behind, upset as motherfuckers could be. When the van started driving, a few of them ran after it, waving, until we drove too fast for them to run.

Then, like I said, they put me in holding, with my suit on and hot as hell.

III

FROM THE JUNGLE TO GEORGETOWN

Freedom

That all ended with me going to jail. So let me tell you about freedom real quick.

It's getting out on the basketball court. It's pulling up to shoot a three over someone a foot taller but a step slower. It's hopping the passing lane and coasting to the other end and jamming it. It's playing in front of a crowd the first time and leaving them speechless.

It's waking up next to Tawanna. Or hanging with my friends and family until the late hours.

It's listening to my music. Rapping with my friends. Partying.

It's returning from jail to my own damn house, with my mom, my friends, everyone waiting there. Fucking exonerated.

It's me wearing a Bethel sweatshirt, oversized, hugging my family for dear life.

It's starting again, knowing that I've been released and unleashed.

SIXTEEN

CITY FARM

They sent me to the Newport News City Farm. I knew about the place. I'm not going to lie. I knew people who had been sent there. I knew people who had gone to much worse prisons than that. The City Farm was minimum security.

Once I got there, it was a new life. I couldn't hang out with my friends. I couldn't be with Iiesha or the rest of my family. I couldn't see Tawanna alone. That one hurt. I couldn't attend school. That one didn't hurt so much!

But regardless of school, I did have to get up early. There wasn't any sleeping-in at the City Farm. Some of the inmates had jobs on the outside, like a halfway house. For the rest of us, they gave everyone a job on the Farm. A lot of inmates would be outside doing the farm work. The job they gave me was inside, in the kitchen bakery. Every day I had to be up at four in the damn morning. Since I wasn't out at night, though, I could do it.

Before I even got there, everyone at the Farm knew who I was—from sports, from the trial, all that. They put me with the halfway-house guys, who left during the day to work, because they were more chill. No one wanted me to be a target. It was quiet. A routine. Boring. After a few days at the jail, I started feeling like it was over. At that age, I couldn't see far in the future, and when I looked at the weeks stretching in front of me, it was hard. No football, no basketball.

People were telling me, "You going to get an appeal bond, we going to get you out." Literally, motherfuckers were telling me every day, "Tomorrow is the day." But tomorrow came, and it wasn't the day. One of my Newport News guys came and visited me not long after I got there. He asked me what I was doing with my time. I told him I was doing push-ups, going to work, and reading the Bible. He was like, *The Bible?* But I told him how I had to focus on praying to get out, like everyone was saying would happen.

He was like, *Ain't these the same people who told you, "You ain't getting arrested, ain't getting tried as an adult, ain't getting convicted, ain't getting sentenced to jail"?* Then he got serious: *You doing the time, Chuck.* He was from the hood with me. When it came to jail and the authorities, he knew there wasn't any use in hoping and praying. Generally things didn't work out. So when he told me that, it actually made it so much easier. I could relax.

Then, I spoke to Nana. Since I had been reading the Bible, I said to her, "If I wasn't guilty, why would God do this to me?" I was almost crying. It wasn't just my future I was sweating. She had her health issues, and I didn't want this to be her last memory of me. She said something I'll never forget: "Never question God." She had a way of setting me straight. So all of this was telling me I had to be patient.

The Farm was minimum security, but it wasn't like it was soft. There were a lot of young dudes like me, doing their first bids. You had to be careful with them. They tended to hang out in a part of the jail just on the other side of the dining area that they called "the jungle." That's where there was trouble.

The older guys were more chill and protective. Some worked in the bakery with me, and others were able to leave the jail during the day for work, like I said. Some of these dudes made sure the young kids didn't mess with me in the jungle. I remember one time some kid gave me a cigarette. So I lit it up out in the yard, and this old head smacked it out my mouth. "Oh you just giving up, huh? Nah motherfucker, you ain't gonna give up, you gonna get out of here, shit. You'll get out of here and you'll get right. 'Cause you ain't gonna be in this motherfucker, falling into this bullshit like everybody else." I didn't smoke any more cigarettes.

The good thing about working in the bakery was that you got done and it was still the morning. So I'd spend the afternoon getting some sleep—my dorm area would be empty with all the other guys out working—and playing basketball. There was one bent-up hoop, and boys would be playing pretty much most of the day. I remember I first got out there, and a dude fouled the shit out of me, and I was like, "Man, ball!" Motherfucker said, "Ball? Where the fuck you think you at? Do you know where you at?" I was like, *Oh shit.* So the rest of the time I focused on my jump shot.

In the evening, they'd let me shoot by myself sometimes. I would dribble on the cracking concrete, pull up, and shoot at the leaning hoop with a ripped-up net, the farm fields in the background, sometimes a setting sun. I would imagine the Bethel crowds, the sweaty defenders, the girls looking on. I would dream of college, the NBA. Could I take these shots, make these moves, on the same court as Michael Jordan? I knew I could—even when I was in jail with no way out.

More and more jumpers, a way to avoid the outside world pressing in, and yet still a dream, even from the prison yard.

At least I had lots of visitors. My mom came, and she would bring Brandy or Iiesha. My lawyers visited. At this point I was represented by new counsel. Tawanna and I could sit outside talking. My friends—Ra and Arnie and E and others—would make the trip and hang out outside the gates showing their support. And that support wasn't just visiting. They helped my mom with the bills. Arnie's beeper was constantly going off when my mom needed anything. And he or Ra always took care of it. They all helped Brandy with getting what she needed for school. A lot of people abandoned me, but those dudes stuck with me—supported my whole family—through those dark days.

The colleges disappeared though. Every university in the country had been recruiting me. Like I told you, some recruiters even came to my trial. I guess they were hoping for an acquittal. Because when the judge locked me up, the interest ended. No more college mail flooding the mailbox. Maybe the college coaches were following the press, article after article telling everyone what a bad guy I was, how *lucky* I was to get such a *short* sentence.

While the recruiting letters weren't coming in, I still got all kinds of mail. Letters arrived at the City Farm from people around the globe. The staff would save them for me and let me look at them. I'm thinking, *If you read these stories in the papers about me, you would think I must be the worst person in the world.* But damn if I didn't get letters talking about how people believed in me, were inspired by my story, saw the injustice in it. Maybe the negative letters were removed, but I didn't get any mail from angry motherfuckers. It was a lesson I always tried to remember. The press ain't the same as the people.

Some of my family and friends wrote to me too. Almost every week I got a letter from Mike Jackson. He was in college at Virginia Military Institute, and he was miserable as a motherfucker could be. He said it was like a jail over there, with the early mornings, the officers yelling at you all day. He hated it. He also expressed guilt that he wasn't there at the bowling alley and then he wasn't there when I got locked up. Hearing from him meant the world to me, how concerned he was. I wrote him back and let him know I was alright. He saved the letter. I wrote, "All these people are supporting me and I'm not going to let them down. But most of all, I'm not going to let myself, God, and family down."

It's hard to believe, but people really cared about my predicament. The Black leaders of Hampton and Newport News—politicians, ministers, teachers—fought for me. The SWIS group kept organizing protests. And the press, not all bad, covered that side of it too.

The goal of my new lawyer, James Ellenson, was to get an appeal bond—let me get out while my case was still open. Then I could go to school, work on sports, rejoin my family. And if I won the appeal later, I wouldn't have spent the time in jail already.

Ellenson kept going to different courts seeking that bond. And if you believe it, the DA claimed they would go along with a bond pending appeal. They would recommend a $15,000 bond, they said, something that at this point the community would be able to raise for me. But the DA never actually signed on in court. That was just some bullshit.

So first a different judge, then Judge Overton again, and then the appeals court on two occasions all denied me that bond. Ellenson kept trying and failing and getting yelled at—he was good at pissing them off. I didn't see any of that (because I was in jail!) but I wasn't surprised when I got the bad news after each setback. People kept saying, "We'll win the next one, Chuck." But I just remembered what my friend had told me. *You doing the time.*

It wasn't just the local media that took an interest. A few days after I got to the City Farm, I think it was the warden who came and told me I would have a visitor the next day. It was Tom Brokaw. I was so young and in my own world, I didn't even really know who that man was. But I learned he was from NBC News, and people were impressed. When I talked to my family before the interview, they were all saying, "Damn Chuck, this is going to be what gets you out!"

So Tom Brokaw flew in from Los Angeles on his private jet and spent the morning with me at the City Farm. He interviewed my mom, the prosecutor, a dude from the local press, and a few others. He just had this way about him, like he was the real shit and in control. He sat down with the cameras rolling and busted a couple jokes about what he had been like as a basketball player. Evidence that white men can't jump, he said. I laughed.

There weren't any gotcha questions. No, he did not ask me about practice, if that's what you're wondering. He did ask me if I thought race was a factor in what happened.

How do you answer that?

I said, "I think so." I didn't say much more than that. And to me at that time, it wasn't complicated. It was a bowling alley brawl between like fifty people, mostly white adults and Black kids. Four people got arrested, and they were all Black kids. The kids, including me, got prosecuted as adults. They prosecuted us under a law originally passed to protect Black people from white mobs, and yet it was used against us so that they could send us to prison.

So yes, I thought race was a factor.

That race question, of course, was what everyone in the press talked about in the days after. That was when I first began to realize no matter how much something might be about race, better not to talk about it if you want to go about your business. People who know me know that I don't really talk about race. I love people of all races. When Black Lives Matter first became a thing, I said I believed all lives matter, and of course that got me in some other kind of trouble.

People really took it personally that I told Tom Brokaw that race was a factor. Maybe that's why the courts kept denying me a bond—*He thinks we're racist. We will show him.* Regardless of what I said, my supporters on the outside centered the conversation around race. They marched. They graffitied "Free Iverson" on the walls. They wore shirts. (Schools disciplined teachers who came to my defense in the classroom!) Everyone was talking about it. The local paper did a poll and found that 81 percent of the white people thought I should be in jail, but just 17 percent of Black people did. So maybe it was a little bit about race.

Truth is, that Brokaw interview elevated the profile of my situation. It's easier to blot out the future of a Black kid when the whole damn country isn't looking on. So while I had my beefs with the press over the years, as you all know, I thank Tom Brokaw for what he did.

As the courtroom defeats piled up, I kneaded dough. I baked bread. I shot hoops.

I figured I would get my chance eventually. One thing I thought about a lot was Nana at home. She was getting older, and she was in and out of the hospital. Uncle Stevie was taking care of her. I didn't want her last memories of me to be as a jailbird. I tried to be patient, but goddammit I wanted to help her, get her whatever hospital she needed, whatever mansion or car she could dream of, everything. But I had to focus on myself before I could get any of that—things for her, my mom, the family.

Of course, I had not graduated from high school. This was supposed to be my senior year. Remember that prosecutor who said of jail, "There is a GED program. Iverson can finish his education"? It's true they had a GED program, but it was also true that the NCAA would not accept a GED for me. So when she said, "I don't think he'd be any worse off," she was talking some bullshit. Back then the only way to pursue basketball, not to mention a college education, was by getting a scholarship and playing in the NCAA first. A GED couldn't help me.

The earliest I could get paroled was the next summer. So we kind of put a plan together. I would first work on the SAT and the ACT with a tutor so I could meet the minimum score (those tests were required by the NCAA) and when I got out, I would enroll at a prep school so I could graduate. Man, we weren't giving up!

Sue Lambiotte ran a tutoring company over in Poquoson. Her son Clay had been a basketball teammate of mine when I was about twelve.

So she knew me. And her husband was a friend of Mr. Payne, the warden at City Farm. She wanted to help. So she visited me and we talked about this plan. She looked me in the eye and told me she believed in me—as a student. She observed me on the bus to games back in the day with her son, she heard me talking, she saw my artwork. She thought I could do it.

So when I was done with the bakery, she worked it out with Mr. Payne that I would spend an hour a day at least prepping for those tests, and come April, I would be ready to take them. Then finish one more year of high school—when I would be nineteen—and I could finally go to college.

SEVENTEEN

FINDING GEORGETOWN

But what college? What college would take me? It was something everyone talked a lot about when they came and visited me. One day, my mom arrived and she just said it: "What about Georgetown? John Thompson could be your coach."

I can laugh now at me being stupid, but I was like, *Nah, that's a big man's school.* If you knew Georgetown back then, that's where Alonzo Mourning and Dikembe Mutombo went, and before that, Patrick Ewing. These guys were centers. John Thompson himself was a big man. The Hoyas played defense like a motherfucker, walked the ball up, and then passed it to the post. It was a slow pace, and I thought no six-foot guard ever came out of that program to the NBA. Plus, Thompson was known to be a hard-ass coach. I didn't think that would work for me.

My mom didn't listen to me, as usual. But what she did when I was in jail wasn't something I could control. So the next part is just the story I heard. I heard it from my mom about a million times, and Coach Thompson liked to tell it too.

It went like this: My mom and Boo Williams agreed Georgetown was worth a shot. Williams had a prior relationship with Coach Thompson because he had coached Mourning in AAU ball and was involved in the recruitment. So Williams called Coach Thompson to talk about me. Coach Thompson said he would be willing to consider it but wanted a meeting with my mom.

So my mom, Boo, Jamil Blackmon (an older dude who had become close with me and my family), and Butch Harper (who ran the Aberdeen sports program) all got in a car and took a drive up to DC. They arrived on campus at McDonough Gymnasium, where Coach's office and the practice facility were at. Once they got there, they started talking. The meeting got off to a terrible start. Somebody in the room questioned whether Coach Thompson could coach a guard, and he was about ready to kick them on out of there. So my mom stopped it, and she asked to speak to Coach Thompson alone. Everyone shuffled out, and it was just the two of them.

Then she got started crying. She basically begged him to take me. Told him about how much she and I had been through. About how I had hopes to bring the whole family out of poverty. And then she got really serious and basically said that if Coach Thompson didn't save me, if I was left down there with everything going on, I could die. It was my life in the balance.

I didn't know Coach Thompson yet. But I can imagine how he was from when I did know him. He probably got all stern and serious. He would agree to help the "child," but the "child" would have to agree to concentrate on his studies and there would be no excuses for any misbehavior. I can see him saying something like that. He said he would send his athletic department academic advisor down to Virginia to check out my work. No promises.

By the time my mom and Coach Thompson walked out of his office, it was arm in arm.

He later said of that day, he saw "the love of a mother who was afraid for the life of her child." And that's why he chose to help me. He focused on her. Her struggles as a single mother. People usually focused on the negative, how my mother supposedly wasn't there for me, or other stories. But Coach Thompson saw in my mom the same thing I learned early on. She believed in me. And she was trying her hardest on her own to help me.

EIGHTEEN

OUT OF JAIL

After we lost all the arguments for a bond pending appeal, we hired new lawyers Larry Woodward and Tom Shuttleworth. We still had the appeal in the works, but that might take years. So the next step was to seek help in getting me out from the Virginia governor. Only he could give me a pardon or clemency. And this new firm had some connections.

The governor at the time was Douglas Wilder. Governor Wilder was Black. He was the grandson of slaves. He was the first Black man ever elected governor of any state in the whole country. And his term was about to end that coming January, of 1994. The lawyers started making calls. The community organized on my behalf and raised the money to pay the legal bills. A whole bunch of celebrities chipped in. I owe thanks to a lot of people.

I was still a teenager. I was in jail—wrongly, I felt—and all that work people were doing, I couldn't really see it. Now that I'm older, I know how much all these community members did for me. I always say now that I didn't make it by myself. There was my family, my teammates, of course. And I like to always thank the training staffs, the people who work at the arena—everybody involved. They are all a part of my legacy. But it goes back so much further. It goes to those community members out there protesting. To the people who donated money to my legal fund. To the lawyers who fought on my behalf. And to the governor of Virginia, who stepped in. And I think sometimes I was so focused on getting out and getting back on track that I didn't always show my appreciation enough at the time.

December came, and I was still locked up. At that point I was happy to be working in the kitchen instead of outside in the winter cold. My family and lawyers were optimistic that the governor might do something. *Before Christmas,* they said, after I spent Thanksgiving at the Farm. As the weeks went by, the media attention started to dry out. After Brokaw interviewed me, ESPN came and did a segment. *Sport Illustrated* wrote a big-ass story as well. The state head of the NAACP visited with me, and they offered to coordinate my legal fight. But come that December, the attention was dying down.

I'll never forget Christmas morning at the Farm (yeah, "before Christmas" hadn't happened). We all got up early to do our jobs. The bakery was doing Christmas baking. Everybody had a little bit of that Christmas spirit, even if no one was with their families. How was it not to be with the family on Christmas? I wanted to be home of course. I reflect now on what Christmas was like as a kid. We had so much love. But in those days, there was disappointment. You know how in the lead-up to Christmas when you write that Christmas list and you're thinking Santa is coming and that everything on that list would be there? Then to wake up and there ain't nothing there, might not even be a damn tree in the house, or ain't nothing in them stockings. "This shit is just for the decoration. That's what makes Christmas"—to hear that every year. Now I get my kids all the shit they want. And when my friends, my family, come to me saying they need money to buy gifts for their kids, what can I do but make sure they have what they need? I remember being that kid.

So at the City Farm, on Christmas, I was okay because it wasn't like all my Christmases had been perfect. We all hung out and had a nice day. The guards didn't give us any shit. We had a good meal.

I was back in the bakery the next morning. And so it went. Until December 30, 1993—four and a half months after getting locked up.

That morning I woke up, went to work, and from the kitchen I heard a little commotion. Mr. Payne, the warden, came to me. He said, "Son, the governor has seen fit to order your release." He told me to pack my shit up and that someone would be there shortly to pick me up.

I just looked at him like he wasn't serious. The guys around me started shouting. All excited. Grabbing me by the back, on the shoulders. I was in shock. Like I said, I found that the only way I could really get through it was by believing I would have to serve the time. Now, here it was. Over. So I went back to my dorm area, which was empty, what with everyone awake and out working, and I packed up the things I had. The letters from fans, from admirers, from the NAACP, from Mike Jackson. I packed up the drawings I'd done, the schoolwork. They took me to another area of the jail and gave me some of my belongings they took at the beginning, when they first threw me in the van. That suit. I wasn't putting that shit on.

Tom Shuttleworth and Larry Woodward drove to the City Farm personally to pick me up. And they came bearing a gift. Someone in the family had given them clothes for me to wear. I took off the white prison clothes and put on green and gold sweats—Bethel's colors. That was me.

I stepped out into the cold winter air and they handed me a Fila hat, which I put on as we walked to the car. I'm thinking to myself, *I can't believe this is happening*. I was in shock. But on the outside, I played it serious as a motherfucker. Like this was expected. That's how I felt like I should act.

When we pulled up to my house, there were cameras and news crews all up and down the damn block. Goddamn, people wanted to see that.

I got out the car, serious. I opened the door to the house with my mom, my aunt, my sisters all waiting. They all wrapped their fucking arms around me. I can't lie and say I kept that serious face. Man, I let it go, behind those closed doors. That shit was over. But it would always stay with me. And here I am all these years later telling that story.

I thank Governor Wilder for what he did. He gave me another shot at life. If it wasn't for his signature, I might not be writing this book.

The *Daily Press* wrote the next day, "Those who believe Iverson was treated appropriately by the criminal justice system—and that includes us—may wonder about the governor's motives." Motives? He was supposedly trying to get the Black vote for a Senate run, the paper said. You think the first Black governor in the nation's motherfucking history needed help with the Black vote? Nah man.

The *Daily Press* took a poll. *Should the Governor have freed Allen Iverson?* Two hundred eighty-eight people said, *Hell yeah.* Seven hundred and sixty-two said, *That boy should stay in jail.* One person answering the poll wrote in, "If he had been white, he would still be in jail."

I thank Governor Wilder because that shit was brave.

Looking at it now after all these years, getting a chance to think about it, goddammit, it was crazy and I was so fortunate to have the support.

Mike Jackson reminded me once that Governor Wilder was the first Black governor of Virginia. He was also the last Black governor of Virginia to this day. Imagine that.

NINETEEN

BACK HOME

I said when I started this whole part of the book that I was "exonerated" when I walked out of that jail. That's how I felt, but the truth is Governor Wilder didn't just say the case is over, it never happened. Nothing like that. I wasn't quite *free*. First, he said no organized sports. I remember telling some of my teammates at Bethel that I couldn't play no more, and damn, they thought I'd be in the lineup that week. Nah, never again. Second, he technically put me on "furlough," meaning I had to check in with parole. That would last until the next August. And third, he gave me a whole bunch of other conditions that were no joke: "Must use his best efforts to obtain his high school diploma." Counseling. A curfew. Damn. And no "criminal activity of any nature whatsoever."

I wasn't thinking about any of that on December 30. I was celebrating with my family. And I wasn't thinking about it, for damn sure, as we all celebrated the calendar turning to 1994 the next night. I embraced Nana. I was a relieved motherfucker, relieved that her last memories weren't of me locked up. I remember some of my friends came over, including Mike.

And I told them when I stepped away to shower, "Yo, don't leave. Don't leave." I didn't want to be alone. It was like I needed my people around me to make me feel sure this was all true.

One thing I said to my lawyers was not to forget about Michael Simmons and Samuel Wynn. Those two guys were serving time in jail too (they were in Hampton Jail, not the City Farm). The governor said he just got their applications for clemency but was still considering them.

Sure enough, they got released under basically the same conditions a couple weeks later. I'll never forget how they had my back. The press wanted to divide us, interviewing them before they got out and after I did. Did they think I got special treatment? Michael said, "I love Allen to death. I just hope he gets out there and gets his education. And don't let the press get to him." Man, Michael was supposed to be playing football at Hampton University that year. Just like me, he was incarcerated that whole fall, missing the season.

My mom also told the press that her focus was my education. "He's a man now," she said. She couldn't help adding, "I think of my candy-apple-red Jaguar he said he's going to buy me" once I'd made it, "and my house better than Michael Jordan's mother's house."

But like the governor said, before any of that, I had to work on that diploma.

Now that I was out, it was easier to study with Ms. Lambiotte. It wasn't just the SAT that I was studying for; I had to get school credits. We figured out a way that she could be my teacher and an accredited school called Milburn School calculated the credits, reviewed my exams, and hopefully would give me that diploma—to satisfy Governor Wilder and Coach Thompson.

All those people that had been contributing to my legal fund contributed now to my education fund. And every weekday I met with Ms. Lambiotte. I've always said I didn't like school because the hours didn't agree with me. But I had a hard time paying attention too. Staying still in the classroom and just passively learning was hard for me. My body and mind always wanted action, to interact with the world. To see something and emulate it, like in basketball. Creating art was like that. I could hear about something or see it and then create something. Ms. Lambiotte tried to harness that energy.

I was not always on time, but she kept adapting. She developed the material by putting it into small segments, so I could concentrate. I would love it when we'd get on a topic I liked, and we'd debate it. I couldn't believe how much writing I was doing, math, all that. And she would incorporate art. She tried other things too. One time she took me to a museum, and wandering the halls, I would be lying if I said I didn't find it boring.

I'd bring my homework each day, and she'd be like, *Allen, this isn't even half done!*

What's she talking about? I'd think. *That's more homework than I did my whole life!*

I'm sure I didn't make it easy for her. But she stuck it out.

As promised, Coach Thompson sent his academic counselor, Mary Fenlon, to check up on me. Ms. Lambiotte showed her all the work I'd done. Ms. Fenlon agreed that I was "a diamond in the rough." Now with her approval, all I needed was that diploma.

Getting home meant getting home to my mom and family, getting home to Tawanna, and also getting to hang out with my friends again. Thrilla decided to leave VMI and transferred to Hampton University, so we hung out a lot. We played Monopoly, like old times.

Ra and E and all them also welcomed me back. We would go out to the clubs sometimes. I would *usually* meet my curfew. I remember one time we were at a club, and it was probably later than I was supposed to be out. And my crew had words with some other dudes, and it came to a fight. I reacted, got up to defend them. Ra just grabbed me, man. He literally pulled my shirt up over my head and forced me the hell out of there. He wasn't letting me violate my conditions! Never mind that it was probably past my curfew. But that was the bond we had. They were still doing the shit they were doing, and now I could pursue basketball again. And our goal was fame, fortune, a fucking new way of life.

For Ra, and all of us, music was central, as I said before. Ra was from the Bronx and had come to Virginia and just decided that it fit him, I guess. He brought the New York sound with him. That fall, as I sat in jail, Wu-Tang released its first studio album, *Enter the Wu-Tang*. Each of them dudes got their individual moments, but then it was a collaboration. After it got released, we listened to it on repeat.

It came a year later when Biggie released *Ready to Die*, but after it came out, damn, it was like he was living the same life we had been living. Biggie voiced how we felt from the album's first track, "Things Done Changed": We could seize the success and riches we dreamed of by hustling, creating music, or developing "a wicked jump shot."

That's the way we saw it. My homeboys were out there doing their thing, but also developing their music, and meanwhile I was focusing on the jump shot part of it. We split it that way. The goal was to lift ourselves up out of there, to make it, one way or another. Later, my friends tried to make it in hip-hop. I went along with them. Obviously, I was the one who got famous and opened the doors, and I did my music thing (and got in trouble for it!), but that was really their passion.

That being said, the music did speak to me. Biggie was telling our story: He didn't say sorry for a history dealing ("I was just tryin' to make some money to feed my daughter"). And he didn't worship authority figures ("To all the teachers that told me I'd never amount to nothin'"). And then there was jail, being persecuted. Tupac, years before, had talked about being imprisoned, and rather than being some kind of black mark, it was almost a point of pride.

Me getting out of jail, it kind of elevated the way we saw ourselves.

There was this part of me that felt invincible. Like if I conquered that jail shit and was out now, and I had just dominated all of high school sports, what couldn't I do?

So that's how I passed the time, studying, hanging out, and one more thing.

I couldn't play organized sports, but I could *practice*. And I did!

Coach Kozlowski was the athletic director at Bethel. For all the fighting we had once done, he was so fucking glad I got out of jail. So without telling anyone, because I don't think he was supposed to, he would open the Bethel gym for me, and I'd go there. The gym was quiet without the crowds, but I'd keep working on my handle, my jumper, my conditioning. Shot after shot. Move after move. It wasn't that different than the Farm in that sense.

I also played pickup games. There were good runs at Langley Air Force Base and Hampton University. It was enough to let me know there wasn't anyone who could stop me.

Getting on the even wood floors felt good, the ball obeying my commands. Shooting at straight baskets. It was a little different from the Farm. During the pickup games, I could drive to the hole and get some respect when I called "Ball."

But practice wasn't enough. It wasn't what was important to me. It wasn't what I went out there and died for. I thirsted for the games, the crowds. I needed that energy. To return to the competition and the drama.

For me, it was about the motherfucking games.

Jail had kept me from the games. Now the governor's order was keeping me from the games. And I had no idea if I would ever be able to play the actual games again. Those games, with real stakes, they were my passion. They were also what was going to get me, and my family, and my friends, out of the shit we were in. The games.

*

The press slowly stopped hounding me. With a curfew I mostly followed, a command to commit no crimes that I damn sure followed, and a mandate to complete high school, it was basically boring.

But the effects of my whole situation kept rippling. We were all shocked when early that summer the principal of Bethel decided to fire Coach Bailey. The team had done okay without me. My old partner, Tony Rutland, was the state player of the year! He was going to Wake Forest. Yet they just went and fired Coach Bailey out of nowhere. Two years removed from the only state basketball title Bethel ever had. They never said why, but everyone figured there had to be one reason: Coach Bailey's support of Allen Iverson. The principal did say, "We'll have different kinds of teams next season. We won't have people who can average twenty points per game." Imagine wanting that.

Coach Bailey was devastated. This man had picked me up to bring me to the gym. Had gone out searching for me at times. He had me in his home for parts of one summer. They kicked him to the street. I always believed it was because he supported me.

Even after experiencing that treatment, Coach Bailey never did anything but encourage me. He was so glad I was out of jail, studying, and pursuing the future he had been such a big part of building. While it wasn't what he wanted, he continued his career coaching basketball at other programs, and we stayed close.

That June, my letter of intent with Georgetown became official. After all the recruiting before my incarceration, it was different with Coach Thompson. He told my mom he would accept me with the conditions he set, but he didn't come down to Virginia one single time. I could have gone somewhere else. I had not officially committed to Georgetown, but he did nothing but wait to see if I lived up to my end of the bargain. He later said the last thing I needed was to be coddled. Before signing the letter of intent, all I had was a phone conversation with Coach Thompson. He really didn't ask me much. He just spoke for a few minutes. I can tell you that about every other word was *motherfucker*. In the press, he'd be all professorial. But with me, he put it like he figured I'd understand it. He didn't say he wasn't going to "coddle" me. He said, "Motherfucker, if you motherfucking cross me I will expel your motherfucking ass so fast."

When my commitment got announced, he told the press, "I am not at all interested in judging what has happened or what he has done. I'm more interested in judging what he's committed to. The proof is what you do in the long run." Part of that long run was still me getting my academics done and being eligible by the fall. Coach Thompson admitted he liked what he saw when it came to my game: "I would be hypocritical if I didn't acknowledge the fact that this is someone who is an exceptional basketball player, and I'm a basketball coach."

Another friend of mine was a guy named Jamil Blackmon. I met him my junior year of high school, when my profile was taking shape and everyone wanted to meet me. He was older than me and the rest of the crew, and he didn't grow up in Newport News with us. He was a college guy, at Hampton. He promoted parties, was always at the clubs, so that's how I got to know him. He started chilling with us. He always carried lots of cash, so he would sometimes take care of things, pay a bill, for dinner, let me sleep at his crib. Years later, we had a falling-out, but back then we were tight.

One night that summer, we were at his spot and were talking about my name. "Bubbachuck" was what they called me down there, of course, but it wasn't a name like "Magic" or "Doctor J." And we just started going back and forth. What would my nickname be when I made it big? We were talking about how the league was changing. Michael Jordan had just retired (the first time) and was playing baseball. Larry Bird had hung it up, and Magic Johnson of course had called it quits a couple times after he got sick. For a league with a lot of questions, I would be the answer. That's what we decided. I knew it as soon as I heard it. *The Answer*. That was me.

I got so goddamned excited, I was like, *I got to make a record of this shit.* I went to a tattoo shop that same night, over in Yorktown. And the first ink I ever got was "The Answer" on my left arm. It was the first of many. It was one of those things that at the time people hated me for, yet now, now dudes like JJ Reddick got all kinds of ink, guys from Duke—now a head coach!

I didn't know it, but Coach Thompson didn't allow tattoos. I wasn't at Georgetown yet. So it was the first tattoo I got, and the only one for a minute. The Answer.

TWENTY

BACK TO BASKETBALL

As much as I looked to my future, home was pulling. That spring, my dad had been out of jail, but he caught another drug charge, this time with a gun. So he got locked up again. Then it was E's turn. He got implicated in a shooting, and they locked his ass up, until their case fell apart, but not for a few months after that. This was all regular shit, but it felt more dangerous, and at the same time more reason to fucking figure it out and get me and everyone else on out of there.

I took the SAT that summer. When I got a high enough score to be eligible, I only had one thing left: that diploma. I was studying the best I could, and the Milburn School was satisfied with my progress. It was going to take all summer to get my last credits, but it was looking good.

Still, I was never good at waiting. It had been so long since I played a meaningful basketball game. Since getting convicted basically, as remember, I was put on a curfew the prior summer leading up to my sentencing day. So no AAU, and no senior year of high school. And now the governor was keeping me from organized sports on furlough. Damn, it had been over a year since my last real game, when mid-trial they'd flown me back and forth to the Nike camp.

I just couldn't wait any longer. I talked to my lawyers, who talked to the parole office, and they said I was doing good enough that they could make an exception. There was a league in DC called the Kenner Summer League, and every year Georgetown fielded a team, the Tombs, with some of its young players and recruits. It was already well-known, with guys like Ewing and Mutombo making their initial mark there. I was dying to get on that court, to play a game that meant something, with refs, a crowd.

So they said I could go to DC and join this league's end-of-summer playoff from Thursday, August 4, 1994, through the weekend. One of my friends drove me up there. Ms. Lambiotte set us up with a friend of hers to stay with. And that was it. I didn't tell anyone other than the coach. There wasn't any announcement.

I did my time. I had a motherfucking future and I was ready to begin it.

So that Thursday, for the first game, it was like I snuck into the gym. Nobody knew. There was hardly time for warm-ups, let alone *practice*. We were at McDonough Hall—the same building my mom had visited to ask Coach Thompson to allow me to play for him. The gym fit around 2,500 people. It was more like the size of a high school court, with something like twenty rows of bleachers running along the sides. Only the real basketball heads would come and watch these summer games. It was the first chance to see incoming Georgetown freshmen and other local talent. That day, there were maybe a few hundred people there.

So as I arrived, I ran into this dude, Eddie Saah, who organized the Kenner League. Immediately recognizing me, he was like, *Oh shit, you playing?* He then had to hustle and get me a jersey just before tip-off. This man also did the public address announcements. So the game started, and without so much as a practice shot, a stretch, or a *what's up* to my teammates, I got the ball on our side of the floor, on the perimeter. The crowd was oblivious. A hard dribble and I raised up behind the three-point line, in front of this dude who towered over me. Cash.

Then, over the sound system, an announcement of who made that shot: "Allen Iverson."

You could feel it. The crowd was like, *Wait, what did that man say?*

And just as people were leaning over to whoever was sitting beside them, whispering, I jumped the lane, stole a pass, and jammed it on the other end. At that moment, the crowd understood they heard what they thought they heard. Allen Iverson was in the house.

It was one of those times, boy, when everything flowed. The jumpers. The drives. The steals. It was like I had been freed from jail, I could step right on the floor, and I still had my superpowers. Every time I rose up, the crowd rose on out of their seats with me. And that night, they got to see the ball sliding through the net. Shot after shot. Thirty points in the first half. Forty in the game. A win to make it to the semifinal.

With the ending buzzer, I left. Slipped on out of there.

But let me tell you, it wasn't over. Two days later was the semifinal and as I got to McDonough Gym, there was a line wrapped around the motherfucking block. My appearance had made the papers, was on the radio. People just knew. And they came. I wasn't even accepted to Georgetown yet! No one knew if I had met my academic requirements (I still needed to earn my last credits). No one even knew for sure if I was done with the criminal case.

The public relations people at Georgetown got involved. John Thompson had rules. No freshmen—I wasn't even that yet—could speak to the press at all through the first semester. Not one word. After that first semester, Georgetown players could only speak right after games in the postgame press conference. Coach Thompson had this protective cone of silence. Some didn't like it, but it was exactly what I needed. Just focus on sports, my family, and my education. Keep the press away. Man, I could get with that.

So the PR guy was with me on that second day making sure I didn't get bothered by any reporters. He escorted me through a spot the back way. I walked out on the court, again barely with time to do warm-ups.

The crowd emitted this rumbling little stir of a noise, people recognizing me as I walked on out there. It was a sound I came to know well over the years. People pointing at me. Remember that face I put on when I walked in front of those damn cameras after getting out of jail? It was like that, like no smile, nothing, because that's how I felt I should look. But what I felt inside, it was like *this is where I should be but also like how the hell did I make it to this point?* Two fucking curfews surrounding a stint in jail, and here I was in the nation's capital. And they're stuffing this little gym to see me. Couldn't believe the crowd that crammed in there. It was standing room only. Well over 3,000, they said.

Once again I had my shot and rhythm going. I had a couple crazy dunks, a few three pointers, drives, dishes. And with each one, the crowd got more and more hyped. I scored 34 that night. I had to share the limelight a little with Jerome Williams. Jerome was a junior college transfer who was about to begin at Georgetown. He scored 37. We won 104–90. This time the PR dude ushered me out of the gym before the game even ended.

There was one more to go. By now, word had made it home that I was taking over the Kenner League, and a whole bunch of family and friends came up—Mo, Brandy, Boo Williams, even Ms. Lambiotte came to watch.

People were wrapped around the block again to get in. This time they said they packed 4,000 people into McDonough Hall—1,500 more than the max. There was floor space on either end of the gym behind the baskets, so after all the seats filled up, they just stuffed people in there, left them to stand. Hundreds of people were turned away. In the standing room, I'll never forget one face staring above the others. It was a smile that I got to know much better in Philadelphia, but it was recognizable then. Dikembe Mutombo was looking on. He was the fourth pick in the 1991 draft, three years he'd been in the NBA—and he couldn't get a motherfucking seat for my *Summer League* game.

I only scored 26 points that night, and my shot was not falling like it had been, just conneting on three of fourteen three-pointers. But the energy was there, and I had a couple highlights for them. I remember as the game went on, I even let my guard down. I smiled. I gestured to the crowd. I let my personality show. And they responded.

We won the championship, but it was so much more to me to get out there for the games, the actual games.

There was no time for anything afterward. Once again they moved me right on out of there after the whistle blew. I didn't even get to collect the trophy. Within a few minutes after exiting McDonough Gym through the back way, I was in the car heading south, back home.

I was still not eligible yet. Nope, I had to finish those last credits. Can you imagine how excruciating it was for me to get back into the classroom? After *that.* Knowing now that I could dominate the college game. I mean, I had played tough games, with good players, pickup games with great talent. But you don't know until you know. Now I knew.

It wouldn't mean anything if I couldn't get those last credits. Ms. Lambiotte was on me. I was writing those assignments. Taking the tests. My last classes were US Government and Psychology. And I passed those motherfuckers. The coordinator at the Milburn School approved and said they could give me what I needed a diploma.

When it was official, that's when I got my next tattoo. A Bulldog, the Georgetown mascot, right on underneath "The Answer" on my left arm.

So Ms. Lambiotte, during the first week of September, almost a year to the day since that van had taken me to jail, said, "Bubba, we are going to give you a graduation ceremony." A graduation of one. She invited my family, the Milburn coordinator, and some other friends to her center in Poquoson. She had a cap and gown waiting for me. It was embarrassing. Then she told me that I was the valedictorian—No. 1 in a class of one. So I better make a speech.

I just thanked her and everyone. For making it possible for me to achieve my dreams. By then I understood that I couldn't have done any of this without everyone who helped along the way, beginning with my mother and now everyone else in the room. They were all a part of my legacy.

IV

HE SAVED MY LIFE: COACH JOHN THOMPSON

The Benz

One morning after my sophomore season of college ended, Coach Thompson called me into his office. We needed to have a talk.

I walked on over there from my dorm room. I knew it was serious. As I got to his office at McDonough Hall, he was sitting behind his desk. He had that stern fatherly look. I really didn't like stern motherfuckers, but Coach Thompson saved my life, so I accepted it. I trusted him.

My trust wasn't automatic, and by then I knew better than to trust based on what someone said to my face. You always want to know what someone really thinks. But I knew with Coach. Because of a little moment that happened earlier. See, after our games, Coach Thompson and the assistants used to go in the bathroom and discuss privately how the game went. Coach Thompson would then come out and give us his postgame thoughts. We never knew what they said in there. So, this one day a teammate of mine, Jerry Nichols, was in the bathroom. But they didn't realize he was there. We had just beaten Seton Hall, and I had scored like 40 on Danny Hurley, and had one of my greatest plays I ever had. So Jerry came back and was like, "Coach Thompson was talking about you." Jerry told me he said to the other coaches, "That little motherfucker is bad as hell."

I tried to play it off. But hearing that shit was something I never forgot. When Jerry told me that Coach Thompson said that about me, when he didn't think I could hear, that was it.

So in his office, he cut to it: "You going pro?"

You got to understand, no one in the history of Coach Thompson's Georgetown Hoyas had left early to enter the NBA Draft. Not Dikembe, not Alonzo, and not Patrick.

"Why do you think that?"

"I know everything that goes on around here. I know what you been driving."

I had just gotten a 600 Benz. It was a loaner. I was thinking, How the fuck you know about my ride? *But a dude from the hood like me couldn't be driving a 600 Benz without him hearing about it.*

I expected anger. Or worse, that disappointed face.

He looked at me. "Do what you got to do." I still had not made up my mind. Then he added, "But return the motherfucking car, you little shit."

And so I did.

TWENTY-ONE

ADJUSTING TO GEORGETOWN

In September 1994, I arrived on the Georgetown campus literally just a couple days after my high school "graduation." Classes had begun already, but I made the late registration window. They brought me to the dorm at Copley Hall. Now, I don't know what most freshmen feel when they walk into their dorm, but for me, I was like, *Damn this is dope.* The rooms were set up as doubles, two private bedrooms that shared a bathroom in the middle. We had a view of the Potomac River out the window.

My roommate was a senior, Don Reid. Coach Thompson really thought of everything, man. He put me with Don because Don was a serious motherfucker. I guess they figured he was going to keep me on the right track. Don was tough enough that they didn't need to worry about him getting overwhelmed by all the attention I got. Coach Thompson made him the captain that year, and he was a lead-by-example type. Quiet as hell.

As a player, Don had been fighting for minutes for three years, and the season before, he finally got playing time as an undersized center alongside Othella Harrington. With the two of them on the low block, the Hoyas had a pretty good season. But for the fourth straight year, they had been eliminated in the second round of the NCAA Tournament.

That September, official basketball practice didn't start right away (there were rules about when practice could start), so the seniors would organize pickup games and workouts at McDonough Hall. To get to the gym, I walked from Copley Hall across the campus. There was a lot of walking because Coach Thompson didn't allow his players to have cars, whether it was a Benz or a hooptie. As I walked up the hill to McDonough, on my right was the football field. That fall you could see the guys practicing, working out. And I would cry, man. My eyes would literally get teary. My first love. My passion. The plan was both sports! Notre Dame, remember?

So watching these guys, it hurt, and after a few days I got it in my head that I would ask Coach Thompson if I could play football. I could see it. Me, playing quarterback again. So later, when I was in the weight room (wasn't lifting weights, just in the weight room), I gathered up the courage and I went to Coach Thompson. "I want to play football."

Coach Thompson just stared at me through his glasses, like, *Goddamn, this boy doesn't know what's right for him.*

Man, I can't repeat what he said after that. But here's what he said at the end: "Don't ever come to me with that stupid shit again. Get the hell out of here."

I think I knew already, but it did hurt. I never thought seriously about playing football again.

And I changed up my route to the gym. I walked the long way so I didn't have to see those dudes playing football anymore.

There was one hard part from the beginning. That dorm room was nice, like I said. The lights turned on. The water got hot. All that. And the dining halls had more food than I'd ever seen. Three times a day. If I ever heard someone complain about the food, I would just look at them like they was crazy.

So what was hard?

It was *just me.*

My mom was still on Victoria Boulevard. So were Brandy and Iiesha, and Iiesha was still going to the doctor about her seizures. The house had the same plumbing problems. Electricity and phone service were off as often as on. And then there were my friends out there, some of them still hustling.

During my time at Georgetown, it was always hard feeling like I'd made it, but alone. There wasn't anything yet I could do for them. Back then, the NCAA had much stricter rules about college athletes getting paid. If I took a dollar from the wrong person, it could be the end of my college career—and Coach Thompson reminded me of that all the damn time. Crazy part was I could take a few dollars from my preexisting friends—who knows where they got it from—but I couldn't sign an autograph for a fee. Nowadays, these college kids can do all that. Some make millions of dollars before ever getting drafted. If I could have done that, it would have been completely different.

As we started working out together, I got to know the dudes who would be at my side. Besides Don Reid there was Othella Harrington. He came to Georgetown touted as the next great Hoya big man. During the two seasons before, he led the team in scoring. I can tell you now, it was a little bit of an adjustment for him with me running things. The other main returner was a shooting guard by the name of George Butler. The year before, he was second on the team in scoring after Othella. Two other rising senior guards, John Jacques and Irvin Church, also played big minutes.

Even before I joined, people were saying we had a strong incoming class. The newcomers began with Jerome Williams. He later became known as the Junkyard Dog. The name fit. Jerome was an animal out there. If there was a board to get, it was his. A loose ball, you had to watch your knees. He was someone you hated to play against but loved having on your team.

Boubacar Aw was another. He had recently come over from Africa. He had size and athleticism. Then there was Jahidi White, a freshman center who got to the NBA eventually.

As official practices were about to begin in mid-October, there was another issue with my eligibility. Remember me flying back and forth to the Nike camp for my trial? The rules only allowed for one round-trip flight, so when Nike added a second flight for me, that was a benefit I wasn't allowed to get. We had to repay Nike. I don't know where we got the money—probably my friends from home gave it to me—but we fucking reimbursed the billion-dollar corporation that had me wearing their shoes in the televised final. Georgetown had to suspend me and then send proof of Nike being repaid. The NCAA accepted it, and that October, the university formally reinstated me in time for me to practice.

This was the shit they put you through. To *practice*!

John Thompson focused on defense as we prepared for the season. We worked on man-to-man and zone looks. I didn't mind. I loved defense—remember, I loved playing safety on the football field. Coach Thompson wanted me to guard my man with discipline but also look for opportunities to turn defense into offense, steal the ball, and take it to the other end of the court.

Coach Thompson had this presence in practice. He was a big dude, former center, who like me had come out of the city, but for him it was DC. As a pro, he'd played with Bill Russell, winning two NBA championships. As a coach, he'd done it all. Georgetown won a championship with Patrick Ewing, of course. They lost a heartbreaker to Villanova in 1985. But the one that came up from the first practice was the '82 final, when the Georgetown defense gave Michael Jordan an open look for the game winner. In that moment, our guy had gotten hung up on a screen, and they'd reversed the ball to a wide open Jordan. When your coach teaches you defense by talking about not leaving Jordan open in the NCAA final, damn right you listen.

It wasn't just on the defensive end of the floor he wanted me to embrace my talent. One thing Coach Thompson said about me more than once was "The last thing he needs is structure. He needs to be free as a bird. He needs to fly." Sometimes it felt like he was referring to me having been locked up. We never actually talked about jail. Not once. It wasn't something I liked to bring up, because, shit, who would want to bring that up, but also because I really wasn't thinking about it anymore. That was done. Coach Thompson seemed to only bring it up in the way he harnessed my game, yelling at my ass when I fucked something up, yeah, but granting me freedom on the floor—freedom he never gave any player before, they said.

One time we were in practice working on breaking the press, and after he saw me just catch the ball and break it with ease by running by everyone, he came up to me and put his arm around my shoulder like he always did. He said that he had this method for breaking the press. You pass here, then here, and then work your way on up the floor. *But son, if you get it and can just get by everyone, motherfucker, just go.*

Like all the way back when I was on the Raiders youth football team in Hampton, there was an issue with my jersey number. I had been number 3 since being on varsity at Bethel. But number 3 was taken when I got to Georgetown. Of course I wanted that number, just like it had to be 33 when I was eight. The only time I ever hooped without number 3 the rest of my career was a year I would rather forget, with the Detroit Pistons toward the end of my NBA career. I played with the number 1, and it never felt right. That was my Raiders football number.

So I went to Coach Thompson's office. I politely asked, "Number 3 is special. Can I wear it?"

I might as well have asked to play football again. He was mad as hell. "Motherfucker, you'll take the number I give you." I was like, *damn*, and walked on out of there—a little pissed off, to tell you the truth.

I came to the next practice and hanging in my locker was the number 3 jersey. That's how Coach Thompson was. He'd let you know who the motherfucker in charge was, but he cared so much for us, man. Looking back now, I might never have been number 3 if he hadn't been like that.

Unlike with the jersey I wore in the games, Coach Thompson was less flexible about the pre- and postgame dress code. When I arrived on campus wearing an earring, he made me take it off. He was strict as a motherfucker about it being a suit and tie. He wasn't going to accept anything else. So I surely didn't try. It was also understood that there were no tattoos (no *more* tattoos for me) and no braids. He liked us coming into the arenas dressed like killers, looking professional as hell. And he'd get all serious about it too. *You motherfuckers got to know, at Georgetown we are perceived in a certain way. People see us as representing a certain culture. And we can't feed into their stereotypes.*

Years later I put it like this: "Only half his practices were about basketball. The other half were about life." That's how he was in practice, man, giving it to us straight. I think that was one reason it was top secret in there. They said he would tape the lines in the doors to the practice gym so you couldn't peek in to see what we were doing (I never saw that though). He wanted to shield us—for protection, for focus, but also to create this sanctuary where he could tell us shit straight. *Motherfucker* this, *motherfucker* that. Then we walk out in jackets and ties, ready to kill them dudes on the court.

TWENTY-TWO

THE HOYA SEASON BEGINS

Before the real games began, we had a couple exhibitions. Exhibition games usually weren't that big a deal, but after the Kenner League, there was an energy on the campus. We played our official games at the Capital Centre, an 18,000-seat arena outside the city. But the exhibitions, like the Kenner League, were held in little old McDonough Hall. Once again, they couldn't fit all the motherfuckers who wanted to see the game in that joint. We were playing Fort Hood. It wasn't the best competition, not a real NCAA team, but these dudes knew how to play basketball. Still, they must have been like *What the fuck?* when they walked into our gym, what with the capacity crowd going crazy.

Coach Thompson did do some shit to keep my ego in check. For that first game, he had me coming off the bench. And he had Jerome Williams running the point, in a little experiment that didn't last too long. So I had to wait—for two minutes and seventeen seconds, to be exact. That's when Coach Thompson relented and had me go to the scorer's table to enter the game. The crowd did that little murmur: *Here he comes.* Twenty-seven seconds later I had me my first points. It was 28 by halftime, 36 for the game. Man, the crowd went nuts as I hit threes, stole passes, got fouled again and again, and kept making my free throws.

Coach Thompson tried to play it off, like it wasn't special. "I want him to improve and to help the team," he said after the game. But the man couldn't hide his true feelings in the second half. As I was coming across half-court, the center for the Fort Hood squad gave me a forearm that sent me flying. I was used to bigger guys and this kind of shit—I mean what other option did they have to stop me, so this was normal to me. But Coach Thompson ran out onto the floor and had to be held back, shouting, "Don't hurt my boy! You can't take him out like that!" He got himself a technical. I looked at Coach Thompson like, *Chill, it's all good.*

I would think about that, man, how he always said he agreed to take me on to support my mother. But seeing him all wide-eyed, worried, running out on the court. Like I said, I think him bringing me to Georgetown had a little bit to do with my talent too.

He and everyone knew about my talent after that game. *The Washington Post* had two articles the next day about it. Everyone was talking about this one by Thomas Boswell, a sports columnist at that paper since before I was born. He wrote, "Sometimes I feel like I've spent my life going to little gyms to watch The Next Greatest Basketball Player Who Ever Lived." He'd seen all the legends over the years. "Now, I have two memories on my first-impression top shelf. The man who became Kareem Abdul-Jabbar, and Allen Iverson. Ewing is third." They read that shit to me, and I was like, *Damn, no fucking way Kareem could take me!*

So then we played a second exhibition against a Croatian team, with the same kind of hoopla. This one was a closer game, but we still won. I scored 39, including a late three to send the crowd into a frenzy and put the game out of reach. It really felt like there was nothing I couldn't do. And that we would win them all. But that didn't turn out to be the case.

*

The first official game on the schedule was against the defending national champs, the Arkansas Razorbacks. Our team, the coaches, everyone was fired up about that game. Arkansas had most of the guys from their championship squad returning—Corliss Williamson, Corey Beck, Scotty Thurman. It was a little personal because on their way to the title the previous year, they had beaten us in the second round of the Tournament. It was supposed to be a test for me in particular. Nolan Richardson was their coach, and under him they attacked on defense nonstop, particularly by pressing. Pressing never really bothered me. I always felt like I could get by anyone. So I wasn't too worried.

The game was at the Pyramid, in Memphis, an arena shaped like the Egyptian pyramids, just with 20,000 fans inside. It was packed that day, and the game was televised nationally on CBS. I'm telling you, I never faced greater pressure than facing Hampton High in the Coliseum, but the scale of this was on a whole different level. Seeing Billy Packer and Jim Nantz ready to call the game as I went through warm-ups . . . *Shit, I've arrived.* The Kenner League and those exhibition games at McDonough Hall had been just a taste.

And I loved it. I loved it so much. The anticipation. Calling out the starting lineups, with the spotlights, all that. (Yes, I was starting.) And I didn't care that Memphis was right next to Arkansas, so all their fans had made the trip and were ready to boo my ass.

I will just tell you a little about that game. Because it was a blowout. Some might say humbling, but I wasn't humbled. They beat us 97–79. They pressed, but after I beat the pressure early, they sat back in a zone designed to cut off my driving lanes. When I tried to drive and got by the perimeter defenders, their big guys were physical as hell. I couldn't find passing lanes and my shots just didn't fall. I only made five out of eighteen shots. I had eight turnovers. But as I felt the defending champs adjust, it was like, *Damn, these guys need to change what they're doing just to deal with me?* And so even though I missed my shots, missed my passes, and my team was beaten badly, I had that feeling I'd get as I got to each new level. I was the best motherfucker out there. Twenty thousand fans made no difference. The fact that CBS and Billy Packer were there, that shit didn't do anything but energize me. Corliss Williamson, 6'7", 250 pounds, waiting in the lane, along with other giants. Compared to my six feet and 165 pounds. None of it stopped me from flying above it all.

In the postgame, Nolan Richardson said, "I ain't never seen anything like that in my life. I've been to three calf shows, nine horse ropings—I even saw Elvis once. But I ain't never seen anyone do what Iverson does." Me, all I was thinking about was getting to the next game. I could not wait for that chance again. I'd had it nearly grabbed away from me. Some people in Virginia had tried their best. So that day, after that beating we took, I just couldn't wait to play the next game.

In college, I always felt there was too much time between games, but luckily the next one was just three days later against Morgan State. After receiving some criticism for shooting and turning the ball over too much against Arkansas, I focused on getting the other guys involved. I scored 18 points, but had 10 assists, and Don Reid led the team in scoring with 21. We won easily. It was a start.

We won the rest of our games through the new year. I scored 30-plus points in back-to-back wins against DePaul and Providence (my Big East debut). I was only the second player in Coach Thompson's time as Georgetown coach to score at least 30 in back-to-back games. Pete Gillen, the Providence coach, said that I was better than Isiah Thomas at the same point in his career. I think Coach Thompson tried to make damn sure I didn't hear any of that. But I would read the praise, or other people would tell me about it. We closed out the year by winning the Holiday Classic in Sacramento, California. At that point it was seven straight wins.

While I heard and appreciated the praise and the excitement for

Georgetown basketball, there was also chatter about the other side of me. Every television broadcast mentioned that I had been in jail the previous fall, that Coach Thompson had agreed to take me on in spite of my associations from home. Still, it was so much easier to keep my head on straight when I was prohibited from talking to the media—living under Coach Thompson's protective umbrella.

But remember, his no-interview policy only lasted the first semester. And with the new year came the second semester. Media outlets were sending so many requests for interviews that the university and Coach Thompson decided to hold a little press conference. Man, so many reporters came to talk to us. Coach Thompson was clear: none of that bowling alley shit, only basketball-related questions. He was good at setting boundaries, protecting me. It was my first press conference on such a big stage. I had no idea that me and press conferences would become a source of notoriety later in life.

What I remember is how Coach Thompson talked. They asked if he was impressed. Sitting beside him, I'm thinking, *Damn right he should be impressed.* But he was always sending messages to me. "If you've been in this business for a while, you're not here to be impressed with people. You're here to attempt to help mold them and get them prepared for the next stage of their life. That's what education is about." He always focused on how he was an "educator" first. Of course, the press pushed, asking if I was causing problems. He turned to me and kind of jokingly grabbed my neck. "I grab him by the neck and choke him once in a while, and he responds very well. We're not dealing with a head case or a special project here." He knew how to loosen up for a minute, could give me a little shit in front of the press.

When we got done, and it was just the two of us, he said, "Motherfucker, that's it with the press, now get your ass out of here."

Remember what I said about the hard part being that it was *just* me there at Georgetown? That took on a whole life of its own because something happened that I wasn't really ready for. Tawanna had our first child, Tiaura, on December 16, 1994. I was only nineteen, and while I was in DC, they were still in Hampton living with Tawanna's mother. Look, me and Tawanna been together since we were kids. We eventually got married in 2001, and we got literally divorced in 2013 (for some shit that was all my fault). A month later, we were back together. She's the one. She was then and always.

I told Tawanna when Tiaura was born, "I got to take care of this child by concentrating on making it in basketball." And she never questioned that. Tawanna was confident in our bond, even if I wasn't there. Now with a child, I had more responsibility, more motivation. Couldn't let my mother down. My girl. My daughter. The rest of my family. My homeboys.

I would go down to visit when I could. I would be with Tawanna and Tiaura. Then they'd go to bed, and I might hang out with my dudes, Arnie and Ra, or Jamil, or I might go to Thrilla's crib, wake his ass up, and we'd sit outside just rapping. But during my freshman year I didn't get to do that much. So I missed too much of Tiaura's first years. Of course, when I made it to the NBA, I kept my promise. We eventually got ourselves a mansion in Philly, lived together with Tiaura, and over the years we were joined by four more kids.

One person I wouldn't have had to travel to visit was my dad, Michael Freeman. It was fucked-up, but he had been sent back to prison for another drug charge. When I got to Georgetown, he was imprisoned in Fairfax County, Virginia, just down the road. Man, I'd visited him in jail the summer before, and it was too much to see him locked up like that.

When I was later asked how I felt about what my dad did to get convicted, I told a reporter, "I feel all the jail time he did was for us. He couldn't stand to look at us like that. So he went out and did what he had to do." I added, "I don't feel what he did was right. But, believe me, he will never have to do it again." That's because I was doing what I needed to do to make it. To make it big. I wanted everything, the fame, the fortune, but I also wanted to take everyone with me, including him. Whatever had happened, whatever anyone had done or was still doing to make ends meet, I aimed to end it.

TWENTY-THREE

THE BIG EAST

With the new year, the season shifted. Over were those nonconference games, some of them easy ones against smaller schools with lower-profile basketball programs. We entered the heart of the Big East schedule now, with games against our real rivals: St. John's, Villanova, UConn, Syracuse. This was my first time through that gauntlet, but I felt ready.

The first game of 1995 was against Pitt, and that ended up being a wake up call. Those dudes got down and dirty. We pulled it out 55–46, but what I remember was how hard it was to get points. We shot around 30 percent, and they shot even worse. It felt like my introduction to Big East basketball. Especially that Pitt crowd. Those motherfuckers welcomed my ass. Whenever I got to the line, they started a chant: "Jailbird, Jailbird!"—all drawn out like singing that motherfucker. I remember after my first free throw I just turned to them and smiled. Once you've been in jail, some dudes calling you a "jailbird" ain't the thing that's going to bother you.

A couple days later, we beat Miami. I had 26 points but again struggled with my shot. Still, in the closing minutes, I flipped in a layup that got us within two and sank a jumper that gave us the lead. Then I made some free throws to seal it. But I wasn't thinking that much about the game afterward, because that was the day they announced that George Butler had been dismissed from the team. He had failed to meet the academic standards, they said. That one hurt, man. George was a friend first, but he was also our second leading scorer and a strong defender to handle the bigger guards we faced. Setting aside the team issues, losing George let me know that there weren't any excuses. Coach Thompson didn't mess around.

The next two games were more of the same. We won, but I struggled with my shot, and scoring was not easy. Against Seton Hall they sent two defenders at me, and I just had to pass out of it. I only shot it eight times. It was another battle against Boston College a couple nights later, and while I shot it more, I made only five of nineteen shots. Still, with two more wins, we were 11-1 overall and 5-0 in the Big East.

A few nights later, we made our first trip to Hartford to face off against the University of Connecticut, ranked No. 2 in the nation. They had a dude who I had never played against growing up, but who obviously became one of the greats, Ray Allen. A sophomore, he was making a name for himself that season. And it wasn't no one-man show. They had Kevin Ollie, Doron Sheffer, and Donny Marshall. But Ray was their man, and at that moment me and him were neck-and-neck for Big East scoring lead.

We got up there, and there was so much excitement. It was another nationally televised game, this time with Dick Vitale in the booth. That Arkansas game was now two months in the rearview, and this was our next big one. You can imagine the excitement I felt. I wanted redemption, all that. But it didn't come that day. I sprained my ankle early on. I stayed in the game as long as I could, because there was no way you could keep me out the goddamn games. We were down just three at halftime. But in the second half, they pulled away and won by twenty. That ankle would bother me for a few weeks. The only good part was that I knew I would get at least one more shot against those dudes, since we played each Big East team at least twice.

Because of my ankle, Coach Thompson made me sit out for a week until Villanova—our first game in the City of Brotherly Love, my future home, the spot where I can still walk the streets and feel like I walk on water. But it wasn't like that then!

Preparing was the normal game-day shit. Suit and tie. Just a bus ride up to Philly from DC. We arrived at the Spectrum, the big Philly arena back then. (I'd open the new place less than two years later.) Of course, I was familiar with the Spectrum from watching Doc and Mo Cheeks and fellow Virginian Moses Malone back in the day. Villanova normally played on their campus on the Main Line of Philly, but for the big ones, the games on national TV, they'd move it to the Spectrum in South Philly. Obviously, this was one of the big ones.

So the whole team filed out of the bus behind Coach Thompson, just like always, doing the respectable thing, in our professional threads. But it didn't earn us any respect back.

We got changed into our uniforms and walked out on the floor for warm-ups. As the start neared, just a couple minutes before tip-off, I remember hearing some commotion. I looked up into the student section of the crowd. It wasn't the most diverse student section, I'll put it like that. I landed on the source of the commotion: four dudes wearing orange jumpsuits, like from prison (mind you, we wore white at the City Farm!). They were holding signs saying shit like "CONVICT U." But the one I will never forget said, "THE NEXT JORDAN," but motherfuckers crossed out "JORDAN" and wrote in "O.J." This was less than a year after O.J. had been arrested and charged with murder.

I just smiled at that shit when I first saw it. It reminded me for a second of a lifetime earlier. Back in Virginia when I was awaiting trial—before the murder charges, the Ford Bronco, and all that—this national reporter wrote an article titled "O.J. Has Some Advice for Allen Iverson." Dude wrote that "O.J. is still the best football player and human being I have ever been around." I guess he figured that O.J., who also came from a tough background, might be able to enlighten me. "[Iverson] has to get selfish," he told the reporter. "Does he want to hang out with the boys every night, or does he want to be a rich and famous athlete?" Flash forward to here at the Spectrum in Philly, and I was being compared to the O.J. who was awaiting trial for murdering his wife.

I wasn't about to let those signs affect me, just like I didn't let it affect me with the Pitt crowd chanting "jailbird." I was more worried about my ankle that still hurt like a motherfucker. But Coach Thompson, he saw that shit and was mad as hell. He walked over and talked to some suits on the Villanova sideline, to Steve Lappas, their coach. He basically told them we weren't going to play the game with those signs showing that level of disrespect. He said we wouldn't just "sit there and expect that child to play under that atmosphere." (Coach Thompson probably was the only person, including my mom, who could call me a "child.") Then he went, "We understand that, periodically, someone's going to jump up and say something. It has happened before and Allen is tough enough to deal with that. But in the same token, I can't condone a Christian university sitting and watching that happen."

So they relented and made those Villanova kids put down their signs. I mean, nobody wanted to deal with that Spectrum crowd if they had to cancel the show. And believe me, Coach Thompson was being serious, we weren't going to play if those signs remained. I remember though, because the crowd was an issue, looking away from the 'Nova student section, panning out you could see that there were a lot of other people who came to see the game, to see me, people from the city, and once the tip went up, a lot of that crowd was cheering for us.

Problem was my ankle was still fucked-up. And after a few minutes, Coach Thompson could see me limping and grimacing, and took me out. I was so mad, but he just told me we had to protect it. It was and remained my lowest-scoring college game—just 2 points. The team hung tough.

Othella played a great game getting 21 points, so we kept it respectable, but we lost another one on national TV.

So after that, a lot of people had an opinion about me getting taunted. I heard about this later, but that old columnist from the *Daily Press* on the Peninsula just couldn't help himself. He wrote, "I fear that Iverson won't deal with mockery by feeling remorse. . . . I fear that he won't learn from his mistakes. I fear that he will develop thicker skin. . . . That kind of toughness is the last thing Allen Iverson needs." Thank God Coach Thompson still limited my press access. Blissfully ignorant, man.

As we got the hell out of Philly, the one thing I had to look forward to was that our next game was another big one. We were playing St. John's, and they had the Big East's *other* freshman, a New York kid named Felipe López. It's easy to say now that I appreciated the press limits Coach Thompson put on me, but there was a downside. At the beginning of the season, *Sports Illustrated* wanted to put me and Felipe on their cover. Can you imagine how disappointed I was when Coach Thompson shut that down? So it was just Felipe.

Well, I made sure that it was my image they remembered after the game. About midway through the first half, I went on a rampage that began with a drive and pass over my shoulder to Othella for an easy layup. Then I hit a three, hit the midrange, had it cooking. On one play, Don got a block and hit me with the outlet. In a second I had it on the other end, faked a pass, yanked that shit back, and watched the defender fly away chasing a ball that wasn't there—as I floated in for a layup. Crowd went crazy. Game was over by halftime, as we led by twenty-one, and I had 19 of those points. Coach Thompson was always ready to try to keep the hype in check though: "As far as the Iverson-Felipe Show, I think it's quite obvious they're both great players. I also think it's quite obvious they're both freshmen."

I guess I was a freshman. Over the next couple weeks we struggled, barely beating Pitt before losing to Syracuse. Two more losses—coupled with more taunts—followed, first in Miami ("You criminal!"), and then BC ("Go back to jail, Iverson!"). That made three in a row, heading into a rematch with UConn, this time at our place, and this time them ranked No. 1. And once again they remained above us—though with my ankle healed at least we gave them a game. We led by eight with less than ten minutes to go. But they executed perfectly down the stretch and beat us. I scored 29 points, with 9 assists, 8 rebounds, 3 steals, and a block.

Beyond the losing, me and Othella weren't coalescing. We got along as friends, but on the court it could be tough. Remember what I said about the Georgetown rep, that they slowed it down on offense and looked to work through the big man? That was what Othella was good at. He had been Big East Rookie of the Year two years earlier, and now he was struggling to get touches and points in an offense that flowed through me. Back then, Tony Kornheiser was just a newspaper columnist. His successful ESPN show, *Pardon the Interruption*, was still years away. He wrote in a column, "Considering John Thompson is such a celebrated milk drinker, I'm surprised he hasn't put Othella's face on the carton." And he said I was the reason Othella had gone missing.

Even though a three-game losing streak now stretched to four, and me and Othella were struggling to mesh, it felt like we could turn it around after the UConn game. Coach Thompson was getting on me a little more. I remember one time, he was talking to me about all this shit, how going fast was good, but knowing when to slow down was also important. I heard that a lot. I never heard it from a fast motherfucker. But he was right. Anyway, one time I got a little frustrated, and I asked if he had a problem with me. He said something I'll never forget: "I don't have a problem with you. If I wasn't talking to you, that's when you know I got a problem with you." He never stopped talking to me.

We got off the losing skid against Providence a few days later, setting up a rematch with Villanova at our place. Villanova was ranked No. 9 coming into the game. They'd won eleven straight including their last game, where they blew out Connecticut. Now they were visiting us.

In Philly, the dudes in the crowd wore prison suits. In DC, our crowd wore presidential suits. But during warm-ups, the crowd's murmurs were not for me. A bunch of Secret Service was there and just before tip-off, in walked Bill Clinton. Georgetown was his alma mater. I tried to keep it serious, put my game face on. But goddammit, I was going crazy. It always mattered to me who was watching. So on this night, it was the president of the United States—I had to bring it.

Man look—I was in jail a little over a year earlier, shooting baskets in the prison yard. Now this. At the time, I never gave myself even a second to reflect, the whiplash of being shackled one moment . . . and now free, now fucking grabbing my future by the throat. And with the president here to see it. With hindsight, I can't believe I did it. Back then, I was like, *Of course this is my path.*

The path that day led to destruction. We scored the first eleven points of the game, got to 41–24 at the half, and never looked back. I felt in control and had some of those plays you never forget. An and-one on a little floater right as the game started. A behind-the-back pass on the fast break for a layup (with Dick Vitale yelling, "Ohhhh, showtiiiiime, in front of the Prezzz . . ." to all my friends watching back at home). A hit ahead on the break to Jerome Williams for a dunk. A gliding reverse layup to elude a defender. But it was more than the highlights. Our whole defense made every pass perilous, every shot challenged. They had Kerry Kittles, Alvin Williams, these were serious ballers. But they couldn't do shit that day. Our intensity was just too much. Steve Lappas later said of our energy, "They played as if someone was going to shoot them if they lost."

After the game, President Clinton came into our locker room. He spoke to Coach Thompson first. But I guess he also wanted to meet me. He came over and shook my hand. Someone told me he was on the air with Vitale during the game, and when asked about me, President Clinton said, "He's good. He's really good. He's got *it*."

We followed that Villanova win with one against Syracuse, then ranked 16th. Othella got it going, scoring 27 points, and people calmed down about me and him fitting together. During that losing streak, people started doubting whether we would even make it to the Tournament, but with the win against 'Nova and now Syracuse, we knew we were making it. It was a matter of how far we could get.

While the team was gelling, home kept calling. There were the nights spent on the phone with Tawanna. For home games, I would leave tickets for all the friends and family I could. Ms. Lambiotte came up, Mo came, Thrilla, Arnie and Ra, everyone came up to see the show. I wasn't abandoning anyone. They weren't coming to the dorms or anything like that, but the dream of bringing everyone out the shit they were in, it was starting to come into view.

It was at that time that even my biological father started calling me. We talked. I heard him out. But like I've always said, I had a dad, so it wasn't like I was looking for one. He talked about coming to visit me, but I wasn't too sure about that. I felt a little like he was calling because now I was famous and on my way. But I wasn't cutting him off or anything like that. Mainly, I didn't want to be that kind of father to Tiaura—I was determined to be there for her.

On the last day in February, I had to go back home for a hearing on my appeal. Mr. Shuttleworth and Mr. Woodward, and their associate, Lisa O'Donnell, had filed the appeal, and now the appeals court was set to hear oral arguments. I traveled to the courthouse in Norfolk with one of the Georgetown assistant coaches. My lawyers said it would be good for me to be there, for the judges to see me.

It was like a flashback, hearing what they were talking about. *Was it just a fight? Or had I participated in a mob?* They were talking about a former life, one that was over now. I was done with it. I wasn't a kid being railroaded in my hometown, stuck. I was a budding All-American conquering basketball in the nation's capital.

Afterward, my lawyers tried to get me to meet the judges. But they just shrugged us off. I kind of got the feeling that it hadn't gone well.

*

The next day I was back in DC for a game against Seton Hall. They gave us hell that night, and I did not have a great game, but Jerome Williams came up big with 27 points, John Jacques made a bunch of threes, and once again Othella kept his recent momentum going. Jerome was really elevating his game, gathering his confidence. He and I would feed off each other. He could get a rebound and just go. He didn't have to pass ahead to me. I would just start running, and a lot of times he would be feeding me. He ended up leading the Big East in rebounds with 10 a game. We held on for another narrow win, and our fourth straight.

The regular season ended with a loss against St. John's, but our ranking was set and Coach Thompson played a lot of the bench. It was time for the Big East Tournament, and then the NCAAs.

But first they announced the end-of-season awards. I received the Big East Rookie of the Year award, and to me the bigger honor, I won Big East Defensive Player of the Year. I had averaged over three steals a game, establishing the Big East record for steals in a season. People don't know that—Big East *Defensive* Player of the Year. It was like at Bethel, being thrilled about a tackle I made in the state championship, the interceptions as much a point of pride as any touchdown pass. Defender of the Year.

The Big East Tournament was held in New York City. When I walked in, knowing the legends who'd come before, the arena had this feeling like it was always expecting something great. It comes from the crowd and the history, I guess. I've played there many times since, more with Georgetown and then numerous times with the Sixers.

In a first-round win over Miami, I scored 31 points and in the process broke the Georgetown record for points in a season. Not just for a freshman, for *anyone*. This set us up for our third shot at UConn, but it was not the charm. Until that day, no team had ever beaten Georgetown three times in the same season. Now it was starting to piss me off. Ray Allen led their team with 24 points. I had 27, and just like the last game against them, while we had a lead in the second half, we couldn't find a way to make stops toward the end.

Even though we were mad as hell at losing, we felt like we were close, getting better and better, and ready for the NCAA Tournament.

TWENTY-FOUR

THE BIG DANCE

The next night, they released the bracket—that was what would tell us where we would go and who we would play against in the Big Dance. We all watched to see our seed, our region, our path. The whole campus was excited. At that time, man, college basketball had such a big place on the campus, on TV, everywhere it seemed. It was just a couple years earlier that the Fab Five had shown the world that freshmen could lead a team all the way—to the championship game at least. Me being a freshman, of course that was on my mind.

As the bracket came out, we learned that we were seeded sixth and placed in the Southeast region, where Kentucky was the No. 1 seed, North Carolina No. 2. I remember thinking, *Sixth seed? Damn, we gotta do better.*

Our first game was against Xavier the following Friday in Tallahassee. If we won, we'd play the winner of Weber State and Michigan State.

Like I said, Coach Thompson and the whole team felt like it had been too long since we'd had some tournament success. Five years since even making it to the Sweet Sixteen. Me, I wasn't thinking about all that. I was dying to play the games, get on the floor, feel the crowd, the attention. I just felt like we could beat anyone.

In Tallahassee, I got a call in my hotel room. It was Coach Thompson. He wanted to speak with me. I walked to his room wondering what was up, what kind of trouble I was in. He looked all serious as I entered.

"I'm going to tell you something that I haven't told you all year." It sounded so terrible. Like the man was about to tell me I couldn't play in the game or some shit.

"I'm proud of you," he said. "Regardless of what happens at the end of this year, I want you to know that."

In my head, I was like, *Okay, and . . . ?*

But that was it. He didn't even dismiss me with a couple of "motherfuckers" at the end. Not knowing what to do, I nodded and just shook his hand. Walked right on out of there.

He said later, "My kids are more comfortable with me when I'm fussing at them and cursing at them or being boisterous. I guess he didn't know what the hell's going on with Coach—he's being nice to me." Looking back now with thirty years of hindsight, I can see what he was doing. When I say Coach Thompson saved my life, it wasn't just a scholarship, a chance at basketball. It was the faith he put in me and the confidence that his faith, his belief, gave me.

So the next day, it got tight down the stretch against Xavier. I had to play the last nine minutes with four fouls. When Coach Thompson put me back in, he was like, "Don't commit any more motherfucking fouls, you little shit." He was done being nice to me, with a game we had to finish. I survived the rest of the game without fouling out, and we moved on to the second round.

Weber State was waiting there for us after upsetting Michigan State. Everybody was kind of putting us in the Sweet Sixteen at that point, saying we got lucky to play Weber State. But Coach Thompson was not hearing that shit. As we practiced the day before, Coach Thompson was on us about keeping our focus. It had been too long to just pencil us in there. He was right not to just assume those dudes would roll over.

Man, it was a slugfest. We didn't make a single three-pointer the entire game. We got out to a 10–0 lead, and I felt like we relaxed a little. They responded and scored the next thirteen. The rest of the way, it was back and forth, neither team able to get into an offensive flow.

We were up one when their star player, Ruben Nembhard, got a layup that put them in the lead. The whole game seemed in the balance, so when I got the inbound, I raced down the court, and I got fouled driving to the basket. Down a point, forty seconds left, I went to the line. So far I had made only three of seven foul shots. Sure enough, I missed the first one. I could not fucking believe it. I hit the second one, though, and now we were tied. They took a timeout. In the huddle, Coach Thompson reminded us of all the defensive work we put in. It was going to come down to defense. Nembhard drove, and Don Reid blocked it, but they got the ball back when it went out of bounds. Off the inbound, Nembhard drove to the basket again, and Boubacar blocked it this time, but they called a foul before the shot. With 7.4 seconds left, their star was going to the foul line for a one-and-one.

As he was getting ready to take the shot, Coach Thompson called me over. Make or miss, "get the ball and just go." It was that message. That freedom. That faith.

Sure enough, he missed the first shot. Jerome got the rebound, I came around, and he got me the ball. I ran. Sprinted past half-court. With just a couple ticks on the clock, I had to shoot. So I jumped up on the dead run, on the left side a few feet outside the three-point line. I fired up the shot. As soon as it left my hand I knew it was way short. Then I saw Don streaking down the right side and under the basket. Like an alley-oop, he caught the ball at the apex of his jump, back of his head below the rim. In one motion he turned his body and while still in the air released it over his shoulder and in, as the last tenth of a second expired.

The whole bench fucking exploded, including Coach Thompson. We were in the Sweet Sixteen. It was madness. I felt like all that time Don and I spent living together—me a chatterbox and Don stoic as hell, always serious about getting his sleep—helped him understand where my shot was going, and what to do with it.

We all danced in the locker room. I never saw Coach Thompson as happy as he was that day. He could really move too. Talking some shit, Coach Thompson told Jerome he could dance way better than him. And he was right!

Coach Thompson explained why he celebrated so much: "I'm at the point in my career where I want to enjoy the moment. I was happy for myself and I also was extremely happy for them." We were all in the locker room, hearing him say this. He added, "This team has been a pleasure. I've gone farther with some jackasses but wouldn't admit it. It's nice to do it with these kind of kids. And I got to do my dance." Dancing with that man, bringing him some joy. I accomplished something.

Now we faced North Carolina. I knew a lot of these dudes. It wasn't no Weber State. Jeff McInnis and Jerry Stackhouse, the dudes I'd beaten in that AAU championship—that now seemed like a lifetime ago. They also had Rasheed Wallace. The last time Georgetown had played the Tar Heels in the Tournament was that final in 1982, more than a decade earlier. People remember that one, the motherfucking game that put Michael Jordan on the map.

We had a few days off before traveling to Birmingham, Alabama, and so we were back on campus, the whole school going crazy. I went out, enjoyed the limelight. The hero, my roommate Don Reid, dude was quieter than ever, didn't want to even leave his room but for practice and class.

Come game time, Carolina came at us hard and jumped out to a 23–7 lead, hitting threes as our defense worked to limit the inside game. Wallace had been nursing an ankle injury in the first two rounds. But while he limped and grimaced, it didn't seem to hold him back. Once we adjusted and started extending the defense out to the three-point line, he started dunking it on us. Feeds from Stackhouse, drop steps, offensive boards. We couldn't stop him.

I couldn't get it going at all in the first half. I didn't get my first points until a free throw a couple minutes before the break. Going into halftime, I was 0-6 from the field. I felt like I was letting the team down, like the one place where I could always handle myself, I couldn't get under control. I knew I could do way better than that first half. As always, I felt like I was the best motherfucker on the court. So I went to the seniors on the team, Irvin Church and John Jacques, and the dudes just encouraged me to keep at it. Coach Thompson told me something I didn't expect. He said I was trying too hard to be a point guard and get other people involved. He encouraged me to push the tempo, push the tempo, and get myself involved. He usually was telling me to slow down, distribute, but that day I think he could see I needed to stop thinking about things, and also he just needed me to take over for us to have a chance.

In the second half, I managed to get ahold of my game and take control of the court. Made a three, a couple steals. On one play I skied for the rebound, took it coast to coast in about a second, slid around Jeff McInnis, who was trying to take a charge, and scooped in a layup. After next to nothing in the first half, I got 21 in the second. I was everywhere, playing with speed, recklessly, but still in control. And at one point we worked the lead down to four. But then Rasheed continued his rampage with a little turnaround on the block, a steal and dunk followed, and the game never got close again.

Then I fouled out. There was about a minute left. And the crowd was filled with fans not just of Georgetown and Carolina, but also Kentucky and Arizona State, who played the second game that day. People from all over the country. Most of them had probably never seen me play. They all stood up and cheered as I walked off. This time there weren't any signs talking about jailbirds or O.J. Obviously the ovation wasn't because we'd won.

It was just like, *Damn, this motherfucker came to play and put it out there.* I was so mad we lost, but hearing the people give me that back, it meant something, gave me fuel going forward. It's something I will never forget.

In the locker room afterward, Coach Thompson stayed positive. I think we were glad to give him that trip to the Sweet Sixteen. And me and Othella and Jerome and Boubacar and Jahidi, we all expected to come back. Come back stronger.

So North Carolina ended our run. I had held my own—we had—but it was over. Now I had to suffer through the rest of the spring semester, still required to go to class, but nothing keeping me grounded. I had been so focused since the summer, everything had been one thing after another, from those Summer League games to high school graduation to classes to practice to the exhibitions to the opener to the Big East schedule to the conference tournament to the NCAAs to the Sweet Sixteen. And then, damn, it was over.

I found myself in the dorm with time on my hands. One distraction was watching Michael Jordan's comeback. Five days after we exited the Tournament, I was chilling with my friends watching Mike's return to Madison Square Garden. The greatest's fifth game, and he dropped 55 on the Knicks. I'd missed his first game back because he was playing at the exact same time as we beat Weber State. Watching Mike now, I got more and more hyped with each shot. And then of course he *passed* it for the winning points. You know what I was thinking about with him quitting baseball and rejoining the NBA? *I'm going to get to play on the same court as Mike!*

Goddammit, I wanted to be out there, and by now I knew I could be. The press was speculating about me leaving Georgetown after one year, and of course my family and friends talked to me about it. But at that time, for Coach Thompson in particular, it really wasn't done. And I felt like, *Shit man, I'm a kid. I lost my senior year of high school, so there's no way I'm just going to skip by college like that.* I also felt like there was more left to do. I shot it under 40 percent, we lost in the Sweet Sixteen. I had to work on my game, had to do better, and I owed it to Coach Thompson. My family and friends, my girl and my daughter, they would have to wait at least another year.

I'm not going to lie though. I had trouble making it to class for a minute there.

One time after the season was over, Coach called me in. It wasn't to say how proud of me he was. Instead he told me he heard I'd been missing class. "You go up that hill every day, you eat three times a day, but your mom and sisters are living in a hellhole," he said. "And you just living it up, ain't you? You got heat. You got hot water. But down there, your mom don't got none of that. You got an opportunity to change all that. And you want to fuck around?" That wasn't the last time he gave me that speech. It never failed to put me back on the right path. So I finished off that semester in good academic standing. Then I went home.

TWENTY-FIVE

SUMMERTIME

I got home that summer, confident about my game and my future. That August I would travel to Japan for my first overseas trip. That was because Me, Othella, and Jerome all had been selected to represent the United States in the World University Games, along with guys like Tim Duncan, Ray Allen, and Kerry Kittles. I knew then that I would play at Georgetown at least one more year, but I also knew eventually I would get paid.

I came home to my homeboys, to my family, to Nana. Nana was in Aberdeen still, living with Uncle Stevie. She had been in and out of the hospital for a couple years at this point. Stevie was so close to her. He'd enlisted in the Marines but left early so that he could take care of her. When I was in jail, I remember worrying about her. I just didn't want her last memories of me to be as another neighborhood kid incarcerated. Thank God she survived and got to see my first year at Georgetown. For me, sitting in my dorm room—"living it up," as Coach Thompson had put it—I would imagine all the shit I would get Nana when I got paid. A house, a car, better health care. It would be more than the hospital gave my family when her daughter died in Connecticut, that's for sure.

So when I got home that summer, I spent as much time with her and Stevie as I could. What I remember is walking into her little room. She didn't have much energy anymore. But the walls were covered with articles about me, fixed on there with masking tape: pictures of Coach Thompson with his arm around me, of me skying for a dunk, of the president looking on from the stands. It meant everything to me to see that shit on her wall, knowing I was bringing her some joy and pride.

But she wasn't doing well, and later that summer she passed. I told Stevie and my mom that she just got tired of going back and forth to the hospital. I was fucked-up for a long while after Nana died. I was just missing her presence and feeling like she didn't get to see me fulfill my ultimate dream of getting to the NBA. And then a lot of times I would think that because I had gotten out of jail and gone to Georgetown, she'd gotten to see that. I don't know, I tried to juggle it in different kinds of ways in my mind, you know, the guilt from what she had to go through with the bowling alley shit, but the joy of me getting out and beginning my basketball journey. I just tried to make that pain disappear somehow, telling myself she saw part of it, and with the pictures on her wall, she was proud. I was real, real fucked-up for a while.

On June 20, 1995, I was at home asleep when I heard my mom just starting hollering from the other side of the house, making a commotion. *Yes, yes, yes! They did it!* I'm thinking it's the lottery or some shit.

Wasn't no lottery, but it felt like a miracle. The Virginia Court of Appeals had made its decision: a complete reversal of my conviction. I wasn't a criminal anymore—technically never had been. I had no record. I heard it, smiled, but kept my composure, and just shook my head.

Damn, I knew I got railroaded but I didn't expect any court to agree with me. My only hope had been a Black governor who had got me halfway there. But then those three white dudes—who wouldn't give me the time of day when I came to the oral argument—had gone and reversed Judge Overton. And they did so on the point we had been making from the beginning: There was insufficient evidence of a mob, and if there had been a mob, there was no evidence that I was a part of it. The appeals court sent it back to the trial court, and to the DA's office. They could retry me on misdemeanors, but no felonies. The DA's office quietly gave up and dismissed the whole motherfucking case a few months later.

I remember I spoke to Coach Thompson right after hearing the news. He had just called the Georgetown president, elated. My mom was jumping up and down still. The whole community that had supported me had been completely vindicated, man. I half-expected the prosecutor to call me up and apologize. *Mr. Iverson, we never should have used that antilynching statute to put you in jail, I'm so sorry.* Maybe the motherfucking judge would tell me how sorry he was for getting the whole point of his job—the legal shit—completely wrong. Or the editorial board. *We reconsider our position that the court system treated Iverson fairly, and in a reversal we are so sorry that Iverson missed his senior year of high school—the sports, his senior prom, his graduation—in fucking jail.* Or that motherfucking columnist, *I was wrong*. Nope, no one said any of that. They said I had gotten off on a technicality. As if insufficient evidence was a technicality.

To think, we asked over and over again. Give me that appeal bond before I serve my time. Because if I win an appeal, and I've already done the time, then I was sitting in jail for nothing? No, no, no. The only man with a little bit of power who listened and acted was Governor Wilder. And the man got pilloried. Where were the apologies to him?

Coach Thompson, always managing the audience, said to me, "It is not a time to gloat."

Well, thirty years later, writing my motherfucking book, maybe I can now gloat. *Just Do It?* You didn't do shit but railroad a kid.

That's what goes through my head now. I felt it then probably, but more than anything, that shit was done. I was glad to win. I was glad my family was happy. I was glad it was over, like over over *over*. And I wasn't looking back.

TWENTY-SIX

SEASON TWO

Freed from jail, from that dark cloud, just fucking free, I came back for my second year of college confident as hell. It wasn't just what happened in the court of law that built my confidence. On the basketball court, I had played Summer League in Virginia and lit the place up, scoring over 80 in one game, over 70 in another. I was joined by my old partners Tony Rutland and Joe Smith, who had just been selected with the first pick in the NBA Draft. Capacity crowds greeted the show. Then I went to Japan for the World University Games. As we went through the schedule, I became more and more of a focal point, leading the team in scoring in both the semifinal and the gold medal game. I joined forces with Ray Allen, my rival, and got to see Tim Duncan up close for the first time. And I got to see the world. On a jet to Tokyo. Feeling the love of a totally different crowd. Appreciation for basketball in countries I never dreamed of visiting. We won easily.

So here I was back at Georgetown for a new year, and just sure that my game was ready to grow, expand, help us win.

In the first day of practice I met a freshman who would become my partner in the backcourt, Victor Page. He and I had some things in common. He was from the projects, but in DC, and he'd come from nothing to dominate on the court, averaging over 30 points per game as a senior in high school. But he had his academic issues, and between high school and starting at Georgetown, he spent a year at a prep school. Not everyone wanted to recruit Victor, but Coach Thompson felt like he did with me, I think, like he wanted to help this dude out. Many people know Victor is in jail now, hit with some charges I can't think or talk about, but back then he was just a good running mate from a tough background.

I told you about the scoring I had done in Summer League. But everyone agreed I had to focus more on being a distributor, a normal point guard. I felt that way too. Had to pick my spots better, score but at a higher percentage—40 percent just wasn't good enough. I had an idea that the NBA was next. And with the NBA I had an expectation. First pick in the draft. That was going to take work.

With Don Reid graduated (the dude who couldn't get on the court his first two years was selected by the Pistons with the very last pick in the draft, and then had a long, successful NBA career), Coach Thompson picked Boubacar to be my roommate. Boubacar was from Senegal. One of our coaches discovered him there and found a way to bring him back to the U.S. After a year at a prep school, he was a Hoya. Then, a couple years later, he found himself living with me. Coach Thompson had his methods—he said that Boubacar could work on his English with me, since "Allen talks all the time." Like with Don, Boubacar was often telling me to shut the hell up as he tried to sleep. Sometimes I would wander the dorm in the middle of the night, looking to find someone who I could chill with.

My freshman year, we didn't have "Midnight Madness"—that campus event where right at midnight on the date you're first allowed to practice, you open up the gym to the fans and put on a show for them. We didn't have it because Coach Thompson had always refused to allow it. That fall we had been begging Coach Thompson to have some fun, and even though he said it was the biggest waste of his fucking time, he relented. He shook his head like, *Damn I'm getting soft.* You could feel it, as they let everyone in that night, the whole campus with this energy—we made it to the Sweet Sixteen and now we were ready for more success. Even Coach Thompson basked in it. He told us, "You have one night to act like a fool. Then it's over."

As we started real practice, Coach Thompson focused on defense, like always. But this year, he had some other ideas. Instead of having me bring the ball up the court and start the offense, he talked about having me play off the ball some, let someone else handle some of the point guard responsibilities so I could focus on scoring once I got the ball in my spots. People give Larry Brown all the credit for this idea, and believe me, Larry Brown deserves it, but Coach Thompson was on it too. To do it, though, he needed the right personnel, so he considered having Victor get the offense set, and having me come off the ball.

Without Don Reid or John Jacques or Irvin Church, it was a new team. But even without those seniors, those who remained were more experienced, and as a group more talented. Practices were fierce. Coach Thompson embraced our reckless energy. I remember early on I got a stray elbow and had to get about ten stitches on my face. But before I did, I stayed to scrimmage—scrimmaging was always the best part of practice for me, and I didn't want to miss that time to compete. We all trash-talked with one another. It started with me and Victor, but everyone was talking all kinds of shit. Then when practice ended, we were friends again. I tried to lead by example. Every day, we ran sprints. I won every damn time. Every time. Mike Jackson was still the only dude who'd beaten me in a race.

The games began with another first for Georgetown. We were playing in the preseason National Invitation Tournament (NIT), which meant earlier games in the year against tougher competition than Georgetown teams were accustomed to. In the first game, we easily beat Colgate. I got seven more stitches in that one and also injured my shoulder trying to dunk on their star big man, Adonal Foyle. In spite of stitches now zigzagging my body like Frankenstein, I reentered and finished the game.

Although I was listed as questionable, I played again a couple nights later against Temple. Me and Victor found our rhythm. In the second half we were pulling away, me and him feeding off each other's energy. So I got out with the ball in transition and I saw Victor sprinting to the basket. I hit him with a lob that he caught with both hands and slammed. Less than a minute later, this time Vic got the ball, and, knowing I didn't have to come and get it, I just shot down the floor. Now his turn, he threw one up to me that I jammed home. We won by twenty-five.

That set up the NIT semifinal just before Thanksgiving against Georgia Tech at Madison Square Garden, which hosted the semifinal and the final. It was just what I wanted, and what everyone wanted because Georgia Tech had the most hyped freshman of the new season, making his return to New York—Stephon Marbury.

Here is what I was supposed to say leading up to that game: "It isn't about me and Stephon. It is about two teams." That's what Coach Thompson preached, and their coach, Bobby Cremins, was saying all the stuff that my coach said about me the year before: "Marbury's only a freshman. Give him a chance." All that. But here we were in the Garden. The motherfucking *Garden*. Spike Lee was center court, taping that shit with his camcorder. As the tip went up, what was I was thinking? I can tell you—I was thinking I had to put on a motherfucking show.

Early on, Stephon came at me. In one move he crossed over right to left, hesitated and came back left to right, to get by me on his way to the basket. He got me a couple more times. He showed me that day something I saw from him again and again over the years. He was one of the toughest dudes for me to guard my entire career. He just had so much strength as he got his shoulder by you. And even then as a freshman, you couldn't give him any space because his shot was so deadly. Still, I did block his shot later in the game.

As we pulled away in the game, there were two plays that stick with me. One, I was getting ready to try and take Marbury one-on-one, the crowd buzzing. But before I could, Othella got position in the post so I pulled it back and fed him. He made this old-school hook shot. Then a little later in transition, I got the ball just by half-court. Off the dribble with my right hand, I hit Jerome with a bounce pass that traveled almost the entire half-court into his hands for a layup. The whole crowd got on their feet for that one. These were highlights where I got other dudes involved. We ended up winning by twenty-two points.

It was games like this that I lived for. In the spotlight. Next, we had the NIT final against Arizona. I added an elbow injury to the list, but still played thirty-seven out of forty minutes. Patrick Ewing, Georgetown alum and then Knicks All-Star, was sitting courtside. I couldn't help it if this game turned into a one-man show. I got mine even though as a team we lost. I scored 40 points, but no one else scored more than seven, and Arizona outscored us by ten. Still, they ended up handing me the tournament MVP trophy.

Going back to the locker room, trophy in hand, I was just furious we didn't win the tournament. We all were. But there to greet us was a smiling Coach Thompson. He was smiling because now he had something to be mad about. He said it was the "slap in the face" we needed. He'd be harping on that game for the rest of the year. *You let those motherfuckers shoot sixty percent! So now we are going to work on DEFENSE!* He was smiling, like now he had the upper hand for practice.

TWENTY-SEVEN

CROSSOVER

While Victor would become my partner in the backcourt, another freshman guard, a walk-on, ended up being elemental to the dude I would become. Dean Berry was from Brooklyn, shorter than me, skinnier than me. Without a scholarship, he showed up and made the team, then unheard-of at Georgetown. He probably made it because of how he played against me. See, I had to guard him every day. The motherfucker didn't even have his name on the back of his jersey. He wore number 12, and damn sure he was the twelfth man on the bench. Yet every day he was busting my ass. Every day he would hit me with it: his crossover.

I had done crossovers before. In high school I had learned the Tim Hardaway, where he'd keep it low, dribble through his leg, then back in front—kind of like what Marbury had done to me in the NIT. Though I knew the move, it wasn't yet a focal point for me. I really would use my raw speed, hesitations, and blow-bys. My first step, unguardable because it was so sudden and explosive, was my main method of getting to the rim. If I got some space with that first step, I could either finish at the hoop or pull up for the midrange. Dean wasn't as fast, but he was getting me with his craft, his crossovers. His were more than just what I knew as the Hardaway. He had variations, and no matter what I did on the defensive end, he was getting me. There I was, Big East Defensive Player of Year, and I couldn't stop this walk-on from blowing by me.

So in practice it was pissing me off. But at the same time, I knew I needed to learn what this motherfucker was doing. I was hesitant to ask him to show me. My ego wouldn't let me do it for the longest. That would just add to his bragging rights, as far as telling people he used to cross me up a lot. But the move was so vicious I just had to learn. So I sucked it up and asked him to teach me. Starting late that fall, I would stay after practice with him, and he would show me. We would work on it again and again, every day.

What I learned was that the crossover is a person being scared of your first step. That's what makes it so vicious, so deadly. So I would look into the defender's eyes, could tell by the way his feet moved if he was scared. I might fake him one time with a little right to left or left to right, and then I do the real one and most of the time they go for it. What I added, what became my signature, was I would bring the ball high and away from my body, with a little cradle in my hand, where I could almost pause it, watch the defender, before deciding. Cross him over or use that first step and blow by.

Over and over, me and Dean Berry, working on it. I started adding it in scrimmages and the games. And once I started, not only was it effective, but it generated this fucking energy. I could see the fear in the dude's eyes as he stood between me and the basket, the ball still in my hand. I could also feel the crowd anticipating—the feeling you'd get as you're rising up to jam it right before they go crazy. But this is just while dribbling, and sure enough, if you hit him with it, and he goes one way, you the other, the crowd would go crazy. It became a part of the show.

*

After the NIT was over, as was his usual, Coach Thompson scheduled some cupcakes. So we ran over teams like Sacramento State and St. Leo, and we avoided one scare against West Virginia, who had just joined the Big East.

We developed a pressure defense coupled with an up-tempo offense that fit my game. Othella was working his way in. We got along well after teaming up in the World University Games, but there were still adjustments. In that West Virginia game, for instance, he wasn't getting involved and got benched for some of the second half. Still, he made a key bucket down the stretch. Victor was adjusting as well. He had to defer to me, and he had to learn the college game now, like I did the year before. Coach Thompson benched him at one point to get a lesson across.

But with me, I was winning, and playing with the same abandon that got me all those stitches. Coach Thompson told the press, "Pound for pound, he plays as big as anybody I've seen." He would regularly say now that I was a shooting guard in a point guard's body, and sometimes dribbled too much. But he'd add, "He gives more damn effort. Allen has gotten twenty stitches in his face this season—in practice." That same *Washington Post* reporter I mentioned earlier, Thomas Boswell, said something about watching me in the games that I always came back to: "It's becoming apparent that Iverson's *game* is defined as much by his effort as by his talent."

We had won nine straight coming into a battle with Seton Hall. That was the game I scored forty (tying my Georgetown record from the Arizona game), and Jerry Nichols heard behind closed doors in the bathroom that Coach Thompson said I was a "bad motherfucker." We were playing at the USAir Arena (earlier the Capital Centre), our home court. On a Saturday, over 18,000 fans came to see the show. It was just one of those days that I had it going. We got out to a seventeen-point lead in the first half, and they actually came back on us and tied the score in the second half, only for me to take over at the end, with a three, a jumper, and some foul shots. By that point Coach Thompson had instructed everyone to get me the ball at the end of tight ones. I made seven of thirteen three-pointers.

But there was one play that stood out. Still in the first half, the ball in my hands, isolated, I had Danny Hurley in front of me. It was that moment, watching his feet, searching his eyes, the ball hanging out high in my hand's cradle, and then as he started leaning, I crossed over to the other side. Left him dusted, crowd gasping, the lane open. As I got to the basket, Donnell Williams helped on D. I twisted by him, got hacked, finished with the and-one.

What had been a gasp was now a roar, pandemonium—in the crowd, among my teammates, on the bench. Then when the game stopped for a timeout, they put that joint on the big screen two times. Each time the crowd got more and more hyped, louder than when we sealed the game, louder even than when I'd first done it live. That's the first crossover I can remember that just took over an arena like that. It wasn't my signature yet, but you could see why Coach Thompson had said I had been a bad motherfucker. Danny Hurley said after the game, "People like me so much down here, they replayed it twice. I didn't want to see it. But I could tell by the crowd's reaction that it was pretty bad." He's recovered, of course, coaching UConn to two championships in a row.

TWENTY-EIGHT

MASTERING THE COLLEGE GAME

As the season went along, a dynamic built. If I did too much scoring, that was a bad thing. So I had scored 40 against Arizona in the NIT and we lost. Then I scored 40 again at Seton Hall and we almost lost. Our third loss that season was against St. John's at the Garden, and I scored 39—lit up the place, but didn't get the W. Those were my three highest-scoring games. But the other guys weren't involved. Meanwhile, we beat Miami and I fed Jerry Nichols for the game-sealing three-pointer. It was another key three for Jerry in a win at Notre Dame (I made sure not to look at the football stadium!). In a win against Syracuse, Othella led the team, getting out of a slump. I scored just 18 as we destroyed West Virginia, and far less than 40 as we easily handled Seton Hall the second time we played them.

It was like it was in high school. Because the way I felt was that if my teammates didn't get it going, I would do what I needed to do. But then Coach Thompson, and the commentators, would say their success was my responsibility. I was the point guard, and so it was my job to make sure they got it going.

Come February, we hit a little slump against ranked opponents. After we lost to St. John's, we had one of those marquee matchups against Villanova, both of us ranked in the top ten. I was concentrating my ass off on getting everyone else involved after all the talk, but my teammates made less than 30 percent of their shots. 'Nova defended us the way more and more teams would, the box and one. Four dudes playing zone, and one dedicated individual—mostly Alvin Williams that night—following me wherever I went. In college I always had to deal with these zone defenses. My teammates would be like, *You going to have it good in the NBA*, where zones weren't allowed.

After that, we went up to Syracuse, and I had the worst game of the season. In foul trouble, missing shots, we got whipped. And then it became *They can't beat ranked opponents.*

So the next two games, Boston College and Memphis, both ranked teams, were tests. We went up to BC, where I scored 24, including a clutch three as we got off the skid with a 66–63-win. Then Memphis came to our place. They were a bunch of tough dudes like me, and came into our arena talking all kinds of shit at us. First half was a dunkfest, highlight reel, technicals, all that shit. Like on the Anderson Park courts. It was the kind of game that brought out my best, 30 points and the win, this time with a big, twenty-one-point margin. In both games, Othella brought it too, scoring over 20 and controlling the glass. I joked after the game that maybe we could skip a practice or two now that we'd beaten some ranked opponents.

But that wasn't happening. Instead Coach Thompson doubled it. And that was because next we had the big one. UConn was coming to our place, the only matchup with them that year, unless we faced off in the Big East Tournament. I would be wearing number 3, but they came in ranked three, and the year before they won all three. These dudes had won twenty-three straight games and were trying to be the first team ever to go undefeated in the Big East.

Leading up to the game, me, Jerome, Boubacar, Othella, and Vic were talking about how whenever we got down in a game, we would get back into it by pressing full court. How 'bout we just press from start to finish? Keep our intensity hot the whole game. It wasn't in the game plan, so as a group we went to Coach Thompson with it. He smiled, because when dudes came to talk it wasn't usually asking to play more defense. "I'm for it," he said. And then he played with us: "I don't know that much about offense anyway."

So that's what we did from the tip. We pressed UConn full-court. We got them to turn the ball over again and again. I had eight steals myself, just two off a record I had established a couple weeks before. With Boubacar locking him up most of the time, we shut down Ray Allen. We built a 32–12 lead and it never really got close after that. Jim Calhoun said about me after the game, "I don't know of any great player who works harder. He works like a guy who's trying to get minutes." That's the way I always was in the *games*. Working my ass off.

But it wasn't any hard work or hustle that I remember best. It was in the first minute of the second half, when I just put those motherfuckers to sleep. I got the ball after a turnover and I turned on the jets, sprinting to the other end. No one got in my way, could or wanted to, and I found myself in the lane, a few feet past the foul line. I took flight. Rudy Johnson came over to try and get in my path. I just remember rising higher, over this 6'6" dude who stood arms raised below me, and I threw it down on top of his head. The rim snapped back into place after releasing it. Then I landed on the ground, the viciousness just reverberating along with rim. Jerome was beside me and he threw up his arms, like, *That's it.* The arena shook. Jim Calhoun took a timeout, which gave the video board time to replay it and replay it.

It's still my favorite dunk I ever did. Over the years, at my NBA peak, I played so many minutes and had to conserve my energy, so I stopped dunking. So that there, that was my best.

*

I was able to focus during those two years at Georgetown. Isolated, in the bubble Coach Thompson created. But I can't lie, there were distractions. The number one distraction, as was always the case, was the riches on the horizon. The NBA. As I played each game with Georgetown, my improvement clarified. I had added to my scoring, increasing from 20 to 25 a game. Instead of shooting below 40 percent, I shot 48 percent that year. Instead of 23 percent from three, 37 percent. And I was on the cusp of breaking my steals record. I'd always known I was going to be a top pick, but now everyone knew it.

I would still go home and visit my friends and family. My dad, Michael Freeman, had gotten out of jail that January. He was paroled, had an ankle monitor so he couldn't go too far, and was living with his brothers in Hampton, where he'd been his whole life. I would go see him. I knew what was going on there—what Dad had done before. It wasn't good things happening in that crib.

Even my biological father, as I said, had been calling me. I didn't pay it too much mind, but he said he wanted to come and visit, see a game. Which he never did.

My mom's house still had the smell of sewage. A lot of the time, you couldn't walk around just in your socks because your feet would get nasty, so you had to put your shoes on as you left your bed to the bathroom, and take them off as you got back to bed. Bills didn't get paid. My sister had her medical problems, still having seizures—in that house. I still had my daughter Tiaura living with Tawanna in Hampton. They were still apart from me. So of course I would visit. I would chill with Arnie, Marlon, Ra, Jamil, with Thrilla when he could. I'd be out late, dreaming of all the things I had coming, but didn't yet have.

I could almost touch those things. My boys would come up to DC. In Arlington we had access to a recording studio, so we would chill over there. We recorded some tracks. I'd play them for my teammates. Boubacar was getting sick of it in our dorm room. They tried to take my Biggie tapes away, because I played "Juicy" over and over. Coach Thompson found out about all that "rapping nonsense" and told me to focus. Focus on the real shit.

Fuck if I didn't want to help everyone from home right now—before I couldn't, like what happened with Nana. Never got a chance to buy all the shit she deserved. And then at the same time, help my goddamn self, and enjoy my life.

But first, first I had to finish that season. And one thing with me, I might get distracted dreaming, chattering with anyone who'd listen into the middle of the night, partying, but once the whistle blew, no more distractions. March Madness was coming.

TWENTY-NINE

ANOTHER VILLANOVA CONTROVERSY

After the UConn game, and another win, another loss, we faced 'Nova again. It was on national TV, Billy Packer calling the game, capacity crowd, all that. Kerry Kittles was sitting out the third game of a three-game suspension for making unauthorized phone calls on a calling card. At that time, the NCAA wouldn't let a school pay for you to talk to your family or your girl! That was the threat we lived under. Coach Thompson let us know. *You think the NCAA won't suspend your asses for nothing?* So their team wasn't at full strength, and we destroyed them from the opening tip. It was special because it was the last game on our home court for the seniors, Jerome and Othella. During the game, the Georgetown students started a chant. We'd heard it before, but it was loud and aggressive that day, with a blowout and not much second-half drama to keep them occupied. "Two more years! Two more years!" While home was pulling me hard to do what I had to do, the fans wanted me to come back for my junior and senior years. I caught Coach Thompson scowling at the kids.

He didn't want everybody obsessing over *would I* or *wouldn't I* with the draft. Someone told me he threw a towel in their direction.

After the game we were all celebrating the win (106–68), and then I noticed some whispering, people talking, and I heard what it was about. Turned out, during the broadcast, Billy Packer was analyzing this nasty and-one I had where I showed Alvin Williams the ball then brought it around the other way, threw him off so bad he swatted my head. And I still made it. But the play doesn't matter, what Packer said did. After seeing that shot, he was like, "You're talking about a tough monkey here."

I heard that shit, and I was like, *ooohhhhh*. Fucked-up, but not that big a deal to me. That comment wasn't getting my ass locked up, you know what I mean?

Coach Thompson came right over to me and said it straight. *This is not our problem. We aren't making shit out of this*. Apparently people were calling CBS stations, complaining about "monkey" being a slur. Packer apologized on the air even before the game was over, said he didn't mean it in any kind of way, it was just a saying about a tough ballplayer. So I remember Coach Thompson taking command in front of the press. "One thing I know about Billy Packer is I don't have to explain to anybody about Billy being a racist. Because he's not. Billy Packer might have made a mistake in what he was saying. . . . Billy Packer is a good man. Allen is not offended. I'm not offended, so let's leave that shit alone." I heard that, listened, and then I told the media, "I've been watching CBS games Billy Packer has done all my life. I never heard him say anything offensive. I didn't even take it that way. I've never considered him a racist."

That's what we said to the press. The conversation behind closed doors, among us Hoyas, with tape covering the gaps in the doors, might have been a little different. Coach Thompson knew that it wasn't a debate that was going to help us focus. Looking back, I think what other parts of my life might have been like if I had Coach Thompson advising me. Like before talking to Tom Brokaw about race. I might have said, *Hell no! Race had nothing to do with me getting locked up for that bowling alley brawl.*

Or shit, what about advising me before the infamous "practice" press conference?

So what's the story with practice, Allen?

Well, sir, I got to go to practice on time every day. In fact, me and Larry Brown are going to practice together right after this motherfucker.

I miss Coach Thompson, and I didn't know how much until the man recently passed away. His son, Ronny, called me, told me he might have a week left. He died the next morning. And I didn't get to say goodbye. For the rest of my playing days, I think I was always searching for another Coach Thompson. Never did find one. Now that he's gone, and I'm retired, I think about him more than ever.

Heading into the Big East Tournament, the Billy Packer controversy continued. After apologizing he had to go and make it worse again, saying things like "I don't think of Allen Iverson as a Black player. I think of Allen as a player." Then he went, "I only apologized to those people who have those sensibilities. But I also feel sorry for people like that because I don't see things in terms of black and white." Only a white dude could say that—but it wasn't my problem.

I was fine with the controversy because it wasn't about me, or Coach Thompson, or the Hoyas. Other people got to argue about that shit, get worked up, and leave the world in the same place. Me and my team, we moved on. We were back in the Garden for the Big East Tournament.

After beating Miami in the first round (I had 38 points), we played 'Nova again, this time with Kittles. It wasn't a blowout, and no race controversies got started, but we handled them. I had 28 points. Vic found his rhythm, scoring 34 points from all over. I was so proud of him because after starting the season hot, he had struggled at times, with Coach Thompson benching him on and off. That set up a final against Ray Allen and UConn.

I wanted to beat those motherfuckers so bad, to win the Big East

Championship. Possibly to earn a No. 1 seed in the tournament. Everyone was saying Ray Allen was going to be Big East Player of the Year too, which pissed me off.

It was tight the whole game. With sixteen seconds left, us up one, I was guarding the ball. They were running some screens to get Ray open off the baseline. But we'd denied him. So Ray came around and got like a little dribble handoff at the top of the key. I ended up switching on to Ray. We played it perfectly. Ray raised up, mid-jump, kind of looked to pass, then threw it up at the rim, awkward as hell. Ball bounced around the rim three, four times before going in.

I took it the other way, got a good look a few feet outside the free throw line, but it didn't go in. Jerome couldn't do a Don Reid. He missed the put back after getting the rebound.

I remember getting back to the locker room and it might as well have been after we lost one playing football as a kid in Aberdeen. I was *trying* to hold back tears. That was the toughest loss for me at Georgetown. My last Big East game. Championship on the line, at the Garden, against our bitter rival.

Defeated, downcast, head in my hands and eyes on the ground. Coach Thompson approached and put his arm around me. I looked up at him. He said, "Don't worry about it." He meant don't worry because we still had more games to play. Or maybe he meant don't worry, it was just a game. My mom once said, "I think if you lift up John's arm, you'll see Allen underneath."

THIRTY

A SECOND DANCE

The NCAA Tournament started a few days later. We were the No. 2 seed in the East region, with our first couple of games scheduled in Richmond, Virginia. Pretty much my backyard. It was easy for all my family and friends to come—which they did. We had an open practice the day before the game and everyone was in the stands, shouting, calling me out by "Bubbachuck," a name I didn't bring with me to DC. My teammates and Coach Thompson were laughing at my ass.

Our first game was against Mississippi Valley State. We won by close to forty (31 points for me). My mom showed up at halftime, that's how late she was. She was wearing her Georgetown number 3 jersey, with Ms. Iverson on the back. But it wasn't her, or all the family, or all my friends, that really got my attention in the crowd.

It was a politician who meant even more to me than Bill Clinton. Governor Douglas Wilder showed up—the man who set me free. He said about me that day, "You can't imagine how good it makes you feel when you catch a kid who could have easily slipped off the slope." This man had become the first Black governor in the entire country's history, was the grandson of slaves, and took it upon himself to emancipate *me*. He said strangers came up to him all the time to thank him for what he'd done. That appeals court had shown how right he was. I didn't get to meet him that day, but my mom did. I would have loved to have thanked him that day, shaken his hand. Motherfucking hero.

That win brought us to a game against New Mexico. I came out slow, making only two shots in the first half and missing all six of my three-pointers. But it wasn't just me wearing a Hoyas uniform, and my teammates picked me up. Jahidi White had his best game of the year. Jerome scored and rebounded. We found ourselves down just three at halftime, feeling like it could have been worse. In the locker room, my teammates told me to relax. If they were there, keep taking my shots. On the defensive end, New Mexico had been picking apart our zone. Coach Thompson wanted to stick with it but add some changes he mapped out. Then Boubacar, usually quiet, was like, "Coach, let's go man." And Coach looked at him and just said, "Do it."

In the second half, I made a couple threes, and offensively we started flowing. Defensively, going man-to-man got us our energy, and we locked them down. I remember about three minutes into the second half, after we finally took the lead, Othella turned to one of their dudes. "It's over now," he said. It was. We pulled away as I scored 19 second-half points.

Talking about the defensive adjustments after the game, Coach Thompson said, "I'd like to take credit for the defensive turnaround." He then explained how Boubacar suggested the switch to man-to-man defense. "So much for my knowledge," he said with his chuckle. Coach was known as an authoritarian, my-way-is-the-only-way type. But he wasn't like that at all. He adjusted to my game from the time I stepped on campus, and he listened to all of us, even the dude from Senegal who'd only been playing ball for a few years.

Staring at us in the Sweet Sixteen was Texas Tech. They were 33-1 on the season, but what really impressed us was them killing North Carolina in the previous round—the same team, granted without Sheed and Stack, that ended our last run. Actually, it wasn't even that. What really impressed us was that Darvin Ham had shattered the backboard in that game. It was so crazy. We found out about it when we were still in the locker room after beating New Mexico and had to run back up there to see all the shattered glass getting picked up.

No backboards got broke in our game, but we almost broke the record for most fouls in a game. It wasn't a pretty motherfucker. I got 32 points, but shot it poorly, just ten for twenty-nine from the field. Some of that was me missing shots, but some of it was them running two defenders at me. When we went into one of our favorite sets, four down, meaning me alone at the top of the key and the others down by the baseline waiting for me to break down the perimeter defender, they'd send a second dude, and I'd have to pass out of it.

Othella was the key, particularly in the first half, shooting it well. Vic, who'd been hot ever since the Big East Tournament, had some big shots, and Jerome did the little things. While my shot was cold, I was all over the place on defense. In the key 17–0 second-half run, I had two steals. I made a couple foul shots down the stretch, sealing an ugly victory. Feeling like we survived more than played great, we left for the locker room relieved. Coach Thompson threatened to do the dance again in the locker room. But it was different this year. We were in the Elite Eight, one win from the Final Four. I knew this might be it for me. I loved Coach Thompson so much, I wanted that one Final Four for him—to be held in the Meadowlands, just outside New York.

But that's as far as we got. A couple days later, on March 23, we ran into a team that for one day at least had all the answers, man. They were No. 1 in the country, with the Player of the Year and the Coach of the Year: UMass, Marcus Camby, and John Calipari. I won't waste anyone's time talking too much about that game. We kept it close in the first half, when I scored 17 points, but their backcourt of Carmelo Travieso and

Edgar Padilla could guard like motherfuckers. When I did get past them, Camby was there, one of the best shot blockers I ever played against. I went 1-10 in the second half. Vic didn't make a shot the whole game. It wasn't our night. Season over.

I won me a lot of awards: Big East Defensive Player of the Year again. First-Team All American. Finalist for the Wooden Award. But I didn't win the Big East, didn't win Player of the Year, and didn't make it to the Final Four.

Coach Thompson was disappointed. He wanted it bad, but he had this way of being, like he'd done what he needed to do in his life, won championships and all that, so he could rise above it. He told us he was proud of us. He was, but looking back, I feel like he saw the end. His Hoya teams never made it that far in the Tournament again.

As for me, I had some decisions to make about my future.

THIRTY-ONE

LEAVING GEORGETOWN

I went to the Benz dealership in Arlington. It was called American Service Center Associates. I looked at what they had on the floor, saw this black Mercedes S600 Coupe, used but with just a few thousand miles on it. A salesman came over to me and told me to get in. *Check out the soft leather. The custom features.* Then he's like, *Let's take it for a spin.* We got out on the road, and I felt the V-12 engine.

I asked how much, and he told me it was a little over $100K.

I shook my head because I didn't have shit yet—other than a reputation, a dorm room, and three campus meals a day.

The salesman knew who I was, so he said to me, *Just take it for a little while. And after things get settled with your future, we could settle up.* No papers, no contract, no money.

Hands wrapped around the fine leather steering wheel, I drove on out of there. As the dealership got farther and farther in the rearview, memories came to me of how far I'd come. Getting in Coach Barefield's van, him telling me and Snapper to comb our hair. Trapping crabs in Stuart Gardens. Stealing Skor bars from the store. Mo driving up to take me away from the streets. Waking up with a thousand dollars in my pocket after a weekend where Mo couldn't find me. And shit, when I was in jail, working the morning shift in the bakery, then shooting hoops in the dying light of the fall afternoons.

This here—this car, this success, this freedom—was what we dreamed of. And it was no crime driving off that lot. It was as good as things could be. Life was perfect—just a hard choice between two great options: the National Basketball Association or another year at Georgetown University.

I put on the stereo and turned it UP. I remember Tupac had just released *All Eyez on Me*, so "California Love" filled the speakers. And a track of his that had always spoken to me, "Dear Mama," also played through my daydreams. I just drove.

I drove home to the Peninsula to see my friends and family. It was Easter weekend. The Tournament—without me—was finished (Kentucky took it that year).

I rolled through to see my mom, my dad, my sisters, my daughter, my friends. Everyone gasped at my ride. I had conversations about my decision for the future. But people looked at that car and figured my decision was made.

So at the end of that weekend, my local paper, the *Daily Press*, announced that I would enter the NBA Draft, citing local anonymous sources. Soon the whole world reported that shit. Maybe I knew in my heart what I was doing, but I hadn't even talked to Coach Thompson yet.

Man, I hadn't made a decision, not consciously. Instead I was dealing with home. That same weekend, my dad got in trouble again. They had gone into the house he shared with his brothers and found all kinds of shit. They arrested him (and everyone else that was there) and hit him with another drug charge. A year later, he would go to trial. So, lawyers needed paying. With his record, in and out of prison and still on parole, he wasn't going to be helping the family out, that's for sure.

Then, if you can believe it, that same April my biological father got arrested too, for a domestic violence charge. He ended up serving years in prison. So he never came to a college game and wouldn't ever make any NBA game either. I can't say that affected how I was thinking about going pro or not, but that's how crazy it was just in that one month.

So it was like my family needed me more than ever, but also, like damn, another year in college away from this shit, under Coach Thompson's protective umbrella, that didn't sound too bad either. I drove the Benz back up to Georgetown, the custom Bose system playing the sounds of the streets, but louder and with higher fidelity than I'd ever heard them before. Could I give up this luxury that I was dying to enjoy?

Back at campus, I was still living in the dorm, just a college student. So one day, a week or so after returning, I rode the Benz over to my friend's house in another part of DC. A TV van from a local station followed my ass and put that shit on TV. Charles Mann, a former football player who'd become a TV news guy, came and knocked on the door. So my friend answered and told him I wasn't there. I was trying to avoid the situation. But they wouldn't take no for an answer. Then my friend told him I wasn't talking to anyone, so they left.

And just like back in Virginia, now everyone in DC assumed I had made a decision based on that car. Remember, I didn't pay for it, couldn't, I was just using it.

I did have to make a decision. People had been asking the question all year: Would Allen be the first to leave Coach Thompson's program early? I told you about the Georgetown crowd chanting for "Two More Years." After that game, Coach Thompson was angrier about that chant than what Billy Packer had said calling me a "tough monkey." He felt like I deserved to make a decision without any outside influence and pressure. Michael Wilbon was, like Kornheiser, just a writer back then, and this is how he put it: "Is he ready for the NBA or not? All that was on anybody's lips was Iverson's name. At the barbershop, at Dollar Bill's, in taxis, at the deli."

All that chatter pissed off Coach. So Coach Thompson said, "Allen's not going anywhere unless I tell him it's time to go." Another time he said, "Allen will be ready for the NBA when I tell him he's ready." Then certain people got mad because he was trying to be controlling. But what he was really trying to do was get the pressure off of me. He also let it be known, "I've never had a blanket rule that anybody has to stay for four years."

One thing was for sure, the decision was mine. But of course I valued his advice more than anyone's.

When it came to me leaving for the NBA, everyone was kind of talking about two aspects of "Is he ready?" There was the basketball question and the off-the-court question. As far as basketball, everyone agreed I had the athleticism and talent. But because I was small, they focused on my ability to be a "point guard." As Bucks general manager Mike Dunleavy put it, "I love Allen's game, but he's still learning how to be a point guard." Wilbon said if there was one issue I needed to improve on, "it's got to be the pass. At six feet and 165 pounds, [he's] got one and only one position: point guard." Even Coach Thompson said, "I think learning to control the tempo of the game and knowing all the other things he needs to learn about this game is going to be the thing that dictates his future."

People also talked about me, my past, all that shit. They quoted Boo Williams, who said, "Basketball-wise, he's ready for the NBA. It's more about social skills. He needs to mature a little more." Coach Thompson said he wasn't worried about the two hours I would be on the court. "I'm scared as hell about those other twenty-two hours." I'm hearing all this, one way or another. It's coming back to me on campus, on the phone with my family and friends. It was pissing me off. I knew I would figure it out on the court. My game was ready. Of that much I was sure. As for the other shit, damn, I was about to be twenty-one that June. *Leave my personal shit out of it.* People just didn't want me to enjoy my life, I figured.

So that's when I got that call from Coach Thompson to come in and talk to him, and he confronted me about the car. I will never forget when he said those words: "Do what you got to do." And he told me to return the motherfucking Benz, which I did.

He also said we still had to perform our due diligence. He had me sit down with his agent, David Falk. Falk represented Jordan, everyone knew that, but he also represented Coach Thompson and most of the Georgetown guys once they went pro. Falk was direct. He thought I should stay in school. Refine my game and improve my draft status. He said I wasn't even going in the lottery. When he said that, I knew he must be crazy. I think what he really wanted was for me to come back and win a championship for Coach Thompson. I wanted that too! That was the hardest part for me, feeling like there was unfinished business at Georgetown.

But then I told Falk and the other dudes at the agency about everything going on at home. That was one thing that nobody was really talking about—it was the basketball and the off-the-court—but not the most important shit. I had to take care of my family. In *The Washington Post*, Wilbon said I shouldn't even pay attention to that. "And as far as your family members and close friends, if they haven't driven a new Lexus or lived in a 4,000-square-foot house all these years, 360 days ain't gonna hurt. Tell 'em to drive what they've been driving and live where they've been living a few more months." No disrespect to anyone's opinion, but losing Nana taught me there are only so many days in a person's life, man, and waiting isn't always an option.

So at this meeting with Falk and his agency, I told these guys about my baby. About my little sister and her ongoing seizures. About my dad's legal situation. About my home.

They quieted down then.

Coach Thompson said later he was fine with me going pro after he had a conversation with Isiah Thomas, then the decision-maker for the Toronto Raptors. Coach Thompson told Isiah I was considering entering the draft and asked where he thought I might get drafted. Isiah didn't say a word. He just raised one finger. Coach Thompson was like, *Damn, number one for that little shit?*

David Falk and his crew learned the same thing when they started asking talent evaluators in the league. I was going high, maybe even the top pick overall.

Dad hit with more drug charges. Mom and sisters living in a terrible house struggling to pay the bills. One sister with medical issues that we couldn't afford to treat. My girl living with her family, raising my child without me. Never had no money and dying to let loose. And about to be a top pick, guaranteed millions of dollars.

It wasn't a choice.

"I've decided to enter the NBA Draft."

That was how I started the press conference.

On my left was my mom. On my right was Coach Thompson. To his right was David Falk. In front of us was a whole bunch of reporters. Here we were in the McDonough Gym, where my Georgetown journey began with my mom begging for my life, and then me tearing up the Kenner League. I wore a suit. Yes I did. Just like I had done for two years at Georgetown. It was the biggest press conference of my life.

This was almost a month after my decision had first been reported. And maybe I knew, but now I had discussed it, done my due diligence, signed Falk as my agent, and was ready to announce it.

At this press conference, nobody asked me about practice.

It was a sad motherfucker, to be honest. I had prepared a statement explaining why I had to leave. It all boiled down to this: "I definitely plan to further my education, but my family needs need to be addressed right now." I put my hand on my mom's shoulder, and she leaned in and kissed me. "She raised me for twenty years and did the best she could. Now I just want an opportunity to do something for her, my little sisters, and my daughter."

I remember I was asked about the Benz, and I said I needed to drive it to see my sister. Kornheiser wrote the next day that I "could have driven a Taurus and stayed off the nightly news." I can laugh now. I mean, of course I wanted to live the good life! That was a big part of my decision. But you couldn't say that shit. If you're some dude who grew up without shit, the only thing you could mention was getting out of poverty. So I stuck to that script.

Coach Thompson took the moment to talk about the system. He discussed how wrong it was that they couldn't have Georgetown Hospital help my little sister. That would be an improper benefit that would make me ineligible. "How could they expect a young man to stay in school," he said in his old-school way, "if going to the NBA was the only way to provide for life's necessities?"

At the end, it went from emotional to some joking around. Coach Thompson was like, "Ironically, from a recruiting standpoint, it has helped us. That's the sickness of all of this. I don't know how many kids that I have lost by going into their homes, and they tell me that they don't want to go here because I'll make them stay for four. So now I can bust through the door and say, 'I let one go!'"

Out from under his arm. But he never did let me go. I didn't speak to him about basketball ever again. But we talked all the time. About life. About making the right decisions. He was always there for me, even after I chose to walk away.

V

FROM THE DRAFT TO ROOKIE OF THE YEAR

Self-Expression

When I was inducted into the Hall of Fame, my whole family—Tawanna and all my kids—were getting ready to go to the ceremony.

It was one of those times when I knew I had to keep it straight, we all did. I wore a tuxedo like I was supposed to. Everyone had something formal. So we were getting ready, and we had this big, beautiful dress for my baby girl, Dream, who was the youngest. She was also the one who most reminded me of myself. Mini-me, *I sometimes called her. She was still just seven then. So when we showed her the dress, she was like, "No, I'm not wearing that."*

I said to her, "Well what are you wearing then? It's Daddy's big night, you got to wear a dress."

The girl just disappeared. Me and Tawanna looked at each other. She went to her room and was rustling around in the closet. She came back on down after a couple minutes, and she had put on these Reebok Sweats, custom joints, that said IVERSON *down the side.*

"You can't wear that, baby girl!" But she was insistent.

The whole family, it was one of those times, man, we all started laughing and couldn't stop. And here is what I was thinking: This girl is just like her daddy—she just wants to wear her sweats. *She could draw like me, this girl, she had a crossover boy, and here she was being stubborn as hell about her style.*

I said to her, "Dream, baby, why you going to wear a sweat suit to the Hall of Fame?"

She was just like, "It's what I like to wear. They have my name on them."

My heart nearly broke, man. Hearing her proud of that name. Hearing her dead-set on being herself no matter the occasion. She's my legacy. All my kids are. And really, all the dudes who are out there playing in the NBA, free to be themselves. They are my legacy, too. Because when I think back to the beginning of my NBA career, especially that first year, man, my success, my survival, it was all just as much about me staying true to myself as it was about what I did on the court. Because damn, didn't a lot of people express a lot of hate each and every step of the way.

But I don't want you to think I'm some perfect, laid-back father. We still made Dream wear a dress! I was only going to be inducted to the Hall of Fame once.

THIRTY-TWO

THE 76ERS

Back home, about two weeks after leaving Georgetown, I was with my Uncle Stevie. We were watching the lottery on NBC. This was where the order of the draft would be determined. No way to even guess where you're going until you can see who is drafting where.

I'll never forget it. All the teams had a representative there, waiting to see if they were the lucky winner. The picks went from 13 to 1, and as it got closer, NBA executive Russ Granik announced the third pick went to Vancouver, the second pick to Toronto, and "that means the first pick of the 1996 draft goes to the Philadelphia 76ers."

Then the man who was representing the 76ers jumps up and starts pumping his fists, high-fiving the dudes he just got the better of. You could tell he couldn't contain himself. He had to celebrate right then and there. And everyone went along with it, people who had lost out in the lottery, slapping this dude's hand.

"Who the fuck is that?" I asked Stevie.

Bob Costas answered from the TV. "So Pat Croce whoops it up."

Pat Croce?

*

Couldn't have scripted it any better. Philly. It made so much sense. My dad's team was always Philly. The city was not too far from home. Legends had played there: Doctor J, Mo Cheeks, Moses, Barkley. Recently they'd been getting their asses beat (that's what put them in position to draft so high), but they had Derrick Coleman and Clarence Weatherspoon, and they'd drafted Jerry Stackhouse the year before.

What were they missing? A point guard.

I learned that Croce was part of the new ownership group. They'd bought the team that year. Croce was a fitness freak, had sold his personal training business and formed a partnership with Ed Snider, who already owned the Flyers. Croce was the minority owner, but he was president and the face of the franchise.

It wasn't just ownership. Everything was new. They had a new general manager, Brad Greenberg. They were about to hire a new coach, Johnny Davis. They had also just completed a new arena, the CoreStates Center, right next to the Spectrum. Maybe it was a relief that I didn't have to go back to where those Villanova students had said I was the next O.J.

Nana had always said that everything happened for a reason. When I saw the 76ers get the first pick, I knew it had to be them. And I will be honest, I didn't like the look of the next few teams. Vancouver and Toronto? Wasn't any way I wanted to live and play in Canada. Milwaukee and Minnesota picked fourth and fifth. Cold weather and small markets.

So after we had kind of begun to see that I would be one of the top picks, we decided on a strategy where I would go work out for one team and one team only—the Philadelphia 76ers. David Falk, my agent, knew if I became the first overall pick, that would raise my profile and my value.

But I had to earn it. I remember going to Philly the first time. They hosted me two weeks before the draft that June. While I had gone to the pre-draft camp in Chicago earlier in the month, I had only gotten measured and met with everyone, rather than doing any on-court work.

When I got to Philly, I met with Croce and Greenberg in the hotel. Croce just went straight to questions about my past, the bowling alley, all that shit. So I told them what happened, and they listened. I mean, it was a concern, but the motherfucking appeals court had already said there was insufficient evidence! They also asked me about my mom, rumors of drug shit, my friends, all that. Later I heard some detective from the Sixers was down in Virginia asking questions about my past, my family, my friends.

The first time people started talking about my friends and my family, I was in high school. So these questions weren't new to me. But I wasn't used to being asked directly about it since I got to Georgetown. Coach Thompson had prohibited any questions about my past, from that first press conference my freshman year up until I left Georgetown a couple weeks earlier. During the NCAA Tournament, a reporter asked me about it, and Coach Thompson cut it off quick. The "child" wouldn't be answering those questions. But Coach Thompson wasn't around anymore. Now it came up repeatedly—at the pre-draft camp, when I came to Philly, in other pre-draft settings. I dealt with it. Answered the way I knew how. My friends were my friends, and the case was over and done with.

So after talking to Croce and Greenberg, I went out there and hooped. That's when I felt free, not answering some bullshit questions. Funny part was, at ninety minutes, the basketball was the shortest part. After that it was meeting with the coaches, meeting with Mo Cheeks, who was in the front office then and later became an assistant coach. Then they had me meet with a psychologist for two motherfucking hours. He asked me about how certain things made me feel, watching the way I responded to questions that had nothing to do with being an athlete, taking notes. It was totally foreign to anything I had ever done. I didn't trust that shit at all and only did it because I had to. It almost seemed like basketball was the last thing on their minds.

I heard the next day the Sixers hosted Marbury, and after that, Ray Allen and Marcus Camby got workouts. No one guaranteed me I would be the first pick. When I was leaving, I spoke to the Philly press for the first time and said, "Now it's up to them. I haven't come out and told them this is where I want to be, but they know. The decision rests in their hands now."

If I was the first pick here is what I was going to get: three years and about $9 million. If I was the fourth pick, it would be three years and $6.7 million. So a few million was in the balance. It really wasn't the money though. That's because even before I got picked, I got paid. About a week before the draft even happened, Falk negotiated and I signed my first sneaker deal—$50 million for ten years.

No matter what happened next, I was getting out of the hood. And I was bringing everyone with me.

When I made my deal with Reebok, I began to see and feel my life open up in new ways. As a result of the shit I'd gotten into, and the success people imagined I would achieve, I'd had so many people—good and bad—telling me what to do and how to be.

Going back before I ever got in trouble or was featured in some recruiting magazine, to when I was thirteen or fourteen, I had freedom then. I could do whatever I wanted. I could leave the house when I wanted, and I didn't even go to school much. I hung out with my friends, and I did plenty of shit I shouldn't have done.

That ended. I look at it like when my mom confronted me on the streets, and then when Mo came and got me and took me to his house, from that day forward, it was like, *Motherfucker, you got to do the shit our way or you ain't going to amount to shit.* So I had to be home at a certain time, lights-out at a certain time, I had to speak and dress according to a program.

Then the bowling alley happened and it was so much more. After my arrest, I was out on a bond. Then when the judge convicted me, he put me on curfew that meant I couldn't even play sports. Until he sentenced me to prison. So I was locked up. Even when Governor Wilder released me, he placed restrictions on me, including another curfew.

But it was even more than a time to be home, or a limit on what I could do. It was like, *Yo, you got one chance because you used up all the other ones, and the motherfucking chance is so limited that if you fuck up in the slightest way, you done. That's it.* Like walking on the edge of a cliff. Fuck up one time and your daughter going to grow up in the ghetto. Your baby sister ain't going to get any medical care. And your mom going to be stuck in the same place, in that shitty house, unable to pay her bills. And that's not even talking about all the personal motherfucking disappointment.

So then, within days of getting off those governor's restrictions, I went and lived and played for Coach Thompson. And he told me what to put on my body—suits. And what not to put on—earrings and tattoos. He told me who to talk to and when. And if someone asked the wrong question, he was there telling them to shut the fuck up. Basically telling me I shouldn't say shit. Even after the season when I drove that goddamn Mercedes, it was like, *Boy you done fucked it up*. Walking right on over the edge of the cliff.

Now, before you think I'm talking some shit about Mo, Governor Wilder, or Coach Thompson, these men in my life gave me everything. Not that judge, but these other dudes were positive role models. They were molding me. Whether it was a suit, or going to bed at a certain time, or going to school, or saying "yes sir" and giving all the right motherfucking answers. But the thing is, that shit wasn't *me*. Guidance I could take. Being molded? I wasn't no ball of clay.

So check it out, I got to the meeting with Reebok, along with David Falk and his team. Falk was all excited because he thought they were going to make a big offer. And these two dudes were there from Reebok, Todd Krinsky and Que Gaskins. They asked me what I wanted. And I said I just wanted to be myself. These dudes were excited as hell to hear that, and said that's what they wanted too. And they meant it. They didn't just say that shit; they said who it was they saw when they saw me. And it wasn't Allen Iverson in a motherfucking suit. It was Allen Iverson from Hampton and Newport News. It was Allen Iverson with his family and friends. It was Allen Iverson wearing what he wants, saying shit the way he wants to say it. *Motherfucker, you been to jail, well that's legit as hell, is what that is.* And in terms of my game? They said the two of them had been talking about me, watching me, at Georgetown from the beginning. They saw the fearlessness, the recklessness, the little man among giants. It wasn't about correcting that shit. It was about *embracing* it.

You know how much I revered Michael Jordan. The dude meant everything to me. O*n the court.* But in life, I didn't want to be like Mike. I said this once, and it's been played so many times, "I don't wanna be Jordan, I don't wanna be Bird or Isiah, I don't wanna be any of these guys. I want to look in the mirror and say I did it my way." That's no disrespect. It's just that I was different. And for the first time since I was a kid, I felt like I could be myself. I *would* be myself. And with all that money, I wasn't walking that cliff's edge anymore.

So then Todd and Que started telling me their plans with getting me my own signature shoe in time for my rookie year. And I was sitting there listening to them, remembering my mom finding a way to get me the shoes I felt I needed to have when the goddamn phone didn't work.

These dudes were like, "We want you to help design the shoe, mold it."

A couple days before the draft, I got a call from David Falk. He told me the Sixers were looking to make me their pick, but they wanted to see me one more time. Wasn't going to meet with any other team, but I was willing to do anything for Philly. So I went back up there, this time without the press or the hoopla. They told me, *Just let it roll, real gamelike conditions.* This one was about basketball. That's all I needed to hear. I went out and fucking raced around that court. This time the new coach, Johnny Davis, was there, and he gave me some feedback, and I responded. It was awesome. When I left, I knew it was happening. But I still didn't *know* know.

So then it was time to get ready. First thing I did was got me another gray suit. Obviously I still had to wear a suit for draft night. Someone from the agency took me to get measured. It was my first tailored suit. Putting it on felt like I had arrived. My mom looked at me before we left, big-ass smile on her face. Nobody was going to lock up this handsome motherfucker tonight!

I went to the jewelry store, and I got all kinds of shit. Bracelets, necklaces, rings—for me, the family, my homeboys. The first big chain I got myself was a big diamond studded cross. I ended up wearing it under my suit that night—I wasn't quite ready to let it all hang free yet.

We had a big limo to take us to the Meadowlands Arena in East Rutherford, New Jersey. That's where the Final Four had been at, goddammit. Because we lost in the Elite Eight, I hadn't been there since I dropped forty on Danny Hurley.

We got to the greenroom. All the top players got to sit and watch with their families, waiting to hear their names called. I was with my mom, aunt, and uncles. Arnie, Marlon, and Ra all came, but they couldn't sit with us in the greenroom. What I remember best was my daughter Tiaura. She was dressed up, wearing this little navy and white striped dress. Just one and a half years old. Wasn't any need to live separate from her anymore. One thing about the greenroom is even if you're the first pick in the draft, there's a lot of waiting. I had her on my lap. Playing with her, trying to think about anything else, nervous as hell.

Even then I didn't *know* know.

Finally David Stern, the NBA commissioner—who later had all kinds of problems with me—walked on up to the podium.

"With the first pick in the draft, the Philadelphia 76ers select . . . Allen Iverson from Georgetown University."

I picked up my little baby off my lap and kissed her head. I handed her to my mother and kissed her. I was so elated, I just smiled. I hugged all my family members there. Cheers in the crowd. I had to go shake the commissioner's hand next but first I left our table and went over to the side. Waiting for me were Ra, Marlon, and Arnie. I hugged those dudes. Then I turned back around to go on the stage. I kind of put my game face on, like how I felt I was supposed to be. But when I got on the stage, seeing the commissioner, putting on my Sixers hat, I just had to smile like a little kid.

I had made it.

THIRTY-THREE

FROM VA TO PA

After getting drafted, it was a blur. Philly selected me No. 1 on June 26, 1996. I went home and partied for a couple of days. I played an exhibition at Hampton University in front of more than 7,000. My squad faced off against a team led by Joe Smith, the No. 1 pick the year before out of Norfolk. Two kids from the same part of Virginia, separated by the James River, picked No. 1 in back-to-back years. Then the city of Hampton threw me a parade on July 6.

Of course, the parade had to be a controversy. It was organized by one of the leaders of SWIS (the organization that had formed to advocate for us dudes arrested after the bowling alley fight). The parade began at Aberdeen Elementary—where I'd gone after tearing off that cast so many years before just so I could play pickup. I remember rolling up in my *new* new black Mercedes. Nas was blasting out the windows. My mom came, my sisters, my daughter. As we began the parade, they put me in a convertible. A Poquoson dealership loaned it to us for the occasion. People were lined along the streets, holding up signs, cheering, as we drove.

Some hated that Hampton was celebrating its first-ever number one pick in the draft. One lady held a sign that said, "Millions do not a hero make. Morals do." As the mayor put it, "I know there is going to be a lot of controversy. There are some people who just cannot let it go. But we've got to move on. He's one of ours, and this is the right thing to do." Everyone down there had an opinion, letters to the editor, columnists, the editorial board. Like old times, replaying the same arguments. The parade ended at the Coliseum—where me and my Bethel teammates beat Hampton High the day after I first met the police. I had to make a speech at the end of the parade. People think I'm some tough guy, but it really just meant so much to me to see my own community there paying tribute. So I thanked my family. I thanked God. I thanked everyone who stuck with me during my roughest times.

Then it was done. They were still debating—me the person, the criminal conviction (that the appeals court had overturned), the city's race relations. And so when I left, I kind of felt like I was really leaving all that behind.

It was time to move on. To Philly.

Three days later, on July 9, I was at the Community College of Philadelphia for a three-day minicamp. It was for all the rookies and undrafted dudes trying to make the team. Jerry Stackhouse came even though he wasn't a rookie. I knew him, of course. I'd gotten the better of him in AAU, but he'd gotten the better of me in the NCAAs. We were not always perfect together on the court, but me and him got along. Johnny Davis led the practices, making us work our asses off.

Right after the camp, I got on the court, in public, for the first time as a Sixer. It was an exhibition against a collection of local all-stars. The game was at McGonigle Hall on the Temple University campus in North Philly, and as we got there, everyone was surprised as hell to see people standing, waiting for blocks to get in the joint. Everyone but me. I was used to exhibitions getting a lot of attention. It wasn't my Kenner League explosion, but I scored 22 points.

The next night we were in Westchester County, just north of New York City, and where one of the NBA's summer leagues was played. We faced the Knicks, and their first pick was John Wallace, who I knew from St. John's. I scored 36 in an overtime loss. Two days later it was the Toronto rookie squad. I had 29 points and 7 assists in a win. I always had confidence, but it was just growing with each game. I mean, these guys were bigger, stronger, faster, hungrier than I'd ever played. But the game opened up without any zone defense. I was still just 165 pounds, soaking wet. I was so competitive, I just kept driving and getting knocked down over and over again. The coaches wanted to hold me out of one game, but I wasn't having it! I was not missing the motherfucking games.

Summer League back then wasn't crazy like it is now. It wasn't in Vegas, and not every game was on ESPN. But it was still this time, if you were a top pick, you wanted to make that first impression. The other part of Summer League was that you had all these dudes trying to make the NBA. So after we played a couple more games, and I was out there putting on a show, some of the guys were unhappy that I was taking so many shots. Motherfuckers always complained when I wouldn't pass the ball. There was something about a six-foot dude not passing that really pissed people off. I just wanted to do my thing, perform for the crowd, and win. We won two and lost three. I averaged about 30 points.

But there was always controversy. One local headline asked, "By Shooting, Is Iverson Missing the Point?" To me the *point* was trying to win games! And I was just so happy to make it to this *point* in my life—alive, out of jail, and achieving my dream.

THIRTY-FOUR

LET THE GAMES BEGIN

On November 1, we opened the CoreStates Center against the Milwaukee Bucks. Like I said, everything was new, from ownership, to management, to the arena, to me—the No. 1 pick. The Bucks had their version of new as well. Ray Allen was suiting up for them for the first time. John Thompson was in the crowd. My mom wore her number 3 jersey. I had tickets waiting for twenty or thirty family members and friends. I would be lying to say I wasn't a little nervous. The lights dimmed and my name was called out in the starting lineup.

Then we tipped off, and it was just a basketball game. I took my time, tried to set up my teammates. A couple minutes into the game I had my first chance. I could feel it: This wasn't just financial freedom, or freedom from everyone telling me what to do, it was freedom on the court. So here I was with my first chance. I had Sherman Douglas staring at me on the right side above the three-point line. Derrick Coleman came over to set a screen, but I wanted the isolation, so after DC dove down, I hit Douglas with it. Paused the ball out wide with my left hand, shoulder shifting left, rock hanging until I saw his weight go that way. And bam, crossed over to my right, right around him. A gasp from the crowd. Got to the baseline and rose to jam it. While a defender got a piece of it so I couldn't finish, it was a goaltend. First points of my career.

Later in the first quarter, I did it again, same crossover. This time the crowd went crazy just from seeing the setup, knowing it was coming before I even did it. Didn't matter that I passed after shaking my man. The crowd thundered.

That night, with those moves and the reactions, it was like meeting a girl for the first time and you just know. Like when I literally backed into Tawanna years earlier in Hampton. The Philly crowd was like, *Damn, this motherfucker came to play*. And I was like, *Damn, this crowd knows what I'm all about*. It was like we were linked now. Ready to fall in love.

I scored 30. And there were other highlights. I had a dunk that got the crowd out their seats. Derrick Coleman dominated. And me and Stack hooked up for an alley-oop. It was a loss, but it was one of those times even in a loss, people were excited as hell. The new hope had arrived. Stephen A. Smith was early in his career at *The Philadelphia Inquirer*, and he covered the Sixers for most of my career in Philly. And if you know Stephen A., you know he told it like he saw it—then and now. In the next day's paper, he wrote, "Iverson was simply sensational. It almost seemed as if no one was guarding the mercurial guard from Georgetown."

The second game was different. We were playing the Bulls in Chicago. Before the game even started, their crowd went crazy because those dudes got their rings. The year before, the Bulls won 72 games and the championship. MJ had come back from baseball when I was a freshman at Georgetown. Since then he had won another championship. It was their home opener, and here he was in front of me getting the hardware.

I got out onto the court, and for the first time in my life a human being didn't look real to me. I literally saw his aura. It was like he was glowing. I couldn't stop looking at him. I'm looking at his shoes, *Man he got on the Jordans*. You got to remember, I idolized this man. Had the man's poster on my door. Wore his shoes to the point where we didn't pay for the goddamn heat. I hated the Knicks and the Bad Boys so much for beating him up like they did back in the '80s and early '90s. Right before my eyes, there he was receiving his fourth championship ring. Alongside him were Dennis Rodman and Scottie Pippen. Phil Jackson was behind them with his chin thrust forward. Bulls games were already crazy with the lights and the intros—"Your Chicago BULLLLLLSSSSSS"—all that. It was on a different level that night. Stack was like, *Man, they setting us up here. We have to play them after all this?*

Game wasn't nothing to talk about. The final score was 115–86. I had a bad game, couldn't make any shots. Rodman and Pippen were in my face talking all kinds of shit about how I wasn't a real point guard, shooting too much. I went right back at them. Then my hero walked over to me, that aura around him. He started talking to me about how we got to respect them.

Man, I did more than respect him, I revered him, I revered that team my whole damn life. But what I learned growing up, playing ball in Virginia, in college, everywhere—on the motherfucking court, you didn't respect anybody. And you definitely didn't get told who to respect. So I said it: *I don't have to respect anyone.* What I meant was, *on the motherfucking court.* Like Mo said, *if it's between you and me, it's me.* No matter who "you" is.

After the game, of course the press had to reprint that shit. And it became about me disrespecting Jordan, the greatest of all time. Basketball Jesus. Heresy, or some shit. I was literally watching this man on the court before the game, seeing his aura, and now because I stood up for myself, they were saying I was the symbol of the new age of disrespectful young thugs. It was some shit I'd hear again and again.

I both cared and didn't care. I cared because all the criticism got to me. And can you imagine hearing people say I didn't respect my idol? But I didn't care because I knew myself. I was being myself. So no one, not even MJ, was going to tell me how to act. And no one was going to make me bow down, submit, fail to stand up for myself. And if I had to fight back (on the court), I would. And what I knew is you had those columnists who would write whatever they wanted to write, and you'd have those people in the seats close to the court, especially in some cities, and they'd heckle or boo or whatever, but if you looked higher up in the stands, if you went to my neighborhood, or the streets of Philadelphia, man, people loved what I was about. *Goddammit, this dude stood up to MJ. I'm gonna buy his motherfucking shoe!*

I revered Mike though. Years later, after I retired and he was owner of the Hornets, he invited me up to his suite. I had some of my boys with me. So I got up to his box and I was just hanging out with him, praising him. He was my hero, and I was letting him know how I felt, like some fan. One of my boys came over, took me to the side, said, *Chuck, stop that shit. You a superstar your damn self.* I was like, *Man, I can't help it, I just love this dude.* Mike overheard that and was like, "Motherfucker you don't love me, because you wouldn't have crossed me up like that." (We will get to that later.)

Going back for a second, before the games even started, the team got messages from the league that my shorts were too baggy and my ankle braces, which were black, covered up too much of my white socks. But the real shit was that after just my fourth game, the league issued a memorandum. In it they said that my crossover was a carrying violation. Shit, they couldn't stop it, so they were going to make it illegal?

After the Bulls game, people talked all kinds of shit about my attitude, but they didn't try arguing what I was doing was illegal. Ron Harper was guarding me that game, and he conceded I was the quickest motherfucker he'd seen. In the preseason, I had gone toe-to-toe with Nick Van Exel on the Lakers, who himself had a lightning-quick handle, and he said mine was the best crossover he'd ever seen. The crowds literally leaned in and inhaled their breath when I had the ball out wide, ready to explode when I hit them with it. Shit, now the NBA was telling everyone it was illegal? I remember getting interviewed about the memorandum. "From the beginning they said my shorts were too long, my crossover is a carry . . .

my ankle braces [violate the rules]. They can't frustrate me. They make the calls, I walk away."

Coach Davis had my back. He came to talk to me about it, and he said to take it as a compliment. *It's like you're Wilt Chamberlain.* See, back in the day, they had to make offensive goaltending illegal because he was so dominant above the rim. So I had my own motherfucking rule. The NBA literally couldn't believe I could do what I was doing. In the memo they said they'd watched the video of it, slowed it down, to analyze it. It must be cheating. Coach Davis argued in the press, and management called the league about it, but it did no good. Now, remember what I said about freedom on the court, having it? Not for long.

First game after the memo was against Phoenix, and motherfuckers called me for two carries. Crazy part was neither was even on a crossover. One call was when I was just walking the ball up the damn court. We still won that game though.

So for the next one, I got back to Madison Square Garden. It was our sixth game, and while we had lost our first three, we'd won our last two. I knew MSG from my Big East days, obviously. I'd played in front of Spike Lee, and sure enough he was there that night. But it was different as a professional. I mean, on the other side of the court was Patrick Ewing, an NBA legend and a Georgetown legend. When we'd been in practice and Coach Thompson talked about him, it just seemed like he was giving us a history lesson. It was a time in the 1980s. Now here he was in front of me. Seven feet tall. Still in his prime. The Knicks had added Larry Johnson that summer, they already had Allan Houston and Charles Oakley, and they were 5-1 so far that season.

We came in there and we took it to them. I had my then-career-high 35 points. Had the crossover going, the hesitations, and made five of nine three-pointers. The motherfuckers didn't call me for any carries that game either. Stack scored 28, and it was like, *Damn, this young backcourt is the shit.* There was a dude in the crowd taunting me, saying, "Let's go bowling." Same old shit. I just bided my time, and when I sealed the game with a pair of free throws, I looked at him and said it: "Yeah, let's go bowling." I played forty-four minutes that game, and I was pissed off about the four minutes I didn't play.

You could have Rodman and Pippen in my face, the refs calling shit, an entire league making up rules, but I just wanted to play the game. Reporters were asking me if I was all right after they saw me throwing my body around these giants, and I would just say, *If I could play a game every day I would.* I didn't like college because there weren't enough games.

My health became a worry because of how undersized I was. So look, I was 6' and 165 pounds. Take Patrick Ewing. He was 7' and 250 pounds. Derrick Coleman was 6'10" and weighed 260. Even Jerry Stackhouse, our other *guard*, was 6'6" and 220. So of course people asked, *How is this dude doing it, and how can he stand up to the punishment?* But that shit never occurred to me. I was just used to playing bigger dudes, and I felt like there was nobody that could stop me or outhustle me.

However, when we lost the next game to Toronto, sure enough I injured my shoulder. The training staff said I had to sit out a few games. I felt like I was just getting started. I remember I was so disappointed because one of the games I missed was against Washington in the USAir Arena, where I played at Georgetown. I watched from the bench as we got whipped, all my friends from that time there sitting beside me, watching me not play. I couldn't take it. So the next night, we faced the Knicks again, this time in Philly, and I spent the whole night just telling my friends how I had to play. *I have to play!* I was ready to take the damn bandages off, healed or not, like I did playing pickup as a kid.

Next day, I walked into Pat Croce's office just begging to play. He wanted to follow the training staff, so I went to the orthopedic specialist and begged him to clear me. He checked me out and couldn't really say it was a further risk of injury. So I went to Johnny Davis. I even went to the GM. Nobody wanted to say yes, but no one could say no. When I came into the locker room, the equipment staff looked at me like I was crazy. They hadn't even prepared my uniform or anything. It came time to play the game, and on the first play, I remember Charles Oakley hit me in the shoulder. It hurt like a motherfucker. But I just shook it off. I didn't want to come out, make all those guys think they were right, saying I shouldn't play. I played forty-two minutes (mad as hell, again, about those minutes I was on the bench). I had 26 points, 9 rebounds, and 9 assists. And we won again.

The Philly crowd went crazy. They had come to the game thinking I wouldn't suit up. They walked out of there dreaming of the success to come.

THIRTY-FIVE

PHILLY, MY HOME

I was out from under Coach Thompson's arm and into the embrace of the City of Brotherly Love. I was on my own in the sense that no one was telling me what to do. But just like when I got out of jail, I didn't ever want to be alone. So while I left Virginia behind, I brought my family, my friends, and some of Hampton and Newport News with me.

I bought a house in Conshohocken, just outside Philly. It was a home for all of us. My mom stayed there along with my two sisters, my Aunt Jessie, and Uncles Stevie and Greg. Tawanna and Tiaura weren't with us full-time yet. But they came back and forth. And that first year, my friends crashed there too—among them Arnie, Marlon, E, Ra. Sometimes it was chaotic, so by the next year, I had my friends staying at hotels!

I had brought them all along to live and to enjoy this life. As my mom had willed right after I got out of jail, sure enough I got her the red Jaguar. After I bought myself a new Range Rover that December, I gave the Lexus I had been driving to my aunt. I paid all the bills, took care of everything. I had gotten the fuck out, and taken them all with me.

Like since I was a kid, I was most awake at night. When most people were going to bed, that's when things got going for me. There was no curfew, whether it was the governor's order or Coach Thompson's rules. And no one was telling me to shut the hell up in our dorm rooms like it was with Don Reid or Boubacar Aw. I could go out when I wanted.

Nowadays the Sixers have a huge practice facility in Camden. Whirlpools, beautiful courts, dining facility, even a statue out front of Allen Iverson. Back then, long before I'd earned a statue, it was a little different. We practiced at the College of Osteopathic Medicine, right off of City Line Avenue. That was near the Main Line. Conshohocken was a little farther from the city, up 76.

I don't remember when it was exactly, but at some point I went to a TGI Fridays that was just a little way from the practice gym, down City Line. It became our spot. We'd go out to clubs and whatnot, but that Fridays was the spot where we would go to chill—after practice, after games, our table area always marked off. We'd eat and drink, sometimes until it was about ready to get light. I kept my Monopoly habit, and they kept a Monopoly board there, ready for me. Another spot I would hit up was DiNardo's Seafood. I would get me some crabs there a couple times a week. It was like at home when I was a kid, except I didn't have to catch them off the bridge—and since I could pay for the motherfuckers, dinner was always guaranteed. It broke my heart when they closed their doors a few years ago. Back then they just kept my credit card on file, ready for me and my homeboys.

My friends from home became an issue almost from the beginning. In September, before the season started, down in Hampton, bullets were fired at a car that my friends were driving. It wouldn't normally have made headlines, but they were in *my car* when it happened. Pat Croce supposedly told some of them before the season started that if they got me into trouble, he would burn their house down. Pat knew those dudes, so I didn't mind him joking around like that, but it got reported in the press that he said that shit, and that pissed me off.

Then, just before the new year, a New York paper reported that my "entourage" got into a fight with Stack's "posse" at the practice gym. I wasn't there for anything like that. And me and Stack both vehemently denied that shit. The reporter walked it back later, but no one cared after the fact. It was already like, *Allen Iverson's crew is out of control.*

When someone told me to get rid of my friends, that was the first way you were going to make me stop listening. And people told me that all the time. Charles Barkley said through the press, "Get rid of your entourage. Your team is your entourage, not your friends." The *Inquirer* called them "unsavory." It was to the point where I had to defend them: "We're not a posse. I don't know why people say we're a posse, or that I have an entourage. Maybe the people who say that have no friends. Maybe they're mad because I have friends. Maybe they're scared of my friends." That January, the *Philadelphia Daily News* did two full pages on my "posse," with me and Stack issuing denials. The *Washington Post, New York Times, USA Today*—they all wrote articles about the people I hung out with.

The big two-page *Daily News* story began, "Rahsaan Langford is twenty-four, from New York. . . . Has known Allen Iverson since he was fourteen." Shit, the reporter interviewed my man, Ra, for his story. If you can believe it, that same reporter five years later was the main one bringing up "practice" in the press conference. Phil Jasner was his name. He covered me and the Sixers my whole career. He passed away not too long ago, and honestly I have nothing but love to send his way, even though we didn't always get along. He was doing his job. But damn, he had interviewed my best friend for his big "Iverson Posse" article. So years before that "practice" press conference, he'd met and interviewed the man who got killed, the man who had been heavy in my heart all year, the man I put front and center.

These were my friends, the dudes who helped me get to this point in my life. When I didn't have shit, they had my back. Maybe I was paying the bills now, getting nice shit like jewelry for everyone. But remember, how'd I get my first real chain? It was after I scored 40 at Bethel, and they were in the back with the herringbone in its box for me. And paying the bills? When I was in jail, or at Georgetown with the NCAA prohibiting me from earning a dime, it was them dudes keeping my family's lights on. Loyalty was everything to me. We were going to make it—we *did* make it—together.

My way wasn't just about sticking with my friends. One time I was on a road trip, early on in my rookie year, and I was injured. It might have been after that shoulder injury that kept me out of a few games. Coach Davis came to me, and he said since I was injured and not dressing for the game, I should consider wearing a suit on the sideline. He even talked about how it might make me more marketable. But it wasn't like with Coach Thompson. Coach Davis was a rookie coach like I was a rookie player. And he couldn't just say this is how it had to be, like Coach Thompson could.

I was just like, *Nah man, I ain't doing that. I don't need to do that.* I had my friends and family there. I wasn't going to be someone else around them, that's for damn sure. I was going to be me, dress the way I wanted, act the way I wanted. Something I've always believed is that since everybody else is taken up, the only option is for me to be me. And Coach Davis understood—my style was my choice.

People sometimes say I was some kind of fashion icon, but from the beginning I was just dressing the way people back home dressed. That's the way we did it. I laugh now when I see pictures of me back in the day. I would get all the XXLs. It was like in *Beetlejuice*, like with the small little head and your body so big.

I would go to the big-and-tall and just buy the shit out. I would actually rush out of practice first, so I could get there first. The real big dudes on the team would be like, *Motherfucker, you the smallest dude and you bought all the shit out.* Maybe it was the little-man complex! I always wanted the big old Rolls-Royce. And I wanted the biggest clothes because I didn't want to look like the smallest dude. But it was thought out too. Like with the pants: No matter how big, they would always be tapered and tight at my ankle, because I had to show off the kicks.

I wasn't trying to make any statement. Just like with my daughter Dream years later, I wanted to wear what I was comfortable in, what I felt best expressed myself. But damn if people didn't hate it. From day one, people criticized me for my hood friends and my hood clothes. One reporter described the way I was as "draped in gold and diamond jewelry, wearing a black headband and loose-fitting casual clothes." As I said then, "I'm twenty-one. Why would people want me in suits all day? I'm not going anywhere where I'd need one." My mentality was, I can buy all the clothes I always wanted, all the styles that the dudes from the neighborhood wanted to wear. And that shit wasn't cheap. I could have saved money by wearing suits!

It just seemed fake to dress up any other way. I mean, going to play basketball, it didn't make any sense to dress like a businessman. I wasn't going to wear a suit to the playground or the gym. And when I was leaving the games, I was going to the club. I wasn't going to wear a suit to no club. Where I grew up, you wore a suit to a church or a funeral. Or your goddamn sentencing day. It's true that I wore suits at Georgetown. I didn't have any money to buy the clothes I wanted anyway. So I followed Coach Thompson's rule, of course. But it wasn't until I made it to the NBA that I had any other choice.

The NBA couldn't yet control what I wore to the game, or when I was going out, or even on the sideline (they would try later!), so they targeted the things they could. My game shorts were too baggy and not enough white showed on the socks. I always felt like you played how you dressed. So if I wanted to be some kind of superhero, I had to dress that way. With the socks, I wanted the black look, because to me it was like Mike Tyson in the ring, the way he wore the black boots up past his ankle. That was what I was trying to emulate. Later I would add the headband. And of course the sleeve. Seeing kids in the park now, wearing sleeves just for the look, man, that shit is crazy.

Obviously, the sneakers were the most important thing. Right before the season started, that October of 1996, I traveled to the Reebok headquarters in Massachusetts. They were all excited to show me my first signature shoe. Not many people had a shoe with their name on it. Getting that signature sneaker was a dream, almost as much as making it to the league. And to do it as a rookie. Krinsky and Que were in the meeting, and a bunch of other people. They showed it to me, and I might have made a couple little comments here and there, but the joint was dope. It was red and white, with a blue sole. You could see the flash of blue on the tip and by the heel, "The Answer" written on the bottom, the number *3* above the heel, with a big *Q* above it. That release was called "The Question." Every Allen Iverson Reebok release after that was The Answer. This here was the one and only Question. And it was damn near perfect.

They had it in my hands by the new year, but we had to plan its release for sale to the public. The goal was to get it out February, in time for the All-Star Game.

By then the Reebok people had seen the dynamic with me. You had old-head reporters whining about my posse, guys courtside calling me "jailbird," and it would only get worse. But they also had the vision that the more all these dudes criticized me and called me names, the more I just kept it authentic. And people on the streets loved it. Remember when I first met the Reebok dudes, I told them I just wanted to be me.

So Reebok decided to release The Question that February with a long ad. In it I spoke about my background in the city, who I really was, what I stood for. The first line was "When it's over, I want everyone to know that I play every game like it's my last."

"Every game like it's my last." I said it from the beginning.

The ad had pictures of the streets I'd survived, shots of me in high school, and then achieving my dream with the Sixers. It was the real me we were selling. And without making apologies. When those guys told me this is how it was going to be, I'm not sure I believed it. Now it was here. And it felt like a message to just keep being myself, like I could keep my friends and family close, keep my style my style, like I had to stay authentic—but even more.

THIRTY-SIX

WINNING AND LOSING

After the first fifteen games, we were 7-8. It wasn't great, but that was a big improvement for the Sixers. The city was so excited that we sold out the next game against the Lakers, and they said it was the most people to ever see a basketball game in the state of Pennsylvania. The excitement was high, but it was a loss that was the beginning of a dark-ass period. Over the next two months, we went through hell, man.

December and January tested me like I've never been tested on the court. At its worst, we lost 23 of 24 games. At the beginning of the streak, I could blame it on my shoulder injury. It affected my shot. They even shut me down for a couple more games. But then I came back and the losing continued. We lost every way imaginable. Overtime losses, blowouts. Six in a row on a Christmas road trip, then more on a home stand. Against great teams like the Rockets, and teams with losing records like the Mavs. At a certain point, Derrick Coleman got injured, Stack missed games, Scott Williams got held out, so we didn't have our whole squad most nights. We were picking up dudes who were out of the league to fill in and play minutes. It got worse and worse.

I remember a reporter asked me if I'd ever lost like that. I was like, *Hell no.* I used to cry after every loss. But I couldn't cry twenty-three times in a little more than a month!

At the same time, I felt like I needed time to learn the ropes, and I was only twenty-one and just starting. I was playing well most games, we would have leads and then lose them in the fourth quarter. It was like we hadn't figured out how to handle games down the stretch. The city and the press were getting mad as hell, but while the losses hurt, my life was better than it ever had been. I just got out of jail. I'm in the NBA. I'm making millions of dollars. My mom is good. My child is good. Tawanna is straight. Anyone with eyes could see I could play. I had money. I had fame. And I was just a twenty-one-year-old rookie!

But of course the trade rumors started. The Sixers were not about to trade me, but there was a lot of talk about Stack. See, back then the league had a rookie pay scale, so we didn't make as much as dudes like Big Dog had made coming out of college just a couple years earlier. On the other hand, it was just a three-year contract and then you were a free agent—nowadays, teams control their young players for longer. Anyway, Stack was in year two, so just another year and the Sixers would have to make a decision about giving him tens of millions of dollars. That's why there were trade rumors.

On the court, that shit affects you. And when you lose 23 out of 24, maybe the coaches start thinking about their jobs. And this was the same time that all the articles were coming out about my friends. People were hearing about me going out to the clubs. They saw the pictures of the way I dressed. All that shit is fine until you add to the fact that the team is losing. That's when they really turn on you.

That January, some good news came. I was invited to take part in All-Star Weekend, to be in the slam-dunk contest and the rookie game. Ultimately with the slam-dunk contest, my shoulder injury meant I had to withdraw. Man, that would have been a show.

I was glad to go for All-Star Weekend, but also disappointed not to make the main event. I was averaging 23 points and felt like I'd made my mark (I was the only player in the top ten in scoring not to make the team). At the same time, we hadn't been winning, so I understood. I remember I reached out and spoke to Coach Thompson about it right before the break. He just let me know that my time would come. He was still waiting to become a member of the Basketball Hall of Fame, he reminded me (and he'd wait another decade for that shit). Damn, with all he'd accomplished. So I figured I would make the best of it.

The rookie game was still new. It was played at the beginning of All-Star Weekend, two groups of top rookies, East versus West, facing off. It was a chance to display the young talent. That draft had so much talent too. Kobe, of course, Marcus Camby and Ray Allen, Steve Nash and Kerry Kittles, Shareef Abdur-Rahim and Stephon Marbury (who sat out with an injury), Antoine Walker and Derek Fisher.

I arrived feeling good. We had won the last two games. We beat Milwaukee first, and I had 23 points and 14 assists. Then against the Spurs, I scored another 25 points to go along with 9 assists. With those two wins, we had won 4 of 7 since losing 23 out of 24. My assists were up, turnovers and shot attempts down. What they all wanted, right?

Not exactly.

During that All-Star Weekend, they were celebrating the NBA's fiftieth anniversary. So they picked the fifty greatest players of all time and brought them to the game. Forty-seven out of fifty attended, each one wearing an official blazer with the NBA logo and the logo of the player's team on the lapel. It was the greatest collection of talent, the biggest gathering of the giants in basketball history. I was in awe, of course, but somehow, bringing all these greats, putting them on the pedestal they deserved, became a way to talk about how bad the new guys were. And the symbol for the new guys became me. I had been in the league for half a season, yet somehow all these legends could talk about was the young guys and a lack of respect. Elvin Hayes and Rick Barry criticized the way I played.

Magic and Jordan criticized the younger generation more generally. John Lucas, who had been the Sixers coach the year before, said, "The mugging and the trash-talking of today was not part of the game when I played."

And Charles Barkley kept his criticism of me coming too. It was so crazy that David Stern got asked about Barkley's comments on NBC's *Meet the Press*. Stern later said, "Suddenly Charles Barkley is the elder statesman? Has Charles forgotten what Charles is about? What he did when he was a young man? Our young players will be fine as they mature, as Charles has done." I love David Stern, even though he made his rules about dressing a certain way, and he brought me in to yell at my ass after some shit I got into. He had my back that day.

With Charles, it got to the point that he and Patrick Ewing came and talked to me about it during the weekend. They sought me out in the training room to have a heart-to-heart. Charles wanted to make it clear that he wasn't against me, that he wanted me to play the right way, and that he loved Philly. He was there accepting his spot in the top fifty wearing the Sixers logo on his jacket—not the Suns, who he got to the Finals with, and not the Rockets, his current team. I was glad to have the conversation with him and Patrick, but it didn't change how everyone was talking about me. Every major newspaper had a story about the younger generation: thugs, gangsters, with me as the headliner.

At this point, it was clear that the press and many of the former greats didn't like what I represented. Maybe it was my style. Or the dudes who I hung out with, my friends from home and people in the music industry. Or maybe it was my game, somehow too focused on scoring for a dude as small as me. Or maybe it was my past, a conviction that had been overturned for lack of evidence. Or was it that I had a signature shoe that was about to be the hottest new seller since Jordan first laced them up? Maybe it was all those things and me making no apologies.

Whatever it was, I was pissing off a hell of a lot of people. But the average attendance in Philly was up by about 4,000. At close to 25 percent, it was the biggest jump of any team in the NBA.

*

Before the rookie game, me and Que made a decision together. By that point, Que was Reebok's man in charge of the Iverson account. He had relocated to Philadelphia, and really he had become one of us. He would chill with us. You'd see him at the club or the Fridays. He was just a great friend. But obviously we talked about style and look and all that.

At the time, people back home had started wearing their hair in braids, or cornrows. So I told Que that I wanted to go with it. He was at Reebok, from the inner city himself, but even he was unsure if people were ready for all that. I didn't care. It was more than just a style choice. I was also tired of people fucking up my hair. Half the season we were on the road in different cities, sometimes a week or two at a time. And I'd go get my cut, a fade, and they'd fuck it up, so I figured if I just grew my hair out and got me some cornrows then I wouldn't have to worry about it. Of course that wasn't how it worked out. In the end, I had to have my braider come wherever I was at least twice a week!

So Que and I agreed we'd both do it. We started growing out our hair maybe around December, and come early February, I figured I was ready to rock it. Everyone knows that the NBA All-Star Game is the center of the world for a weekend. Not just the NBA's biggest stars, but hip-hop and Hollywood come out for the event. It was even bigger that year with the fiftieth-anniversary celebration. On the other hand, it was in Cleveland. Karl Malone got booed in the game because he complained about the Cleveland weather.

The rookie game was part of All-Star Saturday Night, right before the three-point and slam-dunk contests. I remember when I showed up, all these dudes saw my hair with the cornrows. They were really short, hair barely long enough to braid.

But dudes were like, *Bro, you know this is the shit you're getting criticized for, right?*

No player ever told me it was a bad look, but *The New York Times* said my hair "did not sit well with veteran players, who privately mocked [my] new hairdo behind [my] back."

You got to understand, not one other player in the league wore them yet. Latrell Sprewell would soon, but it was no one then. I was the first.

As they did the game introductions, I walked out on the floor. I was excited as hell for this stage. And what I heard was some cheers, but also some boos. I didn't really react, but that's when I began to feel that all these stories, all this hate, it was having an effect.

It wasn't just the crowd I was thinking about. My family was there, my friends of course. But you also had a lot of the guys who would play in the main event the next afternoon sitting courtside. And the fifty greatest were there too. Wilt Chamberlain watching. Larry Bird, Isiah, Kevin McHale, Doctor J, Bill Russell. I mean, everyone. So many of them already on the record talking about me and the new wave.

At the tip, that all went out my mind, and I just wanted to perform, to win. I was also determined to set up my teammates. Maybe they could complain about my style, my friends, but I wasn't going to let them complain about my game. So on my first move of the night, I dropped it off to Camby for a layup. Then I fed Erick Dampier for a dunk. Later it was me, as I prepared to hit Derek Fisher with my crossover, ball hanging in my left hand. When he didn't go for it, I blew by him with the simple hesitation and dunked with two hands. I had a no-look alley-oop and a pair of drop-offs over my back, all to Camby for easy baskets.

In the first half I shot it just two times and had 4 points with 8 assists. We built a fifteen-point cushion. In the second half, we stretched out the lead. When they pulled to within seven with about four minutes left, I focused more on my shot. I drove and hit a scoop shot in traffic. Then I closed the game out with some free throws. For the West, Kobe was their man. He had 31 points. He and I had faced off in the preseason and once during the season. I loved that dude, but obviously we were beginning to be rivals.

After the game, they made me MVP. I had done what they wanted, I figured. I only shot it 11 times, scored 19, but led the team with 9 assists. And we won. I got out there to accept the trophy, and that Cleveland crowd booed again, this time much louder. That's when I knew it wasn't my game that made them so mad. And maybe they wanted Kobe to get it, since he'd scored over 30. But his team lost.

After the trophy presentation, TNT legend Craig Sager interviewed me, and he asked about how the Sixers season was going bad, just 12 wins and all that. Then he brought up one of those articles I was talking about. In fact, he had the motherfucking newspaper in his hand, with the headline "Legends Take Iverson, Young Players to Task."

He said, "Would you please clarify how you feel about the fifty greatest players here today?"

I told you, I couldn't shake it. I respected the hell out of them. Of course I did. Yet here I was just having won the game, distributed the ball first and foremost, earned the MVP, and the questions remained the same.

I said how I felt: "Without those players there would be no Allen Iverson. Those guys paved the way for me."

THIRTY-SEVEN

MORE LOSSES AND TRAGEDY

I was back in Cleveland for our first game after the All-Star Break. I had vowed I would show that crowd what's up after they booed me. But I had a terrible game, and they booed me again. I hated the Cleveland fans at that point.

That's how it went for a little while—losses, negativity. For the first time in my life, it almost felt like I had lost my legs. I shot the ball terribly. I tried to distribute, but my teammates weren't making anything either. It was like we had reentered that period where we lost 23 out of 24.

The Sixers fans were getting pissed off at the losing too. The negative stories about me continued. I held a little press gathering a few days later, at a Reebok event, trying to turn the narrative around. I told these guys the same story, that I respected the legends who came before me. But then they switched it up and started asking me about rumors that I owned a gun in my name. I told them that I did, and that I had to protect myself. With that as the new focal point, it became more of Allen Iverson is a bad guy but add guns to the mix.

Feeling like talking just made it worse, I told the media I was done with that shit. No more press availability. I remember a couple days later, after we won one against the Clippers, Pat Croce came up to me in the arena, and he was like, *Chuck, you got to talk to these guys.* So I agreed to do it, but I took one from the Coach Thompson playbook and said I would only answer questions about basketball. And that's how I handled it for the rest of the season.

It wasn't just me feeling the heat. Johnny Davis's job was rumored to be in trouble, and as the trade deadline approached, I think some dudes were actually *hoping* to get traded.

All this shit hurt, but my life kept on being this dream. Reebok officially released The Question. The authentic me was front and center in the marketing campaign. Of course all my family and friends were wearing them. I wore them on the court for the rookie game, the red, white, and blue matching my Sixers uniform.

Seeing them like that—on my feet, family and friends wearing them—was one thing, but I will never forget witnessing them out in the world for the first time. I was in my car, and a kid had the joints on. Just walking down the city streets. After I passed him in my car, I stopped and put the motherfucker in park. I just kept it there as I looked at the kid in my rearview. Kept my eyes on him until he walked out of sight.

It might as well have been me I was looking at. Here I was, exactly a year removed from driving that first Mercedes off the lot. Three years removed from jail. Not even seven years removed from walking up to Bethel High, just hoping my name was on the list. Seven years removed from hustling. Eight, maybe nine years removed from swiping worms from the corner store and lifting loose change from cars in the mall parking lot. Here I was, in my Benz or my Rolls or whatever it was that day, watching my shoes accompanying this anonymous kid down the city streets.

In spite of all the losing that season, I was loving my life. Makes me think of a conversation I had with my mom—years later, but I think about it a lot. I said to her, "I'm getting scared."

And she was like, "About what?"

I said, "Everything is perfect right now. As good as it could be."

"What do you mean?"

So I tried to explain it. "You know, I been with Tawanna, shit, my whole fucking life. If her day ain't good, my day ain't good. Everything is great with us, my kids are doing fine, my family is fine. All the money we have coming in. Everything is cool. But I'm scared."

"That don't make no sense."

"Everything just seems too goddamn perfect. I feel like something bad is going to happen."

She just said, "Don't you ever live your life like that. That's a blessing, man, God is blessing you, that's a part of being blessed: things going well in your life. Don't get scared of that, don't fucking jinx yourself to where something bad gotta be happening or feel like you got used to bad shit happening in life. You know, life is supposed to be fucking *great.* I know life is hard at times. But when it's going good, that's a blessing. It don't always have to be bad."

So I always tried to enjoy the good times. But I admit, I was never confident they would continue. That's one reason I think I played like I did, and maybe why I partied that way too. Like you never know how long it's going to last. It seemed like it wasn't supposed to happen in the first place.

The Reebok Questions got released as planned, but they were hard to get your hands on at first. Everybody wanted them. I will never forget when I was in LA, and after a game, I heard I had a visitor.

Came out the locker room, and there he was. Biggie.

I was just like, "What the fuck you doing here?"

He went, "I came to see you. I need to get me the Questions."

I had to act cool, having this idol waiting for me, to ask me for something. I was like, "I got you." Then we chilled that night. And I made sure we sent them kicks, obviously.

Man, when I got to the league, it was like a world opened up to me. When I tell you that I was going out with my friends to clubs, out late into the night, many times it wasn't just us. I was chilling with the dudes I idolized, who, like I said, provided the soundtrack of my life.

It started before the draft even. I had gone to hoop at Rucker Park, in Harlem, because you had to play there back then. You weren't the real shit unless you did. When I showed up, all kinds of people came to see the show. That's when I first met Biggie and Lil' Cease from Junior M.A.F.I.A., dudes who'd already done exactly what we were dreaming of doing, conquering, getting rich, and bringing everyone with them. They'd made records. I was playing basketball. So after that with Biggie, we'd chill when I was in New York, or when he was in the same city I happened to be in.

One night earlier that year, when I was in New York, me and some of my friends were invited to his recording studio. It's one of those times it felt like I was dreaming. Everyone was smoking, chilling. At that particular point, I only smoked here and there, and even then, I only started from when I was at Georgetown. So I smoked a little that night, but then I started tripping. I remember I went to the bathroom, and I was wearing this Janet Jackson shirt, and the reflection just started freaking me out. Then I couldn't find my way back down the hallway to the recording studio. Turned out what I smoked was some fucking hash. I really didn't know what I was doing.

So eventually I made it back after some worker found my ass and took me. Me and Ra and E were just sitting there, tripping, as we watched Biggie work on a couple tracks from *Life After Death*. At that point, it had been a minute since his last release, so this was going to be his next big one. That night, Biggie recorded parts of "You're Nobody (Til Somebody Kills You)" and "My Downfall." Ra and E were imagining making it in that world. I was just a fan watching this genius work, man.

Flash forward to March 9, about a month after the All-Star Game, and we had a game in Washington. My mom came to DC to watch my homecoming. Remember, I had missed our first game in DC earlier that year, so now I got to play in front of everyone—the USAir Arena was as close as any NBA basketball arena was to Newport News and Hampton. My mom stayed in my hotel. I went out that night until late. After I had gotten to bed, my mom came and woke my ass up.

"They killed your man!"

I didn't know what she was talking about.

"Biggie dead."

I got up, shook. I had watched him record, gotten him my shoes. He'd been a model for us as we'd plotted getting out the shit. It was crushing. If anyone had been prepared for death, it was me. From all the dudes I'd seen get killed, Tony Clark and too many others to count, it's fucked-up to say I was used to it. But I was used to it.

Still, when you get the fuck out, like I did, and like Biggie had done before me, and it *still* goes that way? I thought about that shit all the time after that. And I always remembered when I was a kid, in Glen Gardens, with a barrel pressed to my head.

Right before he died, they released "Hypnotize," the first single off *Ready to Die*. Then at the end of that month, after his death, the "Hypnotize" video came out. It was so fucking epic, filmed with speedboats and helicopters in Miami Bay. The man had made it, was doing it over the top, just crushing it. Before it all got snatched away. They said he never got to watch the whole video. He definitely never got to see the whole album released. But if you watch that video close, you can see it. He's wearing the motherfucking Questions.

THIRTY-EIGHT

BREAKING RECORDS

There was all the criticism of me—my friends, my style, my hair. There were all the losses—they just piled up after the All-Star Game. And there was this now: death. But out of all that difficult shit, I began to, I don't know how to explain, just move that baggage to the side, and put my game first.

Three days after that terrible night, we had the Bulls on our home floor. The same old shit got repeated. *He doesn't respect Jordan.* And as I always said to anybody with a tape recorder and a pen, I revered the man and the player. But on the court, I said it best back then: "I feel like when you over-respect somebody, the battle is already lost." I didn't over-respect anyone that night.

As I got to the arena, you could feel it wasn't some regular game. The Bulls were different. It was a sellout, and this night they stuffed more people into the CoreStates Center than ever before. Our whole squad was healthy for once, but we were mad as hell. We had played in Minnesota the night before and played well until we blew a late lead. It was my first professional matchup against Marbury. I was so pissed off with that loss and what it meant for the conversation about who should have gone No. 1, who should win the 1996–97 Rookie of the Year. So the bad taste of that was giving me extra motivation.

When the ball went in the air, just like always, everything else disappeared. I had it going early, getting to my spots, making a couple threes, connecting on the midrange, getting steals, setting up my teammates. In the third quarter though, I took it to the next level. I will admit, I was hot enough that I focused on me, my scoring—I just wanted to beat them so bad at that point. The only problem was I got into foul trouble. So I only played thirty-six minutes that night.

It got to the late third quarter, the game tight. Clarence Weatherspoon had the ball on the left side outside the three-point line. When he picked up his dribble, I came up from the baseline around him and took the ball, like a dribble handoff. At the same time, he screened my man, so his man switched onto me.

I just remember hearing Phil Jackson. "Michael! Get up on him!"

And there I was. Directly facing the basket, outside the three-point line, with Michael Jordan staring at me from his defensive crouch. I paused, then backed up for a second. I always knew that if he was guarding me, I would try my move. I told my friends, my family. So when he got on me, I was like, *Here we go*. That's why I backed up.

As I retreated, you could hear the crowd respond. Like this is what they came for. Then the volume rose. The anticipation. I gave him a little left-to-right cross first to see if he would bite on it. He did. The crowd reacted. I let him set his feet as I dribbled the ball back to my left hand. Then I hit him with the real one. This time his body went all the way to my left as I crossed over to the right. With space and him almost on the ground (his Jordans saving his ankles), I pulled up just inside the three-point line.

The jumper was cash. The crowd fucking erupted.

I was just glad it went in. Wouldn't have mattered, even if he had fallen on the ground, if the ball didn't go in. But I didn't have time to appreciate it more than a second. Had to get back on D. Mike came right back at us, missed a little jumper, and after Bill Wennington got the offensive rebound, I got called for my fourth foul. Seconds after changing my entire legacy, I was mad as hell they called that shit on me. I had to sit the rest of the third quarter.

Now, I wish I could tell you we won, but it was another close loss. (The Bulls went 69-13 that year and secured the second title in their three-peat.) I scored what was then my career high of 37 points. But they were just too good down the stretch. Scottie was the one that killed us, as he made everything and scored 31. Rodman controlled the inside with 17 boards.

I was just playing basketball that night. I had done my move on Mike. I didn't really pay attention to it, realize the gravity, until the aftermath, once I got the response from everybody else. I remember getting out the locker room pissed off because we lost. My friends were like, *Bro that shit was crazy. You did that shit on Michael Jordan.* When I went to my normal spot, the Fridays on City Line Avenue, it began to sink in, what I'd done. ESPN showed it over and over. They had all the angles. My friends back home were letting us know—that night all of Newport News and Hampton was on the phone, recounting that shit, celebrating that moment. I got the GOAT.

But just let me tell you how bad and how great Mike was. I hit him with my best move, and he *still* almost blocked it. If you look, he recovered quick and got his hand up to contest. I got him, and he still almost blocked it.

But he didn't. Even now little kids don't say, *You're Allen Iverson.* They say, *You're the guy who crossed over Michael Jordan.*

My confidence built after that. After all the losing, I just decided I needed to do everything I could, and if that meant me scoring, then that's what it would be. Couple days later, we played the Timberwolves again, and this time we finished. I had 24 points and 8 assists, as we beat them by fourteen. While we weren't going to make the playoffs, I felt like I was figuring it out.

As the calendar turned to April and the end of the season approached, it started to seem more and more like it was just me and Stack. We got hit with more injuries. Derrick Coleman missed the last month of the season, Scott Williams was out . . . it went on and on. We had so many guys sitting, we only dressed nine dudes for a few games. With so little to play for, what motivation was there? The *games*, goddammit. And I admit it meant a lot to me to try and win the Rookie of the Year. That award also motivated the Sixers, who wanted something positive to sell as the season drew to a close. The last few weeks of the season, that rookie year, encapsulated the shit I faced, the man I became. By the end of that season, I just embraced my way of being both on the court—putting on a show, trying my hardest, taking on personal goals—and off the court—sticking with my friends, expressing myself through my style. And because of this expression of myself, I had become a target for a certain type, guardians of basketball tradition, whether it be old-head players retired or still in the league, or out-of-shape reporters pontificating about my me-first game and hood style.

The streak started against the Bulls on April 7. With just eight games left, we were coming off a heartbreaker against the Hornets, where I had scored 32 points, with 10 rebounds and 7 assists, and I played all forty-eight minutes. With only nine guys, Coach Davis didn't have much choice other than to let me play. I'd gone more than forty-four minutes for five straight games. Coach Davis said, "He doesn't want to come out. He'd play forty-eight minutes of all eighty-two games. You can't do that, but he'd try it."

So against the Bulls this time, it was the full forty-eight minutes. I scored 44 points, full throttle start to finish, even when the game was already lost. It was a Sixers rookie record for points in a game. But it was them that throttled us, clinching playoff home-court advantage in the process. We were a long way from that. They said Mike was on the bench watching me fly around, shaking his head. He supposedly asked the reporters during the game, "Was I a one-man offense like that when I was a rookie?"

The next game was against the Hawks at home. Unable to defend down low with all the injuries, we got beat again. With me playing the full forty-eight minutes, I scored 40. I was the first rookie to have back-to-back 40-point games since Elvin Hayes (the man who'd criticized my game for being too selfish!). Mike hadn't done it.

There was excitement but at the same time, as always, there was the criticism. *Dude is scoring forty-plus but can't win.* Most teams out of playoff contention were making travel plans at that point. As the guys would say on *Inside the NBA*, they'd "gone fishing." That wasn't me though. One thing I never did was cheat the *games*. We had six left in a lost season, so the criticism to me sounded like, *He's playing too hard. Don't he know they lost their season?*

Yeah, I was going to try hard even when our season was lost. If that made me selfish, so be it.

So after those two 40-point games, we traveled to Milwaukee. And that night, my shots were falling again. I had 44. Glenn Robinson scored 40 and Ray Allen had 27. It was tight in the last three minutes, but Sherman Douglas—my crossover's first victim way back on opening night—got a couple steals off me that helped them seal it.

I said after the game what I felt, that the stats were "meaningless." "I'm out there playing as hard as I can play, and we just can't get it done." Another goddamn loss. But it was also three 40-point games in a row for me. Only Wilt had done that before as a rookie.

So we left Milwaukee with like half a team, all disappointed motherfuckers. The next day was another road game in my favorite city: Cleveland again. They'd booed my ass at the rookie game, booed me again in the game after the break. And sure enough, they booed me during the introductions of this one. And I started off terribly. We got down by as many as 23 in the first half, and I had just 11 points at the break.

The second half was different. Once it started flowing I felt like I could do anything. On one play I got to the paint and through traffic flipped one in almost with my back to the basket. Later, leading a three-on-one break, I started to pass it around my back to Stack on my left, but when I saw the defender go for it, I yanked it back and coasted in for the layup. That made 31. Of course, they couldn't make it easy. I remember on one play, I had Terrell Brandon on the right side. With the ball in my left hand, paused there for a moment, I hit him with it, left him dusted. Then I heard the whistle behind me. The sound of frustration, man. The motherfucker called palming. I just raced down to the other end mad as hell, but ready to play some defense.

I was going for 40, and I was going for the win. We had worked the lead down to under ten. I just kept driving and shooting and stalking the passing lanes. I reached 40 with a little jumper, then broke my career high with 45. As the time ticked down, I knocked down a pair of free throws to get to 50, 39 of which were in the second half. First rookie to get more than 40 in four consecutive games. Not even Wilt had done that.

As for the game, we kept it close, but we lost. As I made each shot, drove into the lane repeatedly, kept getting up after getting knocked down, the crowd stopped heckling me, the boos dwindled. Beginning in the upper levels and filtering throughout the arena, I started hearing cheers. As I left the court, the crowd stood for me. Even in Cleveland, they saw what I did. Our season was over. Our team was decimated. We were on the back end of back-to-backs in two different Midwest cities. And still, I was playing the game like it was my last.

The next game, we hosted the Bullets and got blown out. With less than a minute left, stuck on 37 points but way, way behind, Coach Davis called a couple of timeouts to run plays for me. With the extra time, and a Bullets defense that didn't care, I made an uncontested three to continue the streak one last game. I'll be honest, it didn't feel great. It was another loss, and this one wasn't close. I remember even Stack was mad about making the streak the main thing. It had been motivation for me and the team in the season's final act, but it wasn't enough if we weren't winning. Five straight 40-point games became part of my legacy. I didn't want my legacy to include the fact that all five went in the L column. But that's what it became. The media talked about it as if instead of an accomplishment, it was just another failure—just another unique aspect of Allen Iverson to pick on. As I told them then, everything I'd tried to do positive was turned into something negative. Half the team was injured and chose not even to travel with us. On the floor, it was me and Stack working our asses off. I led the team in scoring each game, but I also led in assists each and every game, averaging seven and a half during those five games. We had lost more than five games in a row plenty of times that season—and with our whole team out there—but somehow this was worse because I had tried so hard and scored so much.

I had never lost like this in my life, and I never wanted to again.

The streak ended the next game, and I was glad. A few nights later, the season was over. In all, it was 22 wins and 60 losses. Pat fired both Johnny Davis and Brad Greenberg a day later. Me? I needed a break and headed home. It was my first summer rich, and with some time off.

THIRTY-NINE

BACK TO THE COURTROOM

A couple weeks after our last game, I was home when a whole bunch of people I knew started hitting me up. They let me know that some white dude was trying to find me. Evidently he was going around my Virginia neighborhoods asking where I was at. Everyone probably thought it was an FBI agent, so they weren't saying shit. But I made some calls and learned he was from the 76ers. At the time, the team just had my beeper number, but I wasn't really paying attention to it—after that year I'd had, I was trying to escape for a minute. Pat Croce later told me they were going crazy because they kept calling my beeper number and I wasn't responding.

So after figuring out it was the Sixers, I contacted him. It was Bill Bonsiewicz, this great PR guy, and the reason he was looking for me was they got word I was going to be named Rookie of the Year. In all the years that franchise had been around, it was the first time any Sixer had won it. The team planned a press conference for the next day—obviously, I had to be there.

It sounds strange, but that award was one of the reasons I was trying to lay low. The season ended with me getting all those 40-point games, yet it seemed like everyone was talking shit about me more and more. The more points I scored, the more I felt the award slipping away. Charles Barkley summed up what all these guys were saying when he told the press, "Iverson is the playground Rookie of the Year"—as if I was playing the wrong game, on the wrong court. That's something that's hard to shake, man. Like, *You shouldn't be here*. You feel it in your soul, sometimes even after you take flight on the arena floor. You'll be flying around, levitating above the motherfucker, crossing over Jordan, scoring 40-plus points, a tiny man towering over giants—and it's still there when you land. *You shouldn't be here.*

Man, I was on the same arena floors as everyone else as I scored more points than any other rookie, averaging 23.5 per game. I averaged the most steals too, with over two a game. And I was a close second to Marbury in assists, with 7.5 a game compared to his 7.8. *But he's selfish, but he's a bad guy, but his team lost*, they said.

So when I learned that I won the award, this sense of relief . . . it's hard to explain, but I had confidence, swagger, purpose on the court—everything would quiet down there. Then I would come back to the locker room, back home, and hear the racket of negativity. Especially from the press, the same people who voted for Rookie of the Year. So when the motherfuckers finally gave it to me—barely, Marbury was a close second—after all that, it was a relief. It was also vindication. I had not changed who I was, how I dressed, who I chilled with. The dude who was out on the streets in Virginia, winning championships for Bethel, stuck behind bars in jail—that was the same dude who was anointed the greatest rookie in the world.

Of course, I wanted to be there for the announcement. When I say I wanted to be there, I mean I wanted the authentic Allen Iverson to be there. That meant I would bring my homeboys and my mom, because I hadn't done it alone. It also meant I had to think about my look. I had been growing out my hair. After the Rookie Game, I rocked the small cornrows some game days, but most of the time I wore it out, still waiting for it to grow enough to look right braided. It wouldn't be until my second year that I wore the cornrows that people remember. The Reebok team had given me these skullcaps, all white. And we had some matching all-white warm-up suits. So me and my boys decided to rock those joints. I wasn't going to be in a suit for this press conference.

The next day, we arrived together at the CoreStates Center. When I walked out to the podium, with my mom beside me, I think people were a little shocked to see me like that. *First he's got cornrows, now he's doing an official press conference in a skullcap?* I later heard that the NBA chose not to promote that press conference because of my look. Pat Croce said that an NBA official told him, "It looks like something people wear in prison." If anyone asked, I could've told them that you couldn't wear that shit in the prison I was at.

I thanked my mother first, of course, for her belief in me. Then came the questions. There weren't any questions about the games, and none about practice either, lol. That would come later. A lot of it was about the criticism I'd faced. I said, "I didn't expect people to be so hard on me. . . . If someone was to go through what I've been through . . . I would take my hat off to somebody who's trying to do something for himself. It didn't seem like people wanted me to be successful." They asked me about getting 40 points in that fifth game, and how Washington let me shoot the three to get there. I said, "I wished I hadn't even shot it, after all the criticism it got me." But almost thirty years later, I can say, fuck that, I'm glad I scored 40 in five straight games. I'm glad I played every minute like it was my last and never cheated the games.

Holding that award, walking away from the press conference—the podium, the microphones, the reporters—I just stared at the trophy. I felt like it said I belonged and I was accepted—the way I was. Yet years later, at that practice press conference, it seemed like people still didn't understand me.

I really didn't have time to think about it. I had to get on a plane back to Virginia. Home was pulling me back.

*

Now, I mentioned that we were partying at home with family when the Sixers couldn't find me. What nobody knew was the whole family was trying to enjoy what turned out to be my dad's last days of freedom for a minute.

Remember, just before I entered the NBA draft, my dad had been arrested and hit with drug charges. Now, almost a year later, his trial was scheduled for the day after that press conference. So while everyone at the Sixers was worrying about my Rookie of the Year press conference, I was worrying about that trial. People like to laugh like, *We couldn't find AI, his beeper was off, he's stuck in the hood.* I was just trying to take care of my family.

To represent my dad, we had hired Woodward and Shuttleworth, the lawyers who handled my clemency petition to the governor, as well as the successful appeal. My dad's defense was that while he was admittedly in the house with the drugs, it was because he *had* to be there: It was the address he was paroled to. Others were living in that house, some of them arrested along with him. The drugs weren't his and he wasn't part of selling them. At the trial, his parole officer testified that my dad had begged the PO to allow him to move to a new address because he was worried about there being drugs in the house. But the parole office had denied his requests. Would he ask to leave if he was the one dealing drugs?

I had to go there to support the man who raised me. I also planned to testify. The trial date had been set months in advance, so for this, I had time to plan my look. No do-rag. No cornrows. I wore a gray suit. It was criminal court, and for that I would wear a suit.

So the day after accepting the Rookie of the Year award, I walked into that same Hampton Circuit Court courthouse. Shit, man, it was the whiplash of my life. So many memories flooded back to me—remembering the word *guilty* at the end of my trial, then the words *fifteen years* on sentencing day. How the night before my sentencing I spent the time chilling with my friends, sure I'd walk but nervous as a motherfucker, never imagining how bad it would be.

The thing that gave me strength as a junior in high school, a *kid*, was the support I had. So many faces had been there. My mom and sisters. Mo, Coach Bailey, and his wife. Tawanna. Supporters in the community. My boys from the neighborhood—though they weren't in the courtroom, they were in my corner—Thrilla and Ra, Arnie and E.

So here I was, present for the man who raised me. It was different testifying when it wasn't my life on the line. But at the end of the day, I just did the same thing. I told them what I knew. I wasn't a witness to any drugs at that house, or anything Daddy was doing there. I couldn't say what they did or didn't find. All I could tell the courtroom was this: As a family we had been poor. We didn't have shit. But we stuck together, no matter what. He raised me, was there for me when he could be. And before he got arrested, when I was already a star at Georgetown but before I had any money, I had told him—*I got you.* I had told him this many times, including during my second (and last) year at Georgetown when I visited that very house just a few months before he was arrested there. Everyone knew that even though I didn't have any money yet, it was coming. I was going to be a top pick, I was going to make millions of dollars. And I would take care of him, along with everyone else. I didn't survive and flourish by myself, and I wasn't going to keep the riches for myself. He had nothing to worry about. So if he didn't need to worry about money or his future, why would he be selling drugs out of that house?

After I testified, I left. I knew better than to be hopeful. When they told me it was the same word I heard—"guilty"—I wasn't surprised. I was hurt and disappointed. Felt like however much I accomplished, or we accomplished as a family, it wasn't going to matter to a judge, to a certain kind of jury. When Daddy got locked up again, that didn't surprise me either.

Some people in Virginia didn't like what I had to say. One columnist put it like this: "This is how Iverson lived his life as he was finishing up his career at Georgetown: According to testimony, he was in and out of a Hampton crack house several times."

When I was at that Rookie of the Year press conference the day before, in front of everyone, I gave the trophy to my mom. As thanks. But it was a statement too. I belonged in the NBA, I'd proven it, but my loyalty still belonged to my home, my friends, my family. And my sense of self, that still belonged to me too.

I'd gotten so far, and the further I got, I kept getting slapped, but harder and harder. Me being stubborn, I dug deeper. You don't like my style? Gonna do it more—let the joints sag further. You don't like my friends? I'm gonna hold those dudes closer. You think my family should be in jail? I'm gonna be there in court for them. You don't like my partying? I'm gonna stay out later, party harder. It ain't a strategy for life I recommend. It's just how I did it. That loyalty, stubbornness, got me in trouble, got me criticized, and sometimes brought pain, but it wasn't stopping me from reaching for greatness and making my mark in the NBA.

I was who I was then. The man who was the MVP four years later. The man in that press conference a year after that. The man writing this book. That was me.

VI

THE 75TH ANNIVERSARY TEAM AND A RUN TO THE FINALS

An Invitation

Twenty-five years later, I was at home, retired, when I got a call.

The voice on the other end informed me that I had been selected as part of the NBA's 75th Anniversary Team. Seventy-five greatest players for seventy-five years of the NBA's history. The next February, over All-Star Weekend, they wanted me to come for the celebration. Not knowing off the top of my head where it was at, I asked. Of course: Cleveland again.

It had been almost nine years since I had officially retired. That was a sad motherfucker because I wanted it to end better, on my own terms. And it was about five years since I had been inducted into the Hall of Fame. For that I traveled to Springfield, Massachusetts, and was joined on the stage for my induction by Coach Thompson, Coach Brown, and Doctor J. It was a joyful night where I got to thank everyone—from my mom to my five kids; from Mo to Coach Bailey, Coach Thompson, and Coach Larry Brown; from my friends from home to inspirations who became friends like Jadakiss and Biggie.

Since then, I was living my life, still out having fun, making mistakes, being human. There were negative stories about me being out of money, out of my marriage, all kinds of shit. So while I was honored to go, I had not forgotten the fifty-year celebration during my rookie year. I got to Cleveland half-expecting boos to rain down again.

Each dude selected to the team got a blue blazer, NBA logo by the lapel, just like they had for the 50th Anniversary Team. But there were no rules on what else to wear, or how to wear my hair. The day of the celebration, February 20, 2022, I had my braider fix my cornrows, four thick braids shooting back. Since my rookie year, I'd worn cornrows for the rest of my career, sometimes flying out my braider to meet me on longer road trips. Certain styles were named after me in hairdressers around the world. Plenty of other dudes in the league wore cornrows ever since.

I had a whole bunch more tattoos now too. Early on in my Sixers career, I'd added two phrases that summed up my path: "Only the Strong Survive" was on my shoulder just above "The Answer," and "Fear No One" joined it there on my left arm. At a certain point I got addicted, the art working its way around my body. I had tributes to Tawanna, my mother, Nana, and of course to all five of my kids—Tiaura, Allen II, Isaiah, Messiah, and Dream. "Cru Thik" was bold and present on my left forearm. And after he passed, I had "Ra Boogie" emblazoned on my neck—a reminder of our friendship cut short. "Ra Boogie" stood above the Chinese character for loyalty. Loyalty meant so much to me. It kept me connected to my roots as my fame and fortune skyrocketed. I added more and more over the years.

But my body art seemed tame as I compared it to some of those guys in Cleveland. Among the All-Stars that year, just about everyone had tattoos.

Other than that blue blazer, I wore white Reeboks, some jeans, and a red designer sweater. I wore rings and earrings, and four or five chains proudly hung loose around my neck. It was hard to believe that in my fourth year in the league, the NBA's official publication, Hoop *magazine, put me on its cover but literally airbrushed out some of the tattoos and my diamond earrings. Then in 2005, they introduced another Allen Iverson rule. Motherfuckers added a dress code for players when they were at the arenas, making collars and blazers mandatory and prohibiting sneakers, jeans, jerseys, and chains. For the 75th Anniversary celebration in 2022, nobody even stopped to look at me. Dudes were expected to express themselves now.*

At the Cleveland arena, they announced each member of that anniversary team, starting with the forwards and centers, followed by the guards. First up among the guards was me. Like in a pregame intro, they said it, "Eleven-time All-Star and four-time scoring champ, AAAAAAA-llen IIIIIIIII-verson!*" Add to those accomplishments a league MVP and Eastern Conference Championship and it's a hell of a résumé, but it felt like I could hardly remember it, the speed it went by.*

FORTY

COACH LARRY BROWN

Those years sped by as I experienced them too. Triumph and calamity often coming one after the other. When things got good, just like I told my mom, I knew to start worrying.

Sure enough, that next August after winning the Rookie of the Year trophy, I had more to worry about. I was with some dudes I barely knew in Virginia. One of them was driving, but it was my car. We had weed, and I had the gun that was registered in Pennsylvania, the one I felt like I needed for protection. I wasn't paying attention, which is my fault obviously. A cop pulled us over for speeding. He searched the car after he said he smelled marijuana, and he found two roaches and the gun. I got arrested and charged: for the weed because it was 1997, and for the gun because I didn't have a Virginia permit. Man, the press took that shit and ran with it. More evidence that Allen Iverson was out of control. The story was everywhere. It fit their narrative perfectly.

I ended up pleading no contest to a misdemeanor weapon charge and getting two years of probation. The probation was terrible. Besides just being a daily irritation, they constantly tested me for weed. So I gave the shit up, and that's why I really didn't smoke weed during the rest of my career—scared me half to death about it possibly ending my career. Of course, when I told Mo about it, he was like, *Goddammit Chuck, what's the cop supposed to do with you boys driving over 90 miles an hour*. I didn't know it was that fast. So then Croce and my team convinced me to get rid of the gun and hire a bodyguard for protection. For years after that, I had Terry Royster at my side, protection but also a friend.

While all that was going on, the Sixers had a lot of business to take care of. First and foremost, the team had to hire a new head coach. Without consulting me, they landed on Larry Brown, who had just left his position as coach of the Indiana Pacers. In Coach Brown I found the other great coaching relationship of my life—but I didn't realize it right away. No, it would take years for me to fully appreciate the man who pushed me to my motherfucking limits. I just wasn't ready to hear what he had to say, not at first. Instead of putting his arm around me like Coach Thompson had done and telling me, *Motherfucker, just go*, he would stop every practice about a million times to teach us about all the shit we did wrong—*Motherfucker, stop*. I never liked drills. That part of practice never appealed to me. But Coach Brown was obsessed with drills and fundamentals. I had dealt with that in the past, but then I could always look forward to the end of practice, to the chance you get to scrimmage. I was like the kid waiting for that treat at the end. Throw the ball up and let's go. But whenever it was time to "scrimmage," we'd get in our first set, and then—the whistle. The sound of frustration. In the middle of supposedly scrimmaging, Coach Brown would be out there making sure the screens were set a certain way, or defensive rotations were perfect. That was practice. It would be long. I didn't like it, and Coach Brown didn't like me missing it. And I admit, I was late sometimes, and other times, I wasn't there at all.

But the games, he never questioned my effort or heart in the games. Me and him would fight when he tried to take me out, but that's about it during the games. He sometimes said he had to endure me calling him "motherfucker" twice every game: once when he rested me in the first half, and then again when he took me out in the second half. I never liked coming out, I admit. I didn't need rest, and I let him know it. But I don't think I called him "motherfucker" that often. If anything, he appreciated that part of me—my relentless desire to compete.

We never saw eye to eye about practice though. I do sometimes wish I had listened more, and sooner. But I stuck to who I was.

The dynamic between us was kind of set from the beginning. Right after the Sixers hired Coach Brown, the team organized an exhibition where our rookies played against a bunch of Philly all-stars, locals, and college kids. The Sixers asked me to play, and though it wasn't required, I said I'd be there. The game was held on the Temple campus, and just like always they filled the spot up. Game time was 7:30 p.m. So I showed up at 7:27. What was there to do before that? By the time I got my uniform on and walked out, the game had already started. No one in the crowd knew for sure I was going to play, so when I walked on out there, the crowd lit up, man, just went crazy. It was my first time in front of a Philly crowd since the end of my rookie year. And when they went crazy like that, it let me know that all that complaining you heard from the press, from TV shows, after my rookie year and the summer's arrest, all that hadn't changed how the Philly fans felt about me.

Truth is, I already knew that me, my image, my way of being, was being embraced worldwide. Earlier that summer Reebok had taken me on a South American tour. I remember being with Que just looking at all these people running, jostling to get closer to me at event after event. I had no idea it would be like that. When they suggested the trip, I kind of felt like it didn't make any sense, going all the way over there. The NBA was an American sports league—but now I knew it was exploding everywhere, and so was I. And I saw that what they all loved about me was the same thing the guys at Reebok had identified in our first meeting. It was the little man battling giants—literal giants on the court but also facing off with the powers that be, the mainstream media and the NBA brass.

So back on the Temple campus, the crowd hyped, I didn't need to stretch or practice, as was always the case with me. I went right into the game and scored twenty-some points, just entertained all those motherfuckers. By the time I left, four cops had to escort me through the throngs and on out of there. I didn't really pay too much mind to Coach Brown sitting there in the crowd. I hadn't yet spoken to him since he had been hired a few weeks before. It was just an exhibition. But people started saying that I'd disrespected him by not talking to him, that I'd displayed bad habits by showing up late and not warming up. That was the dynamic between us that would build and build.

That first year together, we lost more than we won, but by winning 31 games, we improved. More importantly, Coach Brown and the front office leader he'd handpicked, Billy King (he'd be named general manager later), made some big moves, adding guys that became more than teammates. We became brothers. First they traded Stackhouse (who they were never going to pay), acquiring Aaron McKie and Theo Ratliff in return. Next a second-round pick was sent to Seattle for a benchwarmer from Michigan State named Eric Snow. It wasn't clear in the moment, but getting McKie and Snow made it possible over the next couple of years for Coach Brown to switch it up when it came to me and my position. It took time, but Coach Brown eventually convinced me and himself—the two people that most needed convincing—that I didn't have to be the point guard. To allow me to move off the ball, both McKie and Snow could share the job of initiating the offense and at the same time defend bigger guards on the defensive end. It wasn't an immediate change, but by the time of our second season together (1998–99), I was coming off screens more often than not, getting the ball on the wing, and once I did, I could focus on what I did best. Sure enough, after a lockout delayed its start, we won more than we lost that year, I got me my first scoring title, and we reached the playoffs.

These days, in gyms across the world, they call one of the actions we used to get me the ball where I liked it an "Iverson" cut. Basically, I'd run from one sideline of the court to the other, in a little pattern roughly parallel to the three-point line. One or two of my teammates would set screens around the foul line or a little above, and the ballhandler would hit me with a pass as I got to the other side of the screen. Then I would have the ball just inside the three-point line, my defender usually off balance or trailing behind, with me in a position to shoot or attack. That was Coach Brown's creativity.

Our first two runs in the playoffs, in 1999 and 2000, were cut short in the second round by the Indiana Pacers. In the 1999 playoffs they swept us, and then in 2000, they beat us four games to two.

Losing that second time, in 2000, hurt so bad, man. We had been down three games to nothing, then fought back to win the next two, feeling like we could be the first team ever to come back from a 3–0 deficit. In the locker room after losing game six—and the series—on our home floor, it was like when I lost the Big East Championship at Georgetown my sophomore year. I couldn't hide the tears. My mom was in the locker room consoling me. I hated that Indiana team. Not anything about them personally. I respected Reggie Miller, Rik Smits, Jalen Rose, and Mark Jackson, of course, all those dudes, but at the time, it killed me that they beat us.

But it was more than losing, which was bad enough. In the days leading up to game six, when everyone was still down on us for falling behind three to nothing in the series, the team received death threats naming not just me but my kids. By then Tawanna and I had added another child to the family, Allen II, or "Deuce," we called him. The FBI investigated. The team hired extra security. It felt like all that negativity of my whole career had led to this, like it was getting dangerous. Nothing violent ever happened, but that was part of the emotion that came out in the locker room—the release from that.

And then there was also knowing that the offseason was going to be turmoil. The trade rumors were going to be about me now, I knew. Larry Brown was in control of the franchise (he'd just gotten a contract extension), and I guess he was tired of the two of us fighting, me missing practice, me partying all night with rappers and my homeboys. Me being me.

It was a lot of little things that had been brewing between me and Coach Brown during that 1999–2000 season. When it got bad in December 1999, Stephen A. reported that "Brown continuously gripes about everything from Iverson's behavior during practice"—I "joked around in practice" too much, according to his sources—"to his disregarding rules that the players have agreed to, such as the team's dress code."

There were two big incidents that year that made it feel like me and Coach Brown might be headed for a divorce. The first was in December 1999. We were playing the first of back-to-back games against the Pistons. It was one of those nights where the whole team had no energy. We were losing big, and Coach Brown benched his starters, including me, for the last twenty minutes of the game—mid-third quarter on. I was mad as hell. Humiliated, I sat on the bench the whole fourth quarter. It was something that had never happened to me in college or the NBA. So then after the game I told the press that the team should trade me if they were going to disrespect me that way. It was the first time I had said anything about a trade. It was heated and I didn't mean to go that far. I learned later that Coach Brown began to feel it was me or him, that we couldn't coexist. So the next day, Pat Croce got us together in a room and all the animosity came out. We were yelling at each other, talking past each other. It got real. But then we started listening, and it seemed like we found a place of peace. In the second game against the Pistons two days later, I channeled that energy, scoring 32 points in an overtime thriller (Eric Snow hit the game winner). And I made sure to let the press and people know that I apologized and didn't want to be traded: "It's no secret that I want to be in Philadelphia. It's no secret that this is my second home to Virginia. I love the fans here. I don't want to go anywhere."

Still, that confrontation, and all that led to it, lingered. The second blowup was in Miami toward the end of the season, in March 2000. Like always when I was in Miami, I'd gone out the night before. It was a long night and I was out until *late*. The next morning I called the team and told them I wasn't feeling well and would miss the morning shootaround. It wasn't the right thing to do, obviously. But I didn't feel well, it was just a shootaround, and I let them know in advance that I wouldn't be there. When I got to the arena, in plenty of time to play the game, Pat Croce was there, and he informed me I was being suspended. They knew that was a big step—by now you get that I loved the games, was there for the games, and I especially was there for the games in *Miami*. But they suspended me. Sure enough, we lost, and I was seething, forced to sit there and watch. Goddammit, to suspend me for that game made about as much sense as cutting off your nose to spite your face—making something worse, just because you're mad about something small. Missing the shootaround was small to me. So that's how I felt. We got past it, and just like in Detroit, the insult of sitting fueled me. We won the next seven games. But that resentment between me and Coach Brown didn't just go away.

So as I sat there in the locker room, after that second time losing to Indiana in the playoffs, my future was weighing heavily on me.

FORTY-ONE

STAYING IN PHILLY

During the summer of 2000, a few weeks after being eliminated from the playoffs, I was in Virginia, taking some time off, when I got a call from Pat Croce. I felt this little knot in my stomach answering it, because his calls weren't regular.

"Bubba, I'm sorry," he said. "It looks like you're about to be traded." Traded? *Traded.* To Detroit.

My emotions just came out. It was like when I got out of jail, and I got home, and I couldn't put on that game face anymore, and I just let it go with my family. Or when I got up to shake David Stern's hand after hearing my name called as the top pick in the draft and all I could do was smile like a kid. There was nothing but emotion, raw as shit, that came out—but not the good kind. Shocked and fucking disappointed, I pleaded with Pat, *I'll change! Motherfucker, I'm just twenty-five. Give me one more goddamn chance.* But it was done, he said.

Hearing that—*traded*—felt almost as bad as hearing *fifteen years.* Like, that was it, didn't matter if there was a reason, didn't matter if it made sense, and didn't matter how I felt about it. I just couldn't believe they would do that, that Coach Brown would make that decision—and the team would let him. I thought of Nana's words. "Never question God." That's all I could think, but I was questioning His wisdom, I admit.

Before there was any announcement, before it made the newspapers or *SportsCenter*, God did have a hand in it, I think. The proposed trade involved twenty-some players and three or four teams. One of those players was my teammate, Matt Geiger. He had what was called a "trade kicker" in his contract: Once traded, he was entitled to an additional 15 percent of his salary. The Pistons didn't want to pay that, so they asked him to waive the kicker. He explained his thinking a year later, when the whole situation became public: "I looked at Detroit and didn't think Allen and I would've been better off there." That shit is beautiful. He said no, and that saved my ass, because the whole trade got terminated. And I can say it now: *Thank you, Matt Geiger.*

The trade didn't happen, but it almost happened, and that stuck with me. I was determined to be more committed to what Coach Brown wanted. In fact I spoke to Coach Brown and told him I wanted to be team captain for the first time. He agreed.

FORTY-TWO

THE 2000–2001 REGULAR SEASON

After all that noise of a possible trade, that fall was the first time that I was happy to get to training camp. I needed a place to go to turn down the volume. Me and Eric Snow and Aaron McKie were the leaders of that team. And sure enough, all camp I showed up on time for every goddamn practice. I remember on our first media availability, the press kept asking me questions about the trade rumors, and me and Coach Brown's beef. I was defiant. By then I'd put on my game face, so I said it didn't bother me. If they would have traded me, they just would have come to regret it. But you know now: I was so relieved to still be with this team, in this city, and yes, with this coach.

Sure enough, the season's beginning was perfection. We won our first ten games. The Philly crowds were ready. The two years before, when we lost to the Pacers, it was like the city was just dying to explode but couldn't—the energy was just all pent-up. As our bus came up to the arenas during those playoff runs, mobs were there waiting to greet us, excitement just coursing through the city. Then when we entered the arena for warm-ups, the place would already be full, loud as shit. That carried over during our hot start to the 2000–2001 season—and all year. It was like it was already the playoffs. The city knew we had a destination beyond the second round. The fans were prepared to will us there.

We won those first ten games as a team, and it started with defense. In fact, I couldn't find my shooting touch at all. I shot it well under 40 percent during the streak. Yet our defensive pressure was so aggressive, determined, and infectious. George Lynch and Tyrone Hill had been acquired by then, and those dudes played their hearts out every second they were on the floor. Even I focused on guarding like never before—I was connected to my man, not just looking for steals, but helping, trapping, and sound in my assignments. Late in tight games, we began to believe we could win simply by defending our asses off. For the whole squad, realizing we could have that kind of success without me having great shooting nights, it just gave us confidence.

Of course, the season was never going to be simple. Inevitably we lost a game, but then, much worse, we lost Eric Snow to an injury. Eric was the glue. As the starting point guard, he got me the ball in the exact spots on the floor where he knew I could score, and he hit me in the hands right where I could shoot or attack. So Aaron McKie moved from sixth man to starter while Snow was out. McKie was such a pro, such a great teammate, and of course he's now a great coach. Still, we missed Snow, and with McKie in the starting lineup we missed his contributions as the sixth man leading our bench units.

That December—almost a year to the day after me and Coach Brown had our shouting match in Detroit—we got blown out by the Dallas Mavericks. Walking back to the locker room, we were all disgusted. But we still had the NBA's best record at 17-6, so it wasn't panic time. Coach Brown closed the locker room door and said he wanted to talk to us before we met with the press. In the way he was, all he could see was the negative. It was a bad game, and true we were just 7–6 since the 10–0 start, but he just kept talking about how we were slipping—our focus slipping, our defensive intensity slipping, our execution slipping. It was a half hour of that negativity. It pissed me off.

So the next day, me and the guys were talking about how Coach Brown needed to relax, not be so on top of us about every little failure, every little nitpick, not when we had the best record in the whole damn league.

I was a captain, and I said we should voice this shit to him. So we had another team meeting, and I got up and basically told Coach Brown to chill the fuck out. Stop being so negative, lighten the criticism—it almost seemed like it was worse with us winning. He just sat there and took it. You couldn't tell what he thought in the moment. But now I know. He felt blindsided. Attacked. And by all of us because the rest of the team listened while I expressed the frustration.

After the meeting, Coach Brown left the practice facility. And then he disappeared. It was his turn to miss a couple of practices, I guess. Disappearing was one thing, but the real problem was that his absence was reported in the papers and on TV. By this point the Larry Brown–Allen Iverson relationship was a source of daily intrigue, a topic that could entertain an audience for days. Sources within the team told reporters about his team meeting, then my team meeting, and then the story became that Larry Brown was considering quitting.

Sometimes you don't know the shit you have until you almost lose it. Getting informed I'd been traded, goddammit I never wanted to lose Philly. Now hearing Coach Brown was about to quit. We had the best record in the league—together. I did not want to lose him. The team did not want to lose him.

I don't know what happened as he sat at home. I heard he didn't even return Croce's calls. But on the third day, he came back. I can't say he seemed thrilled. His first practice, and the dude was still focused on the details and assumed the worst was just around the corner. But something was different too. We faced Utah at home the next game. Utah was done making it to the Finals, but they still had John Stockton and Karl Malone.

They were still the shit, in other words. I scored 45 points, and we had a big second-half lead. Yet somehow we blew the game down the stretch.

Afterward, Coach Brown was measured: He spoke to us about how well we played to build that lead. And he told us we needed to tighten it up, of course. We didn't want to waste something so special—a 45-point performance like the one I had, and the team effort that built such a solid lead. So he gave us the good with the bad—even after a terrible loss. It was a different Coach Brown, one who had maybe listened to my plea not to be so negative. I had been more focused all season, but I decided right then that me and him were going to do it together.

It wasn't like we won every game after that, but that January and February, we got back to dominating, with our defensive intensity and cohesion. And my game, my shooting, my scoring, it all elevated to another level. In those two months, I averaged more than 35 points a game. Every game, especially at home, was a show.

The show continued for the All-Star Game that February, which was held in DC, my home away from home. I was the top vote-getter among guards and was set to start for the Eastern Conference. Because the Sixers had the best record, Coach Brown was tapped as Eastern Conference coach. These days you hear all kinds of complaints about All-Star Games. They mess with the format, try to incentivize the guys to take it seriously. As long as I went, it was always primarily a time to get the stars in one place, be among the best, party with the best. Like a celebration. But the thing with me is, once you put me on the floor, man, I just had to play my heart out. Simple scrimmages would be like that for me. So imagine an All-Star Game, national TV, capacity crowd. Another guy like that was Kobe Bryant. Motherfucker would not let go of an opportunity to compete under the bright lights. And he was out there starting on the Western Conference squad.

It was almost a given that the West had the way better team. Hearing that talk just motivated me. But shit, they were filled with talent. To give you an idea, their starting front line was Tim Duncan, Kevin Garnett, and

Chris Webber—all three in their prime. (Shaq sat the game out with an injury.) Sure enough, the West pulled ahead from the jump, leading 30–17 at the end of the first quarter. They built the lead to nineteen points after three quarters. Coach Brown was like me though. If he was there, man, he wanted to win. Brilliant coach and tactician that he was, he realized we couldn't match up to their size, so he adjusted by going smaller. In the fourth quarter he put me and Stephon Marbury in the backcourt together. But if he did that, he needed someone who could clean up on the defensive end. And there on the Eastern Conference bench he had the best defender in the league, Dikembe Mutombo. Somehow that combination of speed and defensive presence helped unleash me. That and the fact that the crowd was dying for a competitive game and it felt like this was my home crowd. I just took off, man. I was jumping the passing lanes, pressuring the ball handlers, and if a teammate got a board—usually Dikembe—I'd go get it and push the tempo. A couple of times, I outran everyone down court, weaving through the giants, finishing acrobatic layups as I got fouled. The lead shrank over the next nine minutes, and we caught them when Marbury hit me with a little pass and I drained a three to take the lead by one with a little less than three minutes to play. The DC crowd erupted.

And here is the thing: It might as well have been Anderson Park, because just like those games, the All-Star Game doesn't matter, supposedly. It doesn't change your chance of being a champion. The game is not an official contest and the results don't become part of your official stats. But it is a game. It is a competition. And like every game I came to win that motherfucker.

The problem was, Kobe was on the other side. After I knocked down that three, he took over. Three possessions in a row, he nailed contested jumpers, the third with Mutombo's hand in his face. After all the scoring I'd done, it was Marbury's turn. Down three with a minute left, he drained a three to tie it. After Kobe's last basket put the West up two again, Marbury hit another three over Kobe's outstretched hands. We had ourselves a one-point win, 111–110, considered one of the greatest All-Star Games ever.

Then they announced that I was the MVP. I had scored 15 of my game-high 25 points in the fourth quarter, as we mounted that furious comeback. David Stern himself presented the trophy, and then Ahmad Rashad interviewed me. Smiling like a little kid again, first thing I said was "Where's my coach?" Coach Brown was nowhere to be seen, probably already in the locker room, hopefully feeling some satisfaction. So, when they asked how it felt, I began by saying, "This is a tribute to Coach Brown." It seemed like our relationship was repaired, secure.

Going back for a second, just a couple weeks before the All-Star Game, Theo Ratliff landed awkwardly on his wrist. The man was leading the league with 3.7 blocks a game. He wasn't a towering giant, but his athleticism, effort, and skill made him one of the league's best defenders—and vital to our defense. It wasn't immediately clear how bad the injury was, but as one missed game stretched to the All-Star Break and beyond, we realized we might not get him back in time for our playoff run. So then it happened—a couple weeks after the All-Star Game, the team traded Theo to the Atlanta Hawks for none other than Dikembe Mutombo. It was almost like that All-Star Game had been an audition. Once Coach Brown saw the way the two of us worked together, shit, he had to go for it.

As excited as I was to play with Dikembe, Theo had been there for our whole rise to the top, he'd become a brother, so losing him that year was crushing. But we had no choice. Because of that wrist injury, Theo didn't play another game that season. Dude had to watch us from Atlanta as we made our run.

I loved Dikembe, the person and the player. The man won Defensive Player of the Year with us, and he was just one of the best people you can imagine. When he passed in 2024, the world lost one of the real good ones. I have to tell one funny story about Dikembe, just to give a sense of the dude my fellow Georgetown alum was. You already know how he was there for my Kenner League debut before my freshman year, a towering presence with that radiant smile. Well, one night the season after he joined our team, not long after Ra died, I was just a mess. I was having trouble getting out of bed, let alone making it to practice. Derrick Coleman was back on our team, and he was like, *Come on Chuck, let's go out, you need to have some fun.* Then he got Dikembe to come with us, which was unusual. Well, I got to the bar, and I was drinking Cristal, and I started feeling it, man. Just thinking about Ra, all the emotion of it. I started crying. People were looking at me, staring, like, *Look at AI over there, he's crying.*

Derrick came over and just cleared everyone out. *Ain't no shit to see here, get the fuck out of here.* Then he went to the bartender and ordered ten more bottles of Cris. He told the bartender to open them all up then and there. I was like, *What the fuck?* He said, *Come on, let's go get Dikembe.* Motherfucker started shaking them joints, we went over to Dikembe and started spraying his ass. It made no sense, but shit, Dikembe was like, *I'm never going to the club with you motherfuckers again!* It was the first laugh I had in a minute.

After we got Dikembe in that trade, we won seven of the first nine games with him. At 48-16, it felt like we hadn't missed a beat. We pretty much had home-court advantage sealed with the best record in the East. Though we finished the season a little bit out of sync—I missed seven games down the stretch—we felt ready for the playoff run to come. As the first seed, we would play the eighth seed, the lowest-rated team to make it to the playoffs. That team? The Indiana Pacers.

FORTY-THREE

FROM THE PLAYOFFS TO THE FINALS

The Indiana Pacers weren't as strong a team as the year before. As the eighth seed, they were the last team to make it into the playoffs. And their previous coach, Larry Bird, had been replaced by Isiah Thomas. They still had Reggie Miller and Jalen Rose—the dudes most responsible for eliminating us two straight times. So maybe we had some nerves there as the series began—or as I put it after game one, "Our asses got tight."

It didn't seem that way as game one began. We built a 35–20 lead early in the second quarter and led by sixteen at halftime. Mutombo was dominating the glass. I was getting my shots. But as the fourth quarter grinded, we stopped scoring, and with a little less than twelve seconds left, they had the ball down two. If you know basketball, you know that Reggie Miller is the man you need to control with the game on the line. Well, we didn't. He got free behind the three-point line with less than three seconds left, and he knocked down the game winner. "Gloom and Doomed," the next day's *Inquirer* headline read. It was as if we were on repeat. *This again?* Panic set in throughout the Philadelphia area.

But Coach Brown looked at the tape, saw that they were swarming me once I had the ball (just like back when I was at Bethel), so he sketched out some ways to get me the ball in a position to attack before their defense came at me. And if they did swarm, I had to pass out of it right away, remain patient. In the second game we put his ideas to use and I scored 45 points—my playoff career high to that point—in an eighteen-point win in front of a delirious home crowd. It felt like a cleansing to beat their asses like that. And our asses could loosen up. We won the next two games, closing out the series in Indiana. This time it was tears of *joy*, and in *their* locker room. I remember telling the Philly press it was the best I ever felt on a basketball court. Not since Bethel *football*, beating Hampton and then winning the state title, had I felt this good. "I'm not acting like I won a championship," I said. "But for a team that has beaten you two years in a row, shattered your dreams, it feels good to beat them."

The following Sunday we began an epic series against the Toronto Raptors and Vince Carter. In game one, we came up short when Vince scored 35 points and they held on for a close win. I guess it felt like we needed a little adversity. Down a game, we had all the pressure on us again. With all I'd been through, I really didn't feel pressure about any game. I just wanted to get back out there, get another chance. Finally, game two arrived, and so did I. There was not a thing I couldn't do. All the times I'd been told to distribute, slow down, and include my teammates—be a point guard—everyone forgot about that shit that night. I had to keep shooting it. Thirty-nine times I put the ball up. I scored 54 of our 97 points, including the last 19, in a game we won by just five points. Just imagine the feedback from the fans as I just kept coming and coming, finishing Toronto off with a jumper up three and less than forty seconds left to extend the lead to five.

Walking off the floor after that win, there was no negativity at all. I remember I was asked where it all came from. "Life," I said. "Going through the things I've been through. Poverty."

I could feel myself coming into my own. Whatever hardship I'd had, whether it was poverty or imprisonment, had become part of my superpower. After all that, how could the pressure of a game overwhelm me? After surviving all that, what could possibly stop me now?

After game four, the series tied at two games apiece, I got the greatest honor of my life. I was named Most Valuable Player. I led the league in points, in steals, in minutes per game. Even now I stop and reflect: In that moment I was the greatest player on the planet, No. 1. Shit, man, my mom said she believed in me, and here I was. At just under six feet, and still barely 165 pounds, I was the smallest MVP in league history. Whatever my physical dimensions, my heart couldn't be measured.

In game five, I harnessed that heart. I scored another 52 points as we took a three games to two lead. We needed everything I had, because beginning there in game five, we were without George Lynch. He broke his foot during game four and was done for the season. *Keep shooting* became the ever-more-urgent message.

The Raptors tied the series in Toronto, so the series would be decided in game seven back in Philly. And that one was tight the whole way. In the end they had the ball on the sideline, down a point, with two seconds left. Vince Carter got the inbound by the three-point line, he pump-faked, earning a clean look. As he raised up, I was on the other side of the floor guarding my man. The ball arced high into the air. Me and the rest of my teammates were helpless as it traveled its long-ass path. When it clanged back-rim, I just raised my right arm in victory and sprinted down the court to celebrate. We had advanced to the conference finals.

During that whole series, that whole season, for every game, for every moment, for all the frustration and all the jubilation, I had my family and friends at my side. My mom was there with her jersey, loudest fan in every arena. My sisters, Aunt Jessie, Uncles Steve and Greg, all there, if not in attendance in spirit. Tawanna and my two kids to that point, Tiaura and Deuce, beside me. Mo had come to Philly to help me full-time that season, managing the day-to-day of being Allen Iverson. Dude was just shaking his head as we shattered expectations. Coach Thompson was there too. He came to Philly for the news conference when I won the MVP. And he came for that playoff run to see the heroics—not just mine, but also Dikembe's. He sat in our crowd alongside Alonzo Mourning and Patrick Ewing, and I can only imagine the pride he felt looking on. Arnie and E and Ra and all my other friends from home were there with me too.

While I starred on the team as we marched through the playoffs, it wasn't just Allen Iverson. It was all of Newport News. All off Hampton. All my family. All my friends. Philly. Every goddamn person who worked in the arena. Every employee from the ball boy to the trainer to ticket sales. And of course Ra was a part of that, my best friend. And he just had a few more months of his life left.

It took another seven games to settle the next series with that rival it never seemed I could get the better of—Ray Allen and the Milwaukee Bucks. We arrived with all kinds of injuries. Lynch was out of course, but also Eric Snow had two bum ankles, and Aaron McKie's shoulder was fucked-up. And then there was me. In game seven against Toronto, I had aggravated one of those lingering injuries, a bruised tailbone. Leading up to game time, there was speculation I might have to sit. But Coach Brown knew: "If he sits, he's going to get stiff—or get mad at me, which is worse."

In the first quarter, I think I was stiff, because I missed my first nine shots. To loosen up, I just kept shooting, making thirteen of my final twenty-six attempts, scoring 34 points for the game. (As I said, I needed to keep shooting, now more than ever.) With a little more than a minute left, the game still in doubt, Dikembe got himself an offensive rebound and passed it out to me. A clean look beyond the arc, I hit the dagger over Ray Allen's hand to go up seven and put them away.

Milwaukee responded with a win in game two. And by the time game three arrived, I could barely walk, the tailbone had gotten so bad. I needed rest, to heal. And so I sat that next one out. I remember watching with Mo in my Milwaukee hotel room as our squad, first missing George Lynch and now me, fought until the end, keeping it close. Jumaine Jones and Raja Bell took on bigger roles. But we just didn't have enough and fell behind in the series two games to one. Still, the rest of the guys playing without me, it seemed like it helped, because they came up big over the next two games despite the fact that I shot a combined 15 for 59. We just grinded, playing the defense that got us there. After aggravating his injured ankle in game four, Eric Snow hit the jumper to win by one in game five.

Even with a lead in the series, it felt like I needed to find my shot if we were going to win one more game and reach the Finals. Yet nothing changed at the outset of game six, as we fell behind big in Toronto. My body was feeling better finally, and in the fourth quarter, down 26 points, I tried single-handedly to will us back. I scored 26 in that quarter alone, put a scare into them, in what ended as a ten-point loss. As I kept shooting, kept connecting, and just kept going until the final buzzer, we could feel a shift—even in defeat.

So it was another game seven. Since we'd earned home-court advantage, it was back in our place, in front of our thirsty-ass fans. The Lakers awaited the winner, having dispatched their conference finals foe days before.

From the start of game seven, my back was loose and my shot felt in rhythm, as I made two out of my first three jumpers in the opening minutes. The Bucks weren't just going away though, and they gained the early momentum, pulling ahead by as much as seven in the second quarter. Ray Allen, Glenn Robinson, and Sam Cassell all scored 20-plus points, each taking turns backing me down and shooting over me. But about midway through the second quarter and all the way through the third, we started feeling it, the crowd started feeling it. Raja Bell gave us energy off the bench. Eric Snow and Aaron McKie steadied us throughout. And Dikembe controlled the glass. I scored 27 points in those two quarters, hitting jumpers off that Iverson cut I told you about, driving to the hoop in the half-court, breaking away in transition, and finally as time expired in the third, pulling up for a thirty-footer that gave us an eleven-point lead.

The fourth quarter was tense, but it never got closer than eleven. As the clock got closer and closer to double zeros, the Philly crowd got louder and louder. At breaks in the action, we could hear chants of "Beat LA"—the crowd turning its attention to what was next. As I took free throws in that final frame, it was "MVP, MVP." Finally, with under a minute left, our lead now eighteen, even I relaxed, and I remember running down the court, my hand at my ear, the crowd's mania building and building as I led the celebration.

That's how we found ourselves in the 2001 NBA Finals against the Los Angeles Lakers, with Kobe Bryant and Shaquille O'Neal. By that point Kobe had become one of my greatest rivals, since he was in the same draft, we'd had that All-Star Game battle, and eventually we'd go back and forth winning scoring titles. Kobe was just the ultimate killer. A guy who would try to beat you and fucking eat your heart out.

At that point, though, Shaq was still their main man, totally unstoppable. Shaq is my brother. Like me, he's been a lifetime Reebok guy. Man, he was so dominant. Didn't matter that we had the Defensive Player of the Year. That Lakers team had come into the Finals winning every single playoff game. No one had ever gone undefeated for an entire playoff run before. So in game one, they were well rested at home and imagining a historic undefeated run to the title. We were visiting their house, coming off back-to-back seven-game series and hobbled by injuries. Nobody thought we had a chance. Flash forward to the fourth quarter. I'll tell you about one more play.

It was a reaction. I cut to the right corner, just behind the three-point line. Raja Bell hit me with a bounce pass, then cleared out. I had the ball with my back to the basket, a hand pushing against my hip. I turned to face him. Looking back at me was Ty Lue. Me and this motherfucker had been going at it since halftime—he was grabbing, clawing, holding, trying to prevent me from even getting the ball. It had been working too, but now I held the rock. I stared at him. Surveyed. There was just a minute left in overtime of game one of those 2001 Finals. I had hit a three in the possession before, giving me 46 points for the game and us a two-point lead. The LA crowd was on its feet, screaming. I stood right in front of the Lakers bench, those dudes a foot or two away, talking shit, shouting in my ear from behind.

The court was still the quietest place I knew.

With the ball in both hands at my left hip, I ripped it to my right side, followed by a quick dribble and a step toward the baseline. Lue reacted and followed. After that one hard bounce, I stopped, hung the ball out high, cradled it in my right hand—paused. He relaxed, just for that beat. Then I hit him with the real one, right to left. Lue off balance, space created, I pulled up. He reached for the contest, but I had plenty of room to release a jump shot that arced up and in. And as he scrambled to recover, he fell below me. But my mind wasn't on him at that moment. I turned to look at those motherfuckers on the bench yapping. *Now what?* And then I did it, he was in front of me on the ground, only way forward was over him. So I stepped on over him. I didn't think about it. I just did it. And like that moment of crossing over Jordan, it became iconic, it repeated over and over on *SportsCenter*, in highlights, in documentaries, and even now it lives on in Instagram, TikTok, and whatever will come next.

After that move and that shot, we held on and won game one, and it was the greatest moment of my career. Everything was as good as it could be.

Then we lost the next four.

The season ended, but no one thought of it as a failure. *Maybe if George Lynch hadn't gotten injured*, we said to ourselves. But we never made it back as far as the Finals again. I never did.

That summer I married Tawanna, my partner since I was sixteen. All my family and friends were at our side. Ra was there in his tux, part of the wedding party. Two months later, he would be dead, murdered. A difficult season later, the trade rumors would begin again. A press conference later, I would be asked about practice. *Practice.*

FORTY-FOUR

AMONG GIANTS

Back in Cleveland, at the 75th Anniversary celebration, the spotlight on me and my name still echoing over the PA, I walked to center court. I saw all the other dudes on that team whose names had already been called, smiling, clapping, waiting for me to join them. And the Cleveland crowd greeted me with a loud, growing, unadulterated cheer. If I can talk some shit, it was one of loudest cheers that night.

The greatest part of that weekend was chilling with the other legends. There were the older guys, some of them the same dudes who talked about the younger generation ruining the game back in 1997. Now they wanted to meet me. I was going up to each of them and saying, *It's an honor to meet you.* I couldn't believe it because they were saying the same thing to me. It was flattering, I'll admit it, to be in the room and you're with the best, the cream of the crop, and they're giving you your props. The closest anyone got to talking some shit to me was bringing up "practice." But it was just a positive thing, like a reference. I have done it in TV ads. So at this point, it's almost like saying, "What's up." Hitting me with a, *Hey Allen, practice!*

Another way it came up was the old-timers would say to me, *Can you believe all the* games *these motherfuckers are missing these days? And they gave you shit for* practice? Of course I'd noticed dudes missing games. "Load management," they call it. Guys might miss fifteen or twenty games a year without any official injury.

But with all the criticism I faced, I always knew I would never criticize the guys who came after me—even for missing motherfucking games. People said to me, *Chuck, why don't you go on* Inside the NBA, *do that TV shit?* I'd be like, *I know it's constructive criticism at times, but I've been through the storm of people talking bad about me, and I never liked it when they did it to me, so I never want to do that shit to nobody else.* They go, *But Chuck, it's just basketball.* But who the fuck am I to sit around and talk shit about another professional? We ain't talking about no little-ass amateur on Instagram. It's like one great surgeon talking shit about another surgeon. What makes that one surgeon better? He's saving more lives or something?

Without disrespecting anyone else's choice, TV wasn't for me because to do it, you got to call out some motherfuckers, let the audience know who is scared, who is fucking up, who is hungover, who just can't play. They had me on this show one time, a fucking debate show, and yes they were debating. They were getting personal but they couldn't get me to talk like that. I know they were thinking, *Man, we gotta get this motherfucker off this camera. This kid ain't gonna talk shit about nobody.*

I look at the NBA today, and they limit the hand-checking, they spread everyone out. There is even more freedom on the court. Imagine all the shit I could have accomplished in that environment. And all these younger guys with crazier styles than I ever had—no one paying it any mind. I'd paid the dues so that these guys could express themselves. And bring home a bag, making millions and millions more than I ever made. But, nah, I can't criticize anyone.

The players that came after me on the 75th Anniversary Team were guys like Chris Paul and Dwyane Wade, dudes who not only exemplified greatness but also wore number 3, following in my footsteps. Then you had Russell Westbrook and James Harden. I'd put them on my TV any time they played. And of course my favorite, Steph Curry, who hit sixteen threes during the All-Star Game that very day. I remember sitting in the crowd watching him go crazy like that and I was just enjoying the show. I don't even like to say a favorite because all those dudes are so great.

Just think about my draft class of 1996. Not long after they called my name, Ray Allen and Steve Nash joined me up there. Of course, the greatest draftee of '96 couldn't attend. When they announced Kobe's spot, we all just stopped celebrating for a minute. Goddammit, it wasn't right that he wasn't there with us.

But when Mike showed up, last of course, it was different. From all the other attendees—myself included—I remember the reaction. Basketball Jesus stepped in there. Just the greatest.

I love LeBron. I love everything he has done on the court and off the court. All the shit he stands for. I love him. He's there on Mount Rushmore. That's enough. He's better than I was as a basketball player. So no disrespect. But Jordan is the greatest.

Standing at center court, reflecting for a minute. *Damn.*

So by now, you get it. The practice press conference wasn't really about practice. That was my whole point. What I was trying to say was that it just seemed wrong to focus on practice then and there. *What about the games? What about my friends and family? What about me, the human being?* That's what I was trying to say. And to explain my reaction, I wanted to tell you about the person I was, the person I am, and how I got here.

From the 50th Anniversary Team to the 75th. From roaming the streets of Newport News and Hampton to entering the Hall of Fame. From selling drugs to selling sneakers. From bunching up a suit in my jail cell to wearing that blazer there on center court. From alone in a jail cell to under the arm of Coach Thompson. From banned tattoos to ink poking out of just about every shirt collar and cuff. From bringing my friends and family with me out the shit to losing my best friend once we'd made it.

From my mom dragging me to my first basketball tryout to being named the MVP. From booed to embraced.

Always human. Always misunderstood. Always myself.

I've made mistakes. Plenty of them. I didn't care for practice. It didn't mean enough, no stakes and boring. But I played every game like it was my last. Because I think I always thought it might be.

So what's the situation with practice?

That's all the answer I have.

ACKNOWLEDGMENTS

I've said it a few times in this book, but I can say it again: My legacy isn't mine alone. So many people helped make me who I am, and made this the book it is. When I gave my Hall of Fame speech, I thanked so many people, but even then I remember my iPad stopped scrolling, I kept swiping, and then I skipped some lines. So I didn't thank everyone. It isn't possible to thank everyone. I guess that's what I'm trying to say. Especially in a life like mine, with ups and downs. I accomplished so much, but if you read this far you know my basketball journey could have ended early many times over, like with a broken ankle, a prison sentence, or a premature trade. This book is an acknowledgment in itself to all those who helped build my legacy.

I thank God for blessing me, first. And next I have to thank my beautiful mom and my late Nana. If this book shows anything, it's how much they meant in my life. My Uncles Steve and Greg, and my Aunt Jessie. I feel like I'm still learning from them, about how much they put into helping me achieve my dreams. My dad, Michael Freeman, and my two sisters, Brandy and Iiesha, and my brother, Mister Allen Iverson.

Of course, Tawanna is the one who deserves the most recognition. Since we backed into one another, just teenagers, she's been there for me.

She got in trouble in school for taking my side when the bowling alley situation happened, and now all these years later she's making sure we spend the time we need to spend as a family. There wouldn't be the Allen Iverson you know without her, and there wouldn't be this book. That goes for my five kids too, who each help me every day, by supporting me, by making me proud, by bringing joy to this life.

My friends and my teammates, from childhood to the present day, they know who they are. If you've read this book, you know how much I cherish my friends and social life, and that goes for my teammates who supported me as a player and as a person.

And then there are the fans. My relationship with the fans of Philadelphia is stronger than any fans with any player, as far as I have seen. I love them to death. And beyond Philly, to China and to the whole world, I couldn't have had the success I've had without the support of everyone.

As for the specifics of this book, Antwuan Clisby is my business manager and a great friend, and he was an intricate part of making this book happen. I thank Ian Kleinert, my book agent who stuck with this project, kept believing in it, throughout the decade-plus it's been in the works. Thanks also to the great team at Gallery Books: Aimee Bell, who carefully edited the manuscript and helped mold it (still letting me be me); Jennifer Bergstrom and Jennifer Robinson; Sierra Fang-Horvath and Hanna Preston; and the entire production team. And to Charles Suitt, my man at 13A publishing, a friend for life who carried this book to the finish line, who willed it there.

And, finally, to my friend and collaborator, Ray Beauchamp. For the last seven years, he's been in my phone as "Ray Book," and that name had my phone vibrating. The dude kept calling and texting. We've spent those years talking about *my* life, but also just talking about *life*. It got emotional at times, and some of the things that are embarrassing in this book we got through because of the trust we developed. He's a friend now, and obviously the book wouldn't be what it is without him.